HOLT PHYSICS

LABORATORY EXPERIMENTS
Teacher's Edition

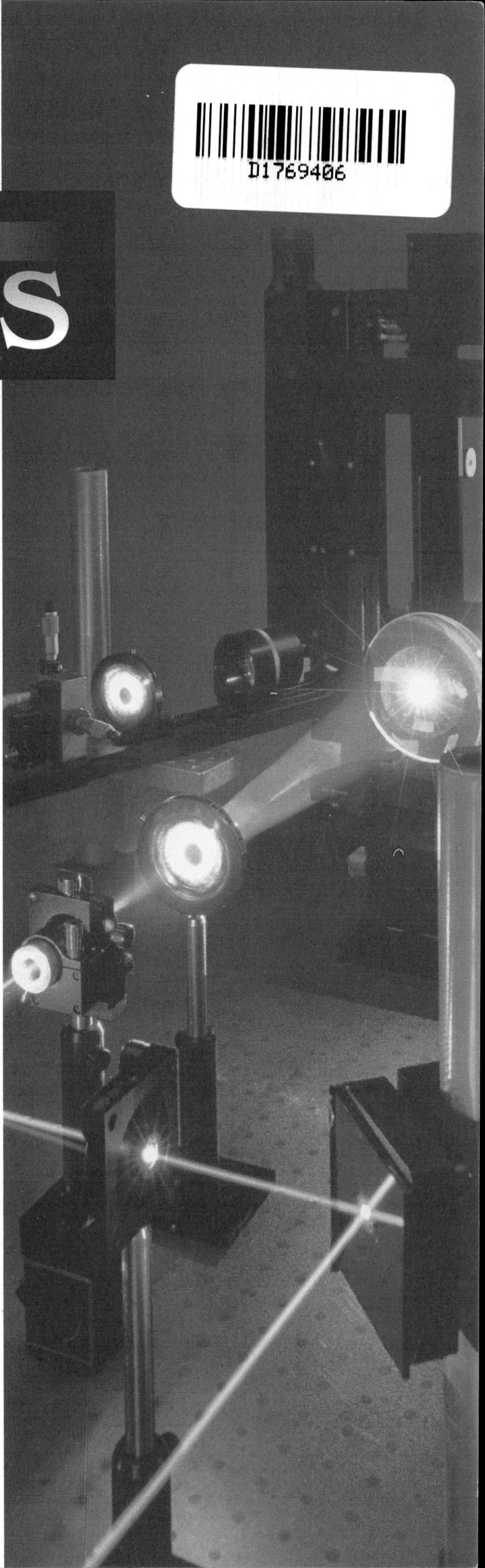

HOLT, RINEHART AND WINSTON
A Harcourt Classroom Education Company

Austin · New York · Orlando · Atlanta · San Francisco · Boston · Dallas · Toronto · London

Holt Physics
Laboratory Experiments Teacher's Edition

Lab Authors

Douglas W. Biedenweg, Ph.D.
Chadwick School
Palos Verdes, CA

Kaye M. Elsner-McCall
Physics Teacher
Riverwood High School
Fulton County Schools
Atlanta, GA

Anthony L. Komon
Physics Teacher
Science Department
Niskayuna High School
Schenectady, NY

Sean P. Lally
Chairman of Science
Sewickley Academy
Sewickley, PA

Safety Reviewer

Gregory Puskar
Laboratory Manager
Physics Department
West Virginia University
Morgantown, WV

Laboratory Reviewers

Lee Sennholtz
Central Scientific Company
Franklin Park, IL

Martin Taylor
Central Scientific Company
Franklin Park, IL

Cover Photo: ©Lawrence Manning/CORBIS

Cover Design: Jason Wilson

Copyright © by Holt, Rinehart and Winston

All rights reserved. No part of this publication may be reproduced or transmitted in any form or by any means, electronic or mechanical, including photocopy, recording, or any information storage and retrieval system, without permission in writing from the publisher.

Requests for permission to make copies of any part of the work should be mailed to the following address: Permissions Department, Holt, Rinehart and Winston, 10801 N. MoPac Expressway, Austin, Texas 78759

Printed in the United States of America

ISBN 0-03-057359-9

2 3 4 5 6 095 04 03 02

Contents

Laboratory Program Overview — T6

Evaluating Lab Work T8
Safety in the Physics Laboratory T17
A Note on Using Electrical Meters T21
Laboratory Experiments Booklet Materials List T22

Student's Introduction — v

Sample Patent Application Lab Report vii
Laboratory Safety ix

Chapter 1
Discovery Lab The Circumference-Diameter Ratio of a Circle 1
Teacher's Notes T26
Invention Lab Bubble Solutions 4
Teacher's Notes T28

Chapter 2
Discovery Lab Motion 7
Teacher's Notes T31
Invention Lab Race Car Construction 10
Teacher's Notes T33

Chapter 3
Discovery Lab Vector Treasure Hunt 13
Teacher's Notes T36
Invention Lab The Path of a Human Cannonball 16
Teacher's Notes T38

Chapter 4
Discovery Lab Discovering Newton's Laws 19
Teacher's Notes T41
Invention Lab Friction: Testing Materials 22
Teacher's Notes T43

Chapter 5
Discovery Lab Exploring Work and Energy 25
Teacher's Notes T45
Invention Lab Bungee Jumping: Energy 28
Teacher's Notes T47

Chapter 7
Discovery Lab Circular Motion **31**
Teacher's Notes **T50**

Chapter 8
Discovery Lab Torque and Center of Mass **35**
Teacher's Notes **T52**
Invention Lab The Rotating Egg Drop **38**
Teacher's Notes **T54**

Chapter 10
Discovery Lab Temperature and Internal Energy **41**
Teacher's Notes **T57**
Invention Lab Thermal Conduction **44**
Teacher's Notes **T59**

Chapter 12
Discovery Lab Pendulums and Spring Waves **47**
Teacher's Notes **T62**
Invention Lab Tensile Strength and Hooke's Law **50**
Teacher's Notes **T64**

Chapter 13
Discovery Lab Resonance and the Nature of Sound **53**
Teacher's Notes **T67**
Invention Lab Building a Musical Instrument **56**
Teacher's Notes **T69**

Chapter 14
Discovery Lab Light and Mirrors **59**
Teacher's Notes **T71**
Invention Lab Designing a Device to Trace Drawings **62**
Teacher's Notes **T73**

Chapter 15
Discovery Lab Refraction and Lenses **65**
Teacher's Notes **T75**
Invention Lab Camera Design **68**
Teacher's Notes **T77**

Chapter 17

Discovery Lab Charges and Electrostatics **71**
Teacher's Notes **T79**
Invention Lab Levitating Toys **74**
Teacher's Notes **T82**

Chapter 19

Discovery Lab Resistors and Current **77**
Teacher's Notes **T84**
Invention Lab Battery-Operated Portable Heater **80**
Teacher's Notes **T86**

Chapter 20

Discovery Lab Exploring Circuit Elements **83**
Teacher's Notes **T89**
Invention Lab Designing a Dimmer Switch **86**
Teacher's Notes **T91**

Chapter 21

Discovery Lab Magnetism **89**
Teacher's Notes **T94**
Invention Lab Designing a Magnetic Spring **92**
Teacher's Notes **T96**

Chapter 22

Discovery Lab Electricity and Magnetism **95**
Teacher's Notes **T99**
Invention Lab Building a Circuit Breaker **98**
Teacher's Notes **T101**

HOLT PHYSICS Laboratory Program Overview

A Wide Variety of Options

Two new kinds of labs provide a complete learning experience for students

The *Holt Physics Laboratory Experiments* booklet contains 33 all-new labs. These labs are designed to guide your students through all the stages of learning physics, from the initial exploration of concepts to the challenge of designing their own experiments.

Tested Procedures
Physics teachers and the staff of CENCO Scientific rigorously bench-tested all procedures for every lab in the *Laboratory Experiments* booklet for ease of use, safety, and practicality. For additional information on safety, **see pages T17–T21.**

Improved Analysis and Interpretation Items
Each section of the Discovery Labs ends with a series of questions designed to lead students step by step through the analysis necessary to develop the physics concepts involved in the lab, just as the steps in the procedure lead students through the techniques of the lab. The questions are designed to challenge common misconceptions and help students build their own understanding of the concepts presented in the chapter.

CENCO Materials Ordering Software
With CENCO's exclusive software-ordering system, specifically designed for use with *Holt Physics*, you can order your materials and supplies quickly and easily. The system lists all required and supplemental materials—per lab group or class size—needed for the full-length labs in the textbook and the labs in the *Laboratory Experiments* booklet. For the printed version of the Master Materials List for the *Laboratory Experiments*, **see pages T22–T25.**

Innovation

New strategies help students take responsibility for their own learning

The 33 new labs in this booklet provide two unique strategies for lab experiences: Discovery Labs for pre-chapter use and Invention Labs for student-designed experiments. Each is designed to further link the key concepts of physics with the students' own experiences and to provide students with the practice they need to build better troubleshooting and problem-solving skills.

HOLT PHYSICS Laboratory Program Overview, continued

Discovery Labs let students develop their own conceptual understanding of physics

Discovery Labs allow students to explore and experience a physics phenomenon before they study the corresponding chapter. The procedures require no prior knowledge of the topic. Instead, they build on students' previous learning to develop new concepts firsthand. Later, as students read the chapter and study the content, they will be able to deepen their understanding drawing upon the concrete examples of the physics concepts they observed.

Flexibility

The lab procedure is broken down into small, self-contained parts to maximize flexibility. Students can either perform the whole lab in one class period or do each part immediately before studying the corresponding topics in the chapter. The lab can even be performed as a confirmatory exercise after the topic has been studied.

Integrated Procedure and Questions

Each part of the procedure is followed by a brief set of questions designed to solidify students' observations and lead students to build their own understanding of the operative physics concepts.

For a rubric to assist you in evaluating student performance on Discovery Labs, **see pages T8–T10.**

Invention Labs challenge students to apply the concepts they've learned to a specific challenge

Invention labs provide an opportunity for open-ended inquiry labs. All the invention labs are set in a working-world scenario in which students are employees of a research and development lab. Students are challenged to invent a device or test materials to solve a specific problem. They are not given a procedure, however, only a list of equipment that could be useful. This way, they can create a unique solution by applying their knowledge of physics.

Initial Plan

Every student must submit an initial plan before they enter the lab. This helps students focus so they can complete their work in the lab period. The rubric on **pages T11–T14** contains useful tips for evaluating student plans.

Final Patent Application

Students submit a final patent application instead of a traditional lab report. Students must make a sketch of their invention, delineate all of the parts, describe how the invention works, and include a discussion of the physics concepts underlying the operation of the invention or process. The rubric on **pages T11–T14** contains useful tips for evaluating patent applications.

A description of the format and a sample patent application lab report is shown on **page T15.**

HOLT PHYSICS Evaluating Lab Work, Scoring rubrics

Scoring rubric for Discovery Labs in the Laboratory Experiments booklet

Lab Assessment in *Holt Physics Laboratory Experiments*

The Discovery Labs in this book are designed to give students an opportunity to gain hands-on experience of the physics concepts presented in each chapter. For these exercises to be meaningful, students must exhibit skillful and careful technique in the lab and must take a logical approach to each exercise.

The following scoring rubric outlines seven levels of students' performance in the laboratory to help you evaluate your students' lab work. Each level describes the scientific skills required in the physics lab and the quality of analysis expected in the written lab report. To use this scale, read the description of each level and choose the level that most accurately reflects each report you grade.

A useful strategy is to keep a file of past reports that seem to exemplify each level. These papers will serve as examples to help you when grading. You might also want to make the file available to students to give them examples of your grading criteria.

▼ Experienced level (6 points)

- Excellent technique was used throughout the lab procedure. Procedures were well-planned and well-executed.
- Data and observations were recorded correctly, descriptively, and completely, with no serious errors.
- Calculations and data analysis were performed clearly, concisely, and correctly, with correct units and properly performed calculations.
- Graphs, if necessary, were drawn accurately and neatly and were clearly labeled.
- Students recognized the connections between their observations and the related physics concepts; this understanding was expressed clearly and completely.
- Good reasoning and logic are evident throughout the report.
- Answers to questions are complete.

HOLT PHYSICS Evaluating Lab Work, Scoring rubrics, continued

▼ Competent level (5 points)

- No errors in technique were observed during the lab procedure. Procedures were well planned and were carried out in an organized fashion.
- Data and observations were recorded correctly, descriptively, and completely, with only minor errors.
- Calculations and data analysis were performed correctly, with correct units and properly performed calculations, but the work may have been slightly unclear or disorganized.
- Graphs, if necessary, were drawn accurately and neatly.
- Students effectively expressed recognition of the connections between their observations and the related physics concepts.
- Good reasoning and logic are evident throughout the report.
- Answers to questions are correct, but may reveal minor misunderstandings.

▼ Intermediate level (4 points)

- Only minor errors in technique were observed during the lab procedure. Procedures are carried out well but may have been slightly disorganized.
- Data and observations were recorded correctly, with only minor errors or omissions.
- Calculations and data analysis were performed correctly, but some minor errors were made either in calculations or in applying correct units.
- Graphs, if necessary, were drawn accurately and neatly.
- Students adequately expressed their recognition of the connections between their observations and the related physics concepts.
- Reasoning is occasionally weak in the report.
- Answers to most questions were correct, but there are some misunderstandings or minor errors.

▼ Transitional level (3 points)

- Only a few errors in technique were observed during the lab procedure, but they were significant. Procedures were not well planned or they were carried out in a disorganized fashion.
- Data and observations were recorded adequately, with only minor errors or omissions.
- Calculations and data analysis were performed correctly, but minor errors were made both in calculations and in applying correct units.
- Graphs, if necessary, are drawn adequately.
- Students recognize connections between their observations and the related physics concepts, but this understanding is very weakly expressed.
- Reasoning is weak throughout much of the report.
- Some answers to questions are incorrect because of misunderstandings, minor errors, or poor data.

Discovery Lab Scoring Rubric

HOLT PHYSICS Evaluating Lab Work, Scoring rubrics, continued

▼ Beginning level (2 points)

- Several serious errors in technique were observed during the lab procedure. Procedures are not well planned and are carried out in a disorganized fashion.
- Most data and observations were recorded adequately but with several significant errors or omissions.
- Calculations and data analysis were performed inaccurately, but correct units were used most of the time.
- Graphs, if necessary, are drawn adequately.
- Students may or may not recognize connections between their observations and the related physics concepts; no expression of understanding is evident in the report.
- Errors in logic are made in the report. Parts of the report were disorganized and unclear.
- Some answers to questions were incorrect or poorly written.

▼ Inexperienced level (1 point)

- Many serious errors in technique were observed during the lab procedure. Procedures were very poorly planned and disorganized, and they show a lack of understanding of the lab.
- Data and observations were incorrect or incomplete.
- Calculations and data analysis were performed incorrectly, with no units or with incorrect units.
- Graphs, if necessary, are drawn incorrectly.
- Students obviously do not recognize connections between their observations and the related physics concepts.
- Errors in logic are made throughout the report.
- Some answers to questions are so incorrect that it is obvious the students did not understand the lab or did not collect any meaningful data.

▼ Unacceptable level (0 points)

- All work is unacceptable.
- No responses are relevant to the lab.
- Major components of the lab report are missing.

HOLT PHYSICS Evaluating Lab Work, Scoring rubrics, continued

Scoring rubric for Invention Labs in the *Laboratory Experiments* booklet

The Invention Labs in this book are designed to give students an opportunity to demonstrate their mastery of the physics concepts presented in each chapter. Students will develop their own procedures for these labs, and it is essential for students to work in an organized and logical manner. Students will turn in an initial plan for your approval before they begin work in the lab, and they will write their final results in the format of a patent application.

Because the Invention Labs challenge students to solve problems on their own, students will often find many different ways of achieving the final result. The teacher's notes for each Invention Lab describe specific criteria that you can use to evaluate the initial plan and the patent application for each activity.

In addition, the following scoring rubric presents descriptions of seven levels of students' performance in the laboratory to help you evaluate your students' lab work. Each level describes the organization and safety requirements for the initial plan, the methods and skills required in the physics lab, and the quality of analysis expected in the written lab report. To use this scale, read the description of each level and decide which most accurately reflects each report you grade.

▼ Experienced level (6 points)

- The plan shows careful and thorough planning with good reasoning and logic. Students express a clear understanding of the physics concepts involved in the lab.

- The plan is complete, appropriate, and safe. It addresses all of the requirements listed in the memorandum for the Invention Lab. The planned procedure is organized and efficient and is presented clearly and concisely.

- Proposed data tables are complete and clearly indicate all measurements that must be made to solve the problem.

- Excellent technique was used throughout the lab procedure.

- Data and observations were recorded correctly, descriptively, and completely, with no errors. The report clearly expresses good reasoning, logic, and understanding of the physics concepts involved in the lab.

- The final report contains all parts of the patent application. Diagrams are correct and neatly drawn and labeled. All apparatus are described in detail.

- The Operation of Invention section includes all necessary diagrams, equations, and graphs. The procedure and results are described clearly and in an organized fashion. Writing is clear, concise, and well organized, with few grammatical or stylistic errors. The connection between the initial problem and the outcome of the lab is clearly expressed.

- Students are successful at solving the problem presented in the lab. The relative error for quantitative answers is less than 15 percent.

HOLT PHYSICS Evaluating Lab Work, Scoring rubrics, continued

▼ Competent level (5 points)

- Plan shows careful planning, although the reasoning and logic behind it may not be clearly expressed. Students express some understanding of the physics concepts involved in the lab.

- The plan is appropriate, safe, and nearly complete. Most of the requirements listed in the memorandum for the Invention Lab are addressed. The planned procedure is organized and fairly efficient. Some parts of the plan could be presented more clearly.

- Proposed data tables indicate all measurements that must be made to solve the problem, but there may be some minor errors or omissions.

- No errors in technique were observed during the lab procedure.

- Data and observations were recorded accurately, and completely, with no serious errors. The report adequately expresses logic and an understanding of the physics concepts involved in the lab.

- The final report contains all parts of the patent application. Diagrams are correct and neatly drawn and labeled. The apparatus are described in some detail.

- The Operation of Invention section includes all necessary diagrams, equations, and graphs. The procedure and results are described clearly and in an organized fashion. Writing is clear, concise, and well organized, with few serious grammatical or stylistic errors. The connection between the initial problem and the outcome of the lab is clearly expressed.

- Students are successful at solving the problem presented in the lab. The relative error for quantitative answers is less than 25 percent.

▼ Intermediate level (4 points)

- The plan shows some logic, but the reasoning could have been more careful, more thorough, or more clearly expressed. The plan reflects a partial understanding of the physics concepts involved in the lab.

- The plan is appropriate and safe, but there are some omissions. The main requirements listed in the memorandum for the Invention Lab are addressed. The planned procedure will work, but it is poorly organized or inefficient. The plan is not presented clearly.

- Proposed data tables indicate all measurements that must be made to solve the problem, but no provision is made for multiple trials.

- Only minor errors in technique were observed during the lab procedure.

- Data and observations are mostly accurate, but they are poorly organized or have some incorrect units. The report expresses some logic and understanding of the physics concepts involved in the lab, but there are several minor errors.

- The final report contains all parts of the patent application. Diagrams are correct, but they may not be complete. The apparatus are not described as clearly as they could be.

- The Operation of Invention section includes all necessary diagrams, equations, and graphs. The procedure and results are described, but the writing is unclear or disorganized. There may be serious grammatical or stylistic errors. Students understand the connection between the initial problem and the outcome of the lab.

- Students are somewhat successful at solving the problem presented by the lab. The relative error for quantitative answers is less than 35 percent.

HOLT PHYSICS Evaluating Lab Work, Scoring rubrics, continued

▼ Transitional level (3 points)

- The plan shows some logic, but not enough to completely solve the problem. The plan reflects a partial understanding of the physics concepts involved in the lab.

- The plan is safe, but it includes inappropriate procedures or omits necessary steps. The problem presented in the Invention Lab is not directly addressed. The planned procedure will probably not work. The plan is poorly written or disorganized.

- Proposed data tables do not include all measurements that must be made to solve the problem.

- Only a few errors in technique were observed during the lab procedure, but they were significant. Procedures were poorly planned, or they were carried out in a disorganized fashion. Students may have made several false starts in solving the problem by trial-and-error.

- Data and observations are adequate but incomplete. The report expresses some logic but does not reflect understanding of the physics concepts involved in the lab. There may be several minor factual errors.

- The final report contains all parts of the patent application, but not every part is completely addressed.

- The Operation of Invention section is unclear or disorganized. There are serious grammatical or stylistic errors. The connection between the initial problem and the outcome of the lab is not expressed in the report.

- Students' results only approximately address the problem presented in the lab. The relative error for quantitative answers is less than 50 percent.

▼ Beginning level (2 points)

- The plan shows very little logic or understanding of necessary procedure and does not reflect understanding of the physics concepts involved in the lab.

- The plan may not be completely safe. The plan is not complete and does not adequately address the problem presented in the Invention Lab. The planned procedure will not work. The plan is poorly written.

- Proposed data tables do not include all of the measurements required to solve the problem.

- Several serious errors in technique were observed during the lab procedure. Procedures are poorly planned and do not indicate an understanding of the physics principles involved. Students attempt to solve the problem by trial-and-error.

- Data and observations are incomplete. The report expresses little logic. There may be several factual errors.

- The final report follows the format of the patent application, but there may be several omissions.

- The Operation of Invention section is unclear or disorganized. There are serious grammatical or stylistic errors. Students do not understand the connection between the initial problem and the outcome of the lab.

- Students' results may not adequately address the problem presented by the lab. The relative error for quantitative answers is less than 65 percent.

HOLT PHYSICS Evaluating Lab Work, Scoring rubrics, continued

▼ Inexperienced level (1 point)

- The plan does not show logic or an understanding of the problem presented in the lab.
- The plan is unsafe. The plan is not complete and does not address the problem presented in the Invention Lab. The planned procedure will definitely not work.
- Proposed data tables are incomplete.
- Many serious errors were observed during the lab procedure. There is no logic in the procedure, and there seems to be no understanding of the physics concepts involved in the lab.
- Data and observations are incomplete and do not address the problem presented in the lab. The report expresses little logic and contains factual errors.
- The final report is incomplete or highly disorganized. There is no attempt to connect the lab and the related physics concepts to draw a conclusion.
- The Operation of Invention section is incomplete. There are serious grammatical or stylistic errors. Students do not understand the connection between the initial problem and the outcome of the lab.
- Students' results do not address the problem presented by the lab. The relative error for quantitative answers is less than 80 percent.

▼ Unacceptable level (0 points)

- All work is unacceptable.
- Major components of the plan are missing. The plan is illogical, unsafe, or irrelevant to the problem presented in the lab.
- Few responses are relevant to the lab.
- Major components of the lab are missing. Students do not understand the connection between the initial problem and the outcome of the lab work. There is no attempt to connect the lab to the physics concepts involved.
- Data and observations are incomplete and do not address the problem presented in the lab. The report expresses little logic and contains factual errors.
- The report does not address the problem presented in the lab. The relative error for quantitative data is more than 80 percent.

HOLT PHYSICS Evaluating Lab Work, Sample Report

Sample Patent Application Lab Report

This sample lab report is provided to give your students a model to follow. Your students' patent applications will not be exactly like this one, but they should contain the same basic parts.

1. **Date:** May 18, 1999
   Title: Doormat Lighting System
   Inventor: Antonia Briggs
   Sinh Ngyuen

2. **Background—Field of Invention:** This invention relates to resistors in direct current circuits, specifically to security lighting.

3. **Drawings:**

4. **Description of Drawings:**

5. **List of Reference Numerals:**
   Drawing A   Top view of the bottom of the doormat
   1. plastic drinking straws, two on ends are 8 cm long, one in center is 4 cm long
   2. flat pieces of cardboard, 20 cm × 10 cm, covered with heavy-duty aluminum foil

   Drawing B   Side view of the doormat
   1. side view of three plastic drinking straws (see Drawing A: 1)
   2. side view of two pieces of cardboard, 20 cm × 10 cm, both covered with aluminum foil
   3. connecting wires, connected to top side of aluminum foil

   Drawing C   Circuit diagram
   1. Doormat (see Drawing B: 1, 2, and 3)
   2. dc battery
   3. light bulb
   4. insulated connecting wires

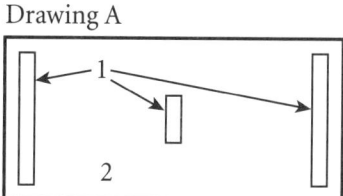
Drawing A

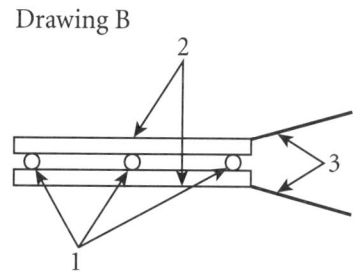
Drawing B

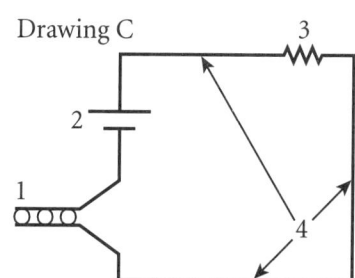
Drawing C

6. **Description of Invention:** The Doormat Lighting System consists of a doormat wired in a series circuit with a dc battery and a light bulb. The doormat is constructed by taking two pieces of cardboard or other firm material and covering them with aluminum foil. The aluminum foil is glued or taped securely to the cardboard. On one piece of cardboard, drinking straws are glued securely, one at each end and one in the middle of the cardboard. The straws on the ends should be almost the same length as the end of the cardboard, and the straw in the middle should be about half that length. All straws should be centered lengthwise on the cardboard, so there is equal distance from the end of the straw to the edge of the cardboard on both sides. See Drawing A.

The second foil-covered piece of cardboard is placed on top of the straws and glued securely. The cardboard pieces should be stacked so that the edges line up exactly, and the straws should prevent them from touching. Insulated connecting wires are attached to the top and bottom of the foil-covered pieces. See Drawing B for a side view.

The insulated connecting wires are used to wire the doormat in series with a dc battery and a light bulb, as shown in Drawing C.

7. **Operation of Invention:** The Doormat Lighting System will light a lightbulb when weight is applied to the doormat. The purpose of this invention is to allow a person to step on the doormat and turn on the light. The dc battery connected in series with the light bulb and the doormat provides a potential difference to the circuit. The doormat acts as a switch in this circuit. When the two surfaces of the doormat are not touching, as when no weight is applied to the doormat, the switch is open and there is no current in the circuit. When weight is applied to the doormat and the two foil-covered surfaces touch, the switch is closed and there is current in the circuit according to the potential difference and the resistance present in the circuit. This relationship is given by the following equation:

$$I = \frac{\Delta V}{R}$$

We developed our circuit using a 9 V dc battery and a 6.3 V, 115 mA light bulb.

When there is current in the circuit, the light bulb, which acts as a resistor in the circuit, will light.

When the weight is removed from the doormat, the plates of the doormat will separate, opening the switch, and there will be no current in the circuit. The light bulb will no longer be lighted.

8. **Conclusion, Ramifications, and Scope of Invention:** The Doormat Lighting System is a security lighting device that uses a resistor in a dc circuit with a battery. The doormat itself operates as a switch in this circuit, and a light bulb operates as a resistor. When the doormat is stepped on, the switch is closed and the light bulb lights. When the weight is removed from the doormat, the switch is opened and the light stops.

In this design, pieces of plastic drinking straws are used to separate the two conducting parts of the doormat. Other items, such as springs, may be used in place of the drinking straws. Any material used for this purpose must be flexible, so that it will compress when weight is applied and will return to its original position when the weight is removed, and it must not conduct electricity. In fact, another type of separator may be better, because the drinking straws become flattened with use and will need to be replaced often to maintain the required distance between the two pieces.

HOLT PHYSICS Evaluating Lab Work, Sample Report, continued

The dimensions of all the parts of this system, from the size of the doormat to the length of the wires, depends upon the desired use. This system may be used to place a doormat outside the door of a house and light a lamp above the door, or it may be used to light a lamp placed inside the house or at another location. The battery and light bulb must be selected so that the battery provides enough potential difference to light the selected bulb but not enough to cause a fire or short circuit.

Another possible use of the design would be to use a resistor other than a light bulb. For example, the circuit could contain a buzzer or some other device. In this way, the circuit could operate as an alarm system or a doorbell. In addition, the switch in the circuit could be designed for use in any device that requires a pressure-sensitive switch. The switch could be placed in the bottom of a mailbox and wired to a light or buzzer inside the house; this system would notify someone inside the house that the mail had been delivered.

Because aluminum foil conducts electricity, it would be necessary to cover the entire switch with insulating material before using this device.

HOLT PHYSICS Safety in the Physics Laboratory

Making your laboratory a safe place to work and learn

Safety should be an integral part of any academic activity, especially in the sciences. Unfortunately, safety tends to be like the speed limit—we are aware of it, but we seldom heed it. We mistakenly believe that accidents will not happen in our laboratory. However, no scientific activity is completely free of risk, and it is rather late to worry about safety after an accident. By reviewing and evaluating safety issues *before* conducting any laboratory activities, teachers can minimize risk to students and prevent most accidents.

Addressing these concerns takes time and effort. Safety must be an integral part of the instructional process, not only to meet legal and ethical standards but also to propagate safe behaviors and attitudes that students can take to their workplaces.

Concern for safety must begin prior to any classroom activity and before students enter the lab. A careful review of the facilities should be a basic part of preparing for each school term. The first steps you should take are to investigate the physical environment, identify any safety risks, and inspect your work areas for compliance to safety regulations.

The review of the lab should be thorough, and all safety issues must be addressed immediately. Keep a file of your review, and add to the list each

HOLT PHYSICS Safety in the Physics Laboratory, continued

year; this will allow you to continue to raise the standard of safety in your classroom. Do not perform any activities in a classroom or laboratory until you can verify that it is safe and you are prepared to respond to emergency situations.

Monitoring activities for safety

Once the laboratory is reviewed and all safety issues are corrected, turn your attention to the activities that will be performed in class. The Invention Labs in this booklet require careful attention to safety, and all initial plans should be reviewed for possible safety concerns. Students should not be allowed to work in the lab until their proposed plans have been reviewed and approved from a safety standpoint. Every teacher should review all experiments, demonstrations, and activities for safety concerns before presenting them to the class. The goal of this review is to identify and eliminate potential safety hazards. In this way, you can maximize learning while minimizing risk and be prepared in case a safety issue arises during the activity.

All reviews should be carried out in the following four stages.

1. Identify the risks

Before introducing any activity to the class, analyze the activity, and ask yourself what could go wrong. Try to consider all possibilities, no matter how unlikely they may seem. Carefully review the list of materials called for to make sure they are safe. Inspect the apparatus in your classroom to make sure they are in good working order. Read the procedures to make sure they are safe. Record any hazards or concerns you identify in a safety log.

2. Evaluate the risks

The focus of this step is to minimize the risks you identified in the last step without sacrificing learning. Weigh the pedagogical value of the activity against the safety risks. Remember that no activity you can perform in the lab is worth risking injury. Thus, extremely hazardous activities or those that violate your school's policies must be eliminated. For activities that present smaller risks, analyze each risk carefully to determine its likelihood. This can be difficult because of the scarcity of documented cases of lab accidents. Using your best judgment and available information, estimate the probability of occurrence for each risk. If the pedagogical value of the activity does not outweigh the risks, the activity must be eliminated.

3. Select controls to address risks

Even low-risk activities require controls to eliminate or minimize the risks. Be careful that in devising controls you do not substitute an equally or more hazardous alternative. If no reasonable controls can be devised, eliminate the activity. Some control methods include the following:

HOLT PHYSICS Safety in the Physics Laboratory, continued

- Explicit verbal and written warnings may be added, signs may be posted and labels attached.
- Apparatus may be rebuilt, relocated, have parts replaced, or be replaced entirely by safer alternatives.
- Risky procedures may be changed or eliminated.
- Student activities can be performed as teacher demonstrations.

4. Implement and review selected controls

Controls do not help if they are forgotten or not enforced. The implementation and review of controls should be as systematic and thorough as the initial analysis of safety concerns in the lab and laboratory activities. This is a constant, ongoing procedure that should take precedence over other concerns.

The following list describes several possible safety hazards and controls that can be implemented to resolve them. This list is not intended to be complete, but it can be used as a starting point to identify some of the known hazards in your laboratory.

Identified safety risk	Preventative control
Lab tables are in disrepair, room is poorly lighted, faucets and electrical outlets do not work or are difficult to use because of their locations.	Work surfaces should be level and stable. There should be adequate lighting. Water supplies, drains, and electrical outlets should be in good working order. Any equipment in a dangerous location should be relocated or rendered inoperable.
Wiring, plumbing, and air circulation systems do not work or do not meet current specifications.	Specifications should be kept on file. Conduct a periodic review of all equipment, and document compliance. Damaged fixtures must be labeled and repaired as soon as possible.
Labs are conducted in multipurpose rooms, and equipment from other courses remains accessible.	Only the items necessary for a given activity should be available to students. All equipment should be locked away when not in use.
Students are permitted to enter or work in the lab without teacher supervision.	Lock all laboratory rooms whenever a teacher is not present. Supervising teachers must be trained in lab safety and emergency procedures.

Safety equipment and emergency procedures

Fire and other emergency drills are infrequent, and no records or measurements are made of the results of the drills.	Implement regular fire and other emergency drills, and conduct careful reviews of each drill. Be sure that plans include alternate routes. Don't wait until an emergency to find the flaws in your plans.

HOLT PHYSICS Safety in the Physics Laboratory, *continued*

Identified safety risk	Preventative control
Emergency evacuation plans do not include instructions for securing the lab in the event of an evacuation during a lab activity.	Plan actions in case of an emergency: establish which devices should be turned off, which escape route to use, and where to meet outside the building.
Fire extinguishers are in inconvenient locations, not on the escape route.	Place fire extinguishers near escape routes, so that they will be useful during an emergency.
Fire extinguishers are not maintained regularly. Teachers are not trained to use extinguishers.	Document the regular maintenance of extinguishers. Train supervisory personnel in the proper use of extinguishers. Instruct students not to use an extinguisher but to call for a teacher.
Teachers in labs and neighboring classrooms are not trained in CPR or first aid.	Teachers should receive training from the local chapter of the American Red Cross. Certifications should be kept current with frequent refresher courses.
Teachers are not aware of their legal responsibilities in case of an injury or accident.	Review your faculty handbook for your responsibilities regarding safety in the classroom and laboratory. Contact the legal counsel for your school district to find out the extent of their support and any rules, regulations, or procedures you must follow. Train all supervisory teachers in the appropriate procedures.
Emergency procedures are not posted. Emergency numbers are kept only at the main switchboard. Instructions are given verbally, at the beginning of each school year, and never reviewed.	Emergency procedures should be posted at all exits and near all safety equipment. Emergency numbers should be posted at all phones, and a script should be provided for the caller to use. Emergency procedures must be reviewed periodically, and students should be reminded of them at the beginning of each activity.
Spills are handled on a case-by-case basis and are cleaned up with whatever materials happen to be on hand.	Have the appropriate equipment and materials available for cleaning up; replace it before expiration dates. Make sure students know to alert you to spilled chemicals, blood, and broken glass.
Work habits and environment	
Safety wear is only used for activities involving chemicals or hot plates.	Aprons and goggles should be worn in the lab at all times. Long hair, loose clothing, and loose jewelry should be secured.

HOLT PHYSICS Safety in the Physics Laboratory, *continued*

Identified safety risk	Preventative control
There is no dress code established for the laboratory; students are allowed to wear sandals or open-toed shoes.	Open-toed shoes should never be worn in the laboratory. Do not allow any footwear in the lab that does not cover feet completely.
Students are required to wear safety gear but teachers and visitors are not.	Always wear safety gear in the lab. Keep extra equipment on hand for visitors.
Safety is emphasized at the beginning of the term but is not mentioned later in the year.	Safety must be the first priority in all lab work. Students should be warned of risks and instructed in emergency procedures for each activity.
There is no assessment of students' knowledge and attitudes regarding safety.	Conduct frequent safety quizzes. Only students with perfect scores should be allowed to work in the lab.
Safety inspections are conducted irregularly and are not documented. Teachers and administrators are unaware of what documentation will be necessary in case of a lawsuit.	Safety reviews should be frequent and regular. All reviews should be documented, and improvements must be implemented immediately. Contact legal counsel for your district to make sure you will be protected in case of a lawsuit.

HOLT PHYSICS A Note on Using Electrical Meters

Several of the activities in this booklet require students to use multimeters or electrical meters to measure current, potential difference (voltage), and resistance. Students should be taught the correct procedure for using the meters in your classroom. To use multimeters to measure current, potential difference, and resistance, use the following setup procedure:

Current: On the front of the multimeter, set the range switch pointer to DC A to read dc amperes. Set the pointer to the 200 mA marker. Use a piece of tape to label this meter *A*. Make sure connections are made to the mA and COM sockets.

Potential difference (voltage): On the front of the multimeter, set the range switch pointer to DC V to read dc volts. Set the pointer to the 20 V marker. Use a piece of tape to label this meter *V*. Make sure connections are made to the V Ω and COM sockets.

Resistance: On the front of the multimeter, set the range switch pointer to Ω to read ohms. Set the pointer to the appropriate marker. Use a piece of tape to label this meter Ω. Make sure connections are made to the sockets V Ω and COM sockets.

Always make sure voltage meters are connected in parallel and current meters are connected in series. When checking students' circuits, always make sure the positive and negative leads are connected to the correct terminals of the meters.

HOLT PHYSICS Laboratory Experiments Materials List

Description	Quantity per group	Sargent-Welch Item Number	Laboratory Exercise Discovery	Laboratory Exercise Invention
Aluminum foil, lab grade	1/class	WLS610-A	17, 21	22
Balance, 400 g × 0.1 g	1/class	WLS2647-20A	7, 10	4
Balance, portable standard, 2000 g	1/class	WLS2646-59	5	
Balance, triple beam, with mass	1/class	WLS3455-02	5	
Ball, solid steel, 20 mm diam.	1	WLS4481-E	2	3
Balloon, round rubber, 13 × 7.5 cm	2/class	WLS71824-05	17	
Balls, steel, drilled, 19 mm	2	CP31450-01	13	
Battery, 6 V dc general purpose	1	WLS30848-30		20
Battery, AA alkaline 1.5 V	2	WLS30841-10		2
Battery, D carbon zinc 1.5 V	6	WLS30840-10	19, 20, 22	19, 20, 22
Battery, dry cell 1.5 V dc	3	WLS30844		20
Battery holder, double D-cell	1	WL2441-01	22	19, 22
Battery holder, single D-cell	6	WL2441A	19, 20	20
Beaker, low form Pyrex, 400 mL	1	WLS4675-L	4	
Beaker, low form Pyrex, 600 mL	2	WLS4675-M	7, 10	
Block with hook, for friction testing	1	WL0977		4
Bottle & cap, glass, 125 mL	1	WLS8240-05CA	13	
CBL™ (Calculator-Based Laboratory)	1	WLS13270		10
Capacitor, 1 F	1	CP32248-50	20	20
Carbon paper, replacement	1/class	WL0852C		3
Chart, eye test	1	WL3539A	14	
Clamp, parallel, 1.3 cm	1/class	CP12242-01		5
Clamp, parallel, 1.9 cm	1/class	CP12242-02		5
Clamp, right-angle, 1.3 cm	3	CP12241-01	5, 8, 13	2, 3, 5
Clamp, right-angle V-groove table	1/class	WLS78430-10		5
Clamp, suspension	1	WLS19501	8, 12	5, 12
Clamp, symmetrical, with holder	1	WLS18975		14, 15
Clamp, V-jaw	2	WL4901		14
Clay, modeling, 454 g	3/class	WL6852	8, 15	3, 21
Compass, magnetic, 16 mm	1/class	CP78430-02	21, 22	
Compass, pocket-sized	1	CP78430-03	21	
Constant motion machine	1	WL0849J	2, 5	
Copper shot, lab grade, 2.5 kg	1/class	WLC3604V	10	
Cord, black nylon pulley, 45 m roll	1/class	CP88066-00	4, 5, 8, 12, 13	5, 21
Cord, thick white braided, 45 m roll	1/class	CP24493-50		21
Cord with alligator clips	9	WLS31121-25B	19, 20, 22	20, 22
Crimper cutter, multipurpose	2/class	WL0195	22	19
Cups, plastic, clear, 300 mL, pkg/50	1/class	CP23145-00	17, 21	
Cups, plastic-foam, 177 mL, pkg/50	1/class	WL8314L	17	17
Disposable wipes, 13 cm × 22 cm, pkg	1/class	WLS19812-A	4	
Dropper, glass medicine, 2 mL	1	WLS69695	15	
Dropper pipet, graduated, 5 mL, pkg/500	1/class	WLS69684-40B		1
Dynamics carts set	1	CP72700-84	4	
Erlenmeyer flask, 1000 mL	1	WLS34107-KE		10

HOLT PHYSICS Laboratory Experiments Materials List

Description	Quantity per group	Sargent-Welch Item Number	Laboratory Exercise Discovery	Laboratory Exercise Invention
Flashlight, 21 cm	1	WLS44220	15	14
Glue, 236 mL tube	1	WLS14935		8
Glycerin (Glycerol), 99.5%, 500 mL	1/class	WLC3841E		1
Graduated cylinder, 500 mL	1	WLS24638-17H		10
Graph paper, 100 sheets	1/class	WLS65181-20	2, 21, 22	
Hammer, soft rubber	1	WL3252	13	
Hot plate	1	WLS41058-70		10
Inclined plane, wooden	1	CP75845-00	5	2
Iron filings, in shaker	1	WL1848	21	
Lamp receptacle on base, infrared	1	CP84182-00		10
Lamp receptacle, miniature, plastic	1/class	CP33008-00	19	
Lamp, infrared 250 W/120 V	1	CP16587-00		10
Lamp, straight filament, and filters	1	CP32944-00		15
Lampboard, five-socket	1	CP32146-01		22
Lampboard, three-socket	1	CP32145-01	20	20
Lens, double concave, 3.75 cm, $f = 5$ cm	1	WL3424	15	
Lens, double convex, 3.75 cm, $f = 10$ cm	1	WL3400	15	14
Lens, double convex, 5 cm, $f = 100$ cm	1	WL3414A		14
Lens, double convex, 3.75 cm, $f = 15$ cm	1	WL3404		15
Lens, double convex, 3.75 cm, $f = 30$ cm	1	WL3409		14
Light bulb, clear 1.3 V, 0.3 A, pkg/10	4/class	CP33001-00		20
Light bulb, clear 2.3 V, 0.3 A, pkg/10	6/class	CP60033-01	20	20, 22
Light bulb, clear 6.3 V, 0.3 A, pkg/10	4/class	CP33002-00	19	20
Magnet set, steel bar, 170 mm × 21 mm × 11 mm	1	WLS44375-40	21	
Magnet, cylindrical, Alnico 1, pair	2	CP78291-01		21
Magnets, neodymium, set of 2	1	CP32209-00		21
Magnets, ring, pkg/16	6/class	WLS44377-30		21
Magnets, replacement set of 3	2	CP32970-00	22	
Magnifier	1	WL8068		15
Marker set, dry erase, pkg/4	1/class	WLS65724-10A		5
Mass hanger, 1300 g capacity	1	WLS4320-30		12
Mass hanger, 500 g capacity	1	CP09611-00	8	5
Mass set, hooked, 1000 g × 10 g	1	WLS4322-11	5	
Mass set, slotted	1	CP33451-00		4
Mass set, slotted, 500 g × 10 g	1	WLS4320-12	8	4, 5, 12, 21
Mass, slotted, 500 g	1	WLS4320-20H		12
Mass, slotted, 1 kg	3	WLS4321-20B	4	
Meter stick, plain wood, 1 meter	1	WLS44685	throughout	throughout
Meter stick, plain wood, 1/2 meter	1	WLS44685-20	8	
Mirror, concave and convex	1	CP85425-00	14	
Mirrors, front surface, 10 cm × 10 cm	1	CP32923-00		14
Mirrors, plane glass, 10 cm × 15 cm	1	WL3512	14	
Mirror support, pkg-6	4/class	WL3514A	14	
Motor, electric 3 V dc	1	WL2454C		2

HOLT PHYSICS Laboratory Experiments Materials List

Description	Quantity per group	Sargent-Welch Item Number	Laboratory Exercise Discovery	Laboratory Exercise Invention
Multitester, digital	2	WLS30712-53	19	19
Pad, silk	1	WL1935	17	
Pad, wool felt	2	WL1937	17	17, 19
Permanent markers, black, pkg/12	1	WLS65723-A	8	
Photogate timing system	1	CP36802-00		3
Plastic straws, colored, 20 cm	1/class	WL5847K	15	1, 2, 21, 22
Plumb bob, 140 g	1	WLS70200		3
Protractors, plain edge	1	WLS44785-20	12–15	3
Pulley, adjustable table clamp	1	CP75665-03	5	
Rectangular cell	1	CP45951-00	15	
Resistor, 10 ohm, 10 W, pkg/5	2/class	CP32995-20		20
Resistor, 68 ohm, 0.5 W, pkg/10	1/class	CP32995-02		20
Resistor, 150 ohm, 0.5 W, pkg/10	1/class	CP32995-04		20
Resistor, 470 ohm, 0.5 W, pkg/10	1	CP32995-06	19	20
Resistor, 2000 ohm, 0.5 W, pkg/10	1/class	CP32995-08	19	
Rod, flint glass, solid	1	WL1926	17	
Rod, lattice, 1.3 cm × 30 cm	1	WLS78454-D	8	3
Rod, threaded, 0.8 cm × 46 cm	2	WLS78311-20A	5, 13	2
Rod, threaded, 1.3 cm × 91 cm	2/class	WLS78311-20D		5
Rubber cement, 121 mL	1/class	WLS14985-20	17	17
Ruler, metric, plastic, 30 cm, pkg/12	1	WLS44675-20	1, 14, 17, 21, 22	1, 3, 12
Second law of motion apparatus	1	WL0877		3
Shears, 11.4 cm	1	WLS74367-A	21	2, 17, 22
Spring and mass holder, replacement	1	CP73955-00		12
Spring scale, pull-type, 2.5 N	1	WLS3679-A	5	4
Spring scale, pull-type, 20 N	1	WLS3679-D	8	
Spring scale, pull-type, 5 N	1	WLS3679-B	5	4
Spring, 5 m stretched length	1	WL3339	12	
Stopwatch, electronic	1	WLA5615	2, 5, 7, 10, 12	2, 10, 12, 19
Support ring, extension, 7.5 cm I.D.	1	WLS73055-B		3, 5
Support ring w/clamp, 11.1 cm I.D.	1	WLS73055-D		3
Support stand with 91 cm rod	2	WLS78306-D	5, 8, 12, 13	throughout
Switch, contact key	1	CP33638-00	19	22
Switch, single pole-double throw	2	WLS31155-B		20
Switch, single pole-single throw	1	WLS31155-A		20
T-pins, 3 cm, 400/box	1/class	WLS723-13A	14	
Tape, black electrical, 19 mm × 21 m, roll	1	WLS79500	15, 22	22
Tape, cellophane, 19 mm × 6.25 m, roll	1	WLS44178-10	13	21
Tape, masking, 13 mm × 55 m, roll	1	WLS44182-80	throughout	throughout
Tape, Teflon™ sealing, 13 mm × 7.6 m, roll	1/class	WLS77345-50		13, 21
Thermometer, red liquid, −20°C to 110°C	2	WLS80035-10B	10	10, 19
TI-83 graphing calculator	1	WLS13283-P		10
TI-Graph Link	1/class	WLS13280		10
Toothpicks, flat wooden, pkg/750	1/class	WL9088-31	17	8

HOLT PHYSICS Laboratory Experiments Materials List

Description	Quantity per group	Sargent-Welch Item Number	Laboratory Exercise Discovery	Laboratory Exercise Invention
Tuning fork set, differential	1	WL3246	13	
Two-can radiation kit	1	WL1732		10
Weighing dishes, disposable	1/class	WLS25725-D	17	
Wire, black, 22 AWG, 100 ft	1/class	WLS85135-50A	22	
Wire, Chromel 24 AWG, 5.1 m	1/class	WLS85125-F		19
Wire, Chromel 26 AWG, 8.2 m	1/class	WLS85125-G		19
Wire, Chromel 28 AWG, 13 m	1/class	WLS85125-H		19
Wire, copper 454 g spool, 18 AWG	1/class	WLS85135-KC		19
Wire, copper enameled, 26 AWG, 454 g	1/class	WLS85135-40J	22	
Wire, copper, 100 g spool, 18 AWG	1/class	WLS85135-C		22
Wooden dowel, 6.5 cm × 90 cm	1	CP23481-00	8	
Wrench, adjustable 25 cm	1	CP88600-46	8	

Many of the experiments in this booklet require materials that should be obtained locally:

- apples
- assorted friction materials
- cans
- cardboard boxes
- coins
- combs, plastic
- construction paper
- cord, fishing-line
- cylindrical objects
- detergent
- disposable cameras
- dolls
- drinking cups and lids
- eggs
- electrical wire, stranded
- erasers
- film canisters and lids
- foam rubber sheet
- funnels
- headphone plugs
- hobby knives
- hot glue guns
- index cards
- light bulbs, 100 W
- magnet wire
- masking tape, black
- matte acetate
- milk
- mounting board
- Mylar film
- nuts, bolts, and screws
- opaque bowls
- paint and brushes
- paper
- paper clips
- pens and pencils
- pie pans
- pipes and pipe fittings
- plastic-foam packing materials
- plates, plastic-foam
- poster board
- roasting pans, aluminum
- rubber bands
- see-through mirror
- skewers
- staples
- stepladder
- stiff card
- tarp, plastic
- thermometer strip, liquid crystal
- tongue depressors
- track, 1/2 in. angle
- transistor radio
- tubing, fine polyethylene
- washers
- wire connectors
- wooden blocks

HOLT PHYSICS Laboratory Experiments Teacher's Edition

Discovery Lab

Pre-Chapter Exploration 1

The Circumference-Diameter Ratio of a Circle

OBJECTIVES

Students will

- develop techniques for measuring the circumference and diameter of a cylinder.
- use data to construct a graph.
- determine the slope of a graph.
- analyze error in an experiment.

Planning

Recommended Time

1 lab period

Materials

[for each lab group]

- ✔ cord
- ✔ masking tape
- ✔ meterstick
- ✔ metric ruler, 15 cm
- ✔ pencil
- ✔ several cylindrical objects of varying size: pencils, soup cans, juice cans, stand rods, wooden cylinders, dowels, etc.
- ✔ 2 sheets white paper

Materials Preparation

Each group will need to have access to several cylinders. Cylinders should be in a wide range of sizes. Make sure cylinders are clean and free of sharp or jagged edges. If possible, label all cylinders before the lab. Use masking tape, and identify each cylinder with a unique label. This will allow students to identify their cylinders in the first part of the lab.

Classroom Organization

- This lab may be performed by students working alone or in pairs. Because groups trade measurements in the first part of the lab, there should be an even number of groups.
- The cylinders may be placed in groups of eight or more for every two groups of students, or they may be placed together in a central location. The cylinders should be placed in a box or other container to keep them from rolling onto the floor. Instruct students to return cylinders to containers when not in use.

Techniques to Demonstrate

If you are using graphing calculators or other graphing software, show students how to use the equipment to graph their data.

Checkpoints

Step 1: Some students will have trouble approaching the question and will wait for you to tell them what to do. It may help to present them with two different cylinders. Ask what information they would need to identify one of the cylinders from a written description.

Step 4: Students should "hide" their cylinder among the others and should trade measurements with a group on the other side of the room. If cylinders are placed in groups around the room, groups should trade stations when they trade measurements.

Step 5: If cylinders are already labeled, students can record the label instead of relabeling the cylinders.

HOLT PHYSICS Laboratory Experiments Teacher's Edition continued

Step 6: Some students may need help finding a second method to measure the cylinder. Check any groups that seem to be stuck, and offer hints. Students may wrap string around the cylinder and mark and measure the string, or they may roll the cylinder along a piece of paper and measure the distance from the initial position to the final position.

Step 10: Students may need help finding the best fit line on the graph. Ask students to explain why the line need not include all data points.

Step 11: Some students may need help finding the coordinates of the chosen points. If using graphing calculators or software, make sure students know how to find the values of the points.

Answers To

Analysis

A. Answers will vary, but many students will measure the length, circumference, and diameter or radius. Some students will realize that they only need to measure the length and the circumference.

B. Answers will vary. Answers should be specific and should demonstrate a concern for accuracy and precision.

C. The answer should be "yes." If not, answers should identify possible causes of the discrepancy, such as incomplete or inaccurate measurements.

D. same as C

E. Answers will vary. Students should explain how differences in methods could cause different measurements.

F. Answers will vary. Students should realize that different methods may give slightly different results.

G. Answers will vary but should describe the strengths and weaknesses of the different methods.

H. Answers will vary but may include taking many measurements, having other people confirm the measurements, and using more precise instruments.

I. It is the same.

J. the diameter (or the circumference) and the length

K. the diameter

L. the circumference

M. The graph should be a straight line pointing up and to the right.

N. Answers will vary but should be close to 3.14. Make sure students use the appropriate number of significant figures based on their measurements.

O. Students should realize that using the graph prevents bad data from affecting the results.

Invention Lab

Post-Chapter Activity 1

Bubble Solutions

OBJECTIVES

Students will

- use appropriate lab safety procedures.
- use the scientific method to solve a problem.
- design and implement their own procedure.
- identify dependent and independent variables in an experiment.
- work quickly to take accurate measurements.

Planning

Recommended Time

2 lab periods

Students should have their plan approved before the class begins.

Materials

[for each class]

- ✔ 24 L water
- ✔ 50 mL glycerin
- ✔ 6 large aluminum pans
- ✔ 6 types of dish soap, 120 mL each
- ✔ newspapers

[for each group]

- ✔ 1 m cord
- ✔ 6 plastic drinking straws
- ✔ adhesive tape
- ✔ construction paper templates (see Proposed Procedure)
- ✔ meterstick
- ✔ metric ruler
- ✔ paper towels
- ✔ rubber bands

Materials Preparation

Use six different types of dish soap for this lab, including several national brands and one or two local or store brands. You may also include one sample of automatic-dishwasher or laundry detergent, for added interest. Prepare detergent mixtures at least 24 h before they will be used to allow the glycerin to dissolve. It is convenient to mix the solutions in the storage bottles. Plastic milk jugs and plastic soda bottles work well. Label each mixture with a letter, and record the identity of each letter in your notebook. You will need about 4 L of each solution. For each liter of solution, use 30 mL of detergent, 2 mL of glycerin, and 1 L of water. Mix the water and detergent first, then add the glycerin using a graduated dropper.

Be careful when mixing and storing glycerin and glycerin solutions. Glycerin is combustible when exposed to heat, flames, or strong oxidizers.

At the beginning of class, pour each mixture into a large pan and label the pan with the letter from the bottle. If you will be using the detergent mixtures for two days, cover the pans to prevent the composition of the mixtures from changing due to evaporation.

Classroom Organization

- Set up the mixtures at six stations so students can move from station to station during the lab.
- Set out newspapers and paper towels on the lab tables and floor to aid in cleaning up spilled detergent mixtures.
- If possible, do this lab outdoors.
- **Safety warnings:** The floor will become very slippery when detergent mixtures are spilled or dripped. Make sure students exercise care when moving around the lab. Remind students to clean up all spills immediately.

HOLT PHYSICS Laboratory Experiments Teacher's Edition continued

Techniques to Demonstrate

Based on the plans students present before the lab, you will be able to determine whether they need to see a sample bubble maker for the second part of the lab. You may prepare one according to the design described in the lab and make it available for students to look at. You may want to demonstrate using the device to make bubbles, especially if you are concerned about time.

Pre-Lab Discussion

Discuss with students how they will know which mixture makes the biggest bubbles. Ask students what they mean by "size" in this lab. Most students will realize that the size of the bubble is directly related to the radius or diameter of the sphere.

Students should realize that they will need to find the average bubble size for each mixture and that they must be consistent in their measurements.

Tips for Evaluating the Pre-Lab Requirements

Students' plans should include both parts of the lab, the dome bubble test and the free-floating bubble activity. Complete plans will include a materials list, a diagram showing the bubble-making apparatus and a method for measuring the bubbles, and a brief description of the procedure for each part. Plans should also explain how students will analyze data to determine which mixture consistently produces the biggest bubbles.

Proposed Procedure

Part I: Domed Bubble Test

Use a plastic drinking straw to blow a dome bubble in the pan of solution. The bubble will be half-spherical in shape, so that the surface of the solution is the base of the domed bubble. Blow several test bubbles to determine how large the bubble can be. Make the bubbles larger and larger until they burst, and use this method to find the largest size of bubble that will not pop.

There are several methods that can be used to measure the bubbles. Students may use templates made from sheets of construction paper with holes of various diameters cut in them. They may also construct a bubble meter using a meterstick with a crossbar made from a drinking straw attached with rubber bands. The crossbar can be moved up and down to gauge the size of the bubbles. A meterstick can be used with two straws, tape, and rubber bands to make calipers to measure the bubbles. One straw is fixed in place at the end of the meterstick, and the other straw is attached with a rubber band so it can be moved up and down.

Students may come up with other methods.

For each method described above, the easiest way to find the maximum bubble size is to set the gauge to a predetermined size and blow bubbles to fill the gauge. Progressively increase the size of the gauge until bubbles pop before reaching the gauge.

For each mixture, repeat the process of finding the largest possible bubbles. Do several trials for each mixture, and take the average of all trials to find the average size of the domed bubble for each solution.

Part II: Free-floating Bubble Test

Design and construct a bubble maker using two plastic drinking straws and a length of cord. Perform several trials to find the best technique for making large bubbles with the device. For some students or some mixtures, it will be easier to make large bubbles by gently blowing through the device than by pulling it through the air. Students should repeat the exercise until they are able to produce consistent results for several trials.

At the same time, test and develop a method of measuring the bubbles using a meterstick. This method must take into account that the bubbles are fragile, round, and in motion.

The meterstick gauge and meterstick calipers methods described above will both work to measure these bubbles.

Students may come up with other methods.

Do several trials for each mixture, and take the average of all trials to find the average size of the free-floating bubble for each solution.

CHAPTER 1 **T29**

Post-Lab

Tips for Evaluating Patent Application Lab Report

Student lab reports should include diagrams of the apparatus used to create bubbles and detailed diagrams of the method used to measure the bubbles. Diagrams should be labeled and clearly drawn, and there should be a section describing each diagram. Reports should include an analysis of the method and of the data. Students should describe how their method of measurement overcame the problems of measuring the bubbles consistently, and they should analyze any error in their results.

Students should identify which mixture(s) produced the largest bubbles and should explain the data analysis they used to compare results for different mixtures. Although individual results will vary, class results on the whole should indicate that one or two of the bubble mixtures produced the largest bubbles.

Additional Notes

HOLT PHYSICS *Laboratory Experiments Teacher's Edition*

Discovery Lab

Pre-Chapter Exploration 2

Motion

OBJECTIVES

Students will

- observe objects moving at a constant speed and objects moving with increasing speed.
- graph the relationships between distance and time for moving objects.
- interpret graphs relating distance and time for moving objects.

Planning

Recommended Time

1 lab period. Alternatively, each section of the lab could be performed separately on different days.

Materials

[for each lab group]

- ✔ battery-operated toy car
- ✔ block, book, or clay
- ✔ graph paper
- ✔ masking tape
- ✔ metal ball
- ✔ meterstick
- ✔ stopwatch
- ✔ grooved track
- ✔ wooden block
- ✔ **Optional:** data analysis and/or graphing software

Materials Preparation

Any slow-moving battery-powered car can be used. Typical speeds for battery-powered toy cars are about 0.35 m/s. Do not use the faster, radio-controlled models. A grooved track is essential for the acceleration experiment because even a small unevenness in a flat track will cause a rolling ball to deviate to one side and usually results in the ball falling off the track. An ideal and inexpensive track can be made from a 1.5 m length of a 2.5 cm extruded aluminum angle, found at any hardware store, propped up by clay to form a v-channel. A steel ball 2.5 cm in diameter will roll well on the track. Place a block or plastic cup at the base of the track to stop the ball when it reaches the bottom. This clarifies when the stopwatch should be stopped and prevents balls from rolling onto the floor and creating a safety hazard.

Classroom Organization

- This lab should be performed by students working in groups of two or three.
- If time permits, have students perform more than one trial for each section.
- **Safety warnings:** If balls roll onto the floor, they will create a safety hazard. All trials should be performed in areas free of obstacles and traffic and where they will not obstruct emergency exits.

Techniques to Demonstrate

If you are using graphing calculators or other graphing software, show students how to use the equipment to graph their data.

Checkpoints

Step 2: The "starting point" and the 0.00 m mark are separate because the car accelerates from rest to a constant velocity. To find the constant velocity, the accelerated motion is disregarded.

Step 9: The track should resemble an inclined plane and should be securely supported by clay, a book, or a block.

Step 12: Students should stop the stopwatch when the ball reaches the block or a plastic cup at the base of the ramp.

Step 13: Students may need help adjusting the track so that the ball reaches the end of the track after 5.0 s. If the ball reaches the end of the ramp before 5.0 s, decrease the angle between the floor and the ramp. If the ball reaches the end of the ramp more than 0.2 s after 5.0 s, increase the angle between the floor and the ramp. Make sure ramps are secured firmly in place for each trial.

Step 15: One student should mark the position of the ball on the ramp while the other student times the movement of the ball. Students clock the longer time interval first so that the ball will not slow down as it crosses over a line of masking tape marking a shorter time interval.

Answers To

Analysis

A. Because the car starts from rest, it speeds up between the starting point and the 0.00 m mark, but it maintains the same speed after the 0.00 m mark. The distance traveled in each time interval is the same.

B. The graph shows a straight diagonal line pointing up and to the right. Make sure students use the appropriate number of significant figures based on their measurements.

C. Answers will vary, but the distance traveled in each time interval should be nearly constant.

D. Answers will vary. Students should base their predictions on the linear trend of the graph by using a ruler to find the point where the line would correspond to the 12.0 s mark on the time axis.

E. Answers will vary, but the graph should be a horizontal line. Some students may realize that this line is horizontal because the change in position was constant in each time interval.

F. Both graphs are linear.

G. The students may have been able to observe that the ball sped up as it traveled. From the graph, students may realize that the distance traveled increased in each time interval.

H. Make sure students use the appropriate number of significant figures based on their measurements. The graph should resemble a parabolic curve.

I. Answers will vary. The distance traveled should increase in each successive time interval.

J. Answers will vary. Students should base their predictions on the parabolic trend of the graph by using a ruler to find the point where the curve would correspond to the 12.0 s mark on the time axis.

K. Answers will vary. The graph should be a straight line pointing up and to the right. Some students may realize that this graph displays constant acceleration of the ball or that the velocity is changing.

L. The ball that sped up has a graph of a parabolic curve, and the car that maintained a constant speed has a linear graph.

Invention Lab

HOLT PHYSICS *Laboratory Experiments Teacher's Edition*

Post-Chapter Activity 2

Race-Car Construction

OBJECTIVES

Students will

- use appropriate lab safety procedures.
- use the scientific method to solve a problem.
- design and implement their procedure.
- construct a model car to meet assigned criteria.
- use concepts in physics to measure the performance of the car.

Planning

Recommended Time

One lab period is necessary to test the car. Students can design and construct the car at home or use one more lab period to design and construct the car. Students should have their plan approved before the class begins.

Materials

[for each lab group]

- ✔ aluminum sheet
- ✔ 2 bamboo skewers
- ✔ drinking straws
- ✔ glue
- ✔ 2 large, wide rubber bands
- ✔ masking tape
- ✔ meterstick
- ✔ 3 plastic film canister lids
- ✔ scissors
- ✔ 4 small rubber bands
- ✔ stopwatch
- ✔ 2 support stands with clamps
- ✔ table clamp
- ✔ 5 tongue depressors
- ✔ inclined plane

Optional

- ✔ 1.5 V–3.0 V dc motor
- ✔ 15 cm insulated wire
- ✔ 2 AA batteries

Materials Preparation

Teachers should specify which motor the class should use to avoid the electric car contest just becoming a question of which motor is largest. Motors can be bought from an electronics store for about $2–$5. This lab was bench tested using the 3 V Mabuchi "Cer-Mag" model RE 280 motor, which is widely available. For the gravity-powered car, a steep incline works well to accelerate the car only if there is a smooth transition between the incline and the floor. A smooth transition can be easily obtained by taping a thin aluminum sheet to the bottom of the incline and to the floor. The type of sheet sold in hardware stores as roof flashing or for air conditioning equipment works well.

Classroom Organization

- This lab may be performed by students working alone or in pairs.
- **Safety warnings:** Students should be especially careful while using sharp objects, as they can cause serious injury. They should wear eye protection and perform this experiment in a clear area. When a sharp tool is not in use, it should always be covered with its protective sheath and kept in a safe place.

CHAPTER 2 **T33**

HOLT PHYSICS Laboratory Experiments Teacher's Edition continued

Techniques to Demonstrate

You may wish to make a sample car of your own in each category to inspire your students. Follow the steps in the Proposed Procedure section.

Pre-Lab Discussion

Discuss with students some of the following issues:

- how the angle of the ramp influences the speed of a nonmotorized car
- how the size of the tires influences a car's speed if it moves at a constant speed
- where friction should be minimized on the car and what materials can be used to decrease friction
- where the force of friction helps the car move faster, and what materials can be used to increase friction
- different ways to design a motorized car (that is, direct drive, belt driven) and how this design would influence the car's speed

For a car to move in a straight path, students should align the center of mass with the drive wheel(s). There are many ways to do this, depending on the design of the car.

Gravity-powered car: mass will not affect the speed, but it might keep it from slowing down as much on the horizontal. However, greater mass increases the normal force, which increases friction.

Car with a motor: there are two common methods to design the car.

Method 1: connect the wheel directly to the motor shaft (as described in the Proposed Procedure section).

Method 2: Wrap a rubber band around the motor shaft that then goes around the wheel axle to power the car.

Tips for Evaluating the Pre-Lab Requirements

Students' plans should include the category they plan to enter, a materials list, a diagram illustrating the design of the car, and the name they have chosen for the car. A procedure should be described for measuring the speed of the car and analyzing the average speed of the car. The direct-drive apparatus is simpler to construct and more reliable than the rubber-band apparatus.

Proposed Procedure

Part I: The Design of the Car

Examples of designs are provided below.

Gravity-powered car: mount and tie a brick to an old roller skate with cord.

Motorized car: cut tongue depressor down to three-fourths its original length. This will serve as the body of the car. Cut one straw in half. Clean the bamboo skewers of loose fibers to reduce friction, and place it inside this straw. Cut the bamboo skewer so that it is 2.5 cm longer than the straw piece. This will serve as an axle of the car. Cut tiny holes directly through the centers of two film canister lids for the rear wheels. Connect a lid to each end of the bamboo skewer, and secure them in place with hot glue. Center the straw perpendicular to the tongue depressor, and hot glue it to one end of the tongue depressor. Mount the motor sideways on the other end of the tongue depressor. The motor shaft should be mounted so that it is parallel to the bamboo skewer at the opposite end. Cut a tiny hole in the middle of the third film canister lid and shove it onto the motor shaft so that it fits tightly. Play around with this lid until it spins evenly on the motor shaft. When this happens, hot glue the lid to the shaft. This will serve as the front drive wheel and the motor of the car. The car should now be able to roll along the floor supported by three wheels, and no parts should drag.

Mount the two AA batteries on top of the tongue depressor using rubber bands. To ensure contact between the batteries and the motor, place a large, wide rubber band end to end around both batteries. This keeps the batteries firmly pressed together and holds the bare ends of the motor wire against the battery terminals. The car will run in a straighter line if the batteries hang over the edge of the tongue depressor on the side opposite the motor.

Tightly mount rubber bands to serve as tires on the wheel perimeters for added traction. Connect wires from the batteries to the motor and you are ready to race. Thread beads through the bamboo skewer axle to help guide it and reduce its friction.

A sample design uses 15 cm wooden plant labeling sticks rather than tongue depressors. The key to having the car run straight is to make sure that the line of thrust of the drive wheel passes through the center of mass of the car. One disadvantage of the direct-drive method is that it places one of the largest masses on the car, the motor, off the line of thrust. This can be balanced by placing the other large mass, the battery pack, on the other side of thrust on an outrigger. For sample data, the motor had a mass of 46 g and the batteries had a mass of 48 g. The rest of the sample car massed 24 g. Using this type of assembly, the car is started by twisting the free ends of the wires together to close the circuit.

Part II: Measuring the Car's Speed

Use tape to mark a starting line at 0.00 m and a finish line at 1.00 m. The stopwatch should be started at the 0.00 m mark and stopped at the 1.00 m mark. Gravity-powered cars should roll down an inclined plane at the steepest angle possible without causing the car to tumble. The 0.00 m mark should be made at the base of the inclined plane and a distance of 1.00 m should be measured from this mark. Motorized cars should follow steps 1–3 in the Chapter 2 Discovery Lab. A distance of 1.00 m should be measured from the 0.00 m mark.

Post-Lab

Tips for Evaluating Patent Application Lab Report

Student lab reports should include clearly drawn and labeled diagrams of the car and the method used to measure the average speed of the car over 1.00 m for three trials. There should be a section describing each diagram and explaining why certain features of the car's design were chosen. Reports should include a detailed procedure and the data, and they should clearly indicate how students calculated the average speed of the car.

Additional Notes

Discovery Lab

Pre-Chapter Exploration 3

Vector Treasure Hunt

OBJECTIVES

Students will

- create a series of directions to lead to a specific object.
- follow directions to locate a specific object.
- develop standard notation for writing direction symbols.
- generate a scale map.

Planning

Recommended time

1 lab period

For a 2-period lab, have students perform the first section one day and the rest of the lab the next.

Materials

[for each lab group]

✔ meterstick or trundle wheel
✔ 16 index cards

Materials Preparation

Students may use metersticks or trundle wheels to measure the distances. A trundle wheel has a circumference of 1 m and can be used to measure distances while walking.

The most important preparation is to define the boundaries of the area students may use. Check with your administration for specific issues relating to student movement around campus. If outside, keep paths away from traffic flow, school shop areas, compressed gas storage areas, and utility entry points. If inside, keep paths away from storage areas for hazardous materials such as chemicals or gas, prep rooms, shop areas, and custodial or utility closets.

Select a starting point and define north. You may use a compass to find north or simply choose a convenient direction.

Classroom Organization

- Students may perform this lab alone or in groups of two or more students.
- Student groups will be switching cards. You may have an even number of groups and do a direct swap or simply make sure each group is given another group's cards in the second part.
- Encourage students to think of the lab as a treasure hunt.
- **Safety warnings:** The safety issues in this lab depend primarily on where students will be working. Make sure students stay within the specified boundaries, and do not allow any disruptive behavior.

Checkpoints

Step 2: If students are counting paces as a measurement, encourage them to take turns pacing out the distance. This will help remind them to convert paces to meters.

Step 3: Some students will be tempted to use degrees to describe direction or to choose directions between specified directions. Unless you wish to modify the lab to include these options, this should be discouraged.

Step 4: Encourage students to be creative in describing the path. Students will develop an understanding of vectors and two-dimensional motion by using a wide range of directions to describe straight-line motion.

HOLT PHYSICS *Laboratory Experiments Teacher's Edition continued*

Step 6: Before handing a pack of cards to a group, shuffle them dramatically. Some students will realize that this is not a problem, but some will be convinced that they will not be able to find the object if the directions are out of order.

Step 7: Some students will add all the distances in each direction and find the object by following the resultant. Others will simply begin following the cards one at a time. Students may need help dealing with obstacles such as walls.

Step 11: If possible, students should work on graph paper or a computer to make the map.

Answers To:
Analysis

A. Answers will vary, based on the object selected and the method used to describe its location.

B. Answers will vary, but most will be longer. Students may realize that the straight-line path can be found by adding distances or by drawing a map and connecting the points.

C. Answers will vary.

D. Answers will vary. Students should realize that using standard notation will allow others to find the object.

E. Answers will vary. Some students may believe that the directions must be followed in a specific order. Other students may realize that the order doesn't matter.

F. Students should realize that it does not matter what order the directions are given in.

G. Answers will vary. Students should realize that the cards identify the same object no matter what order they are in, so they could never be sure they were in original order.

H. Answers will vary.

I. Answers will vary. Some students may have noticed that they could simply add the distances in each direction.

J. Answers will vary.

K. Answers will vary. Differences should be explained by encountering obstacles such as walls or by following a more direct path than described by the cards.

L. Students should realize that shuffling the cards had no affect on the positions of the starting point and the object and that the path described between them was probably not the same as the original description.

M. Answers will vary. Students may realize that they could simply add the distances in each direction and that this would work for any set of directions.

HOLT PHYSICS Laboratory Experiments Teacher's Edition

Invention Lab

Post-Chapter Activity **3**

The Path of a Human Cannonball

OBJECTIVES

Students will

- use appropriate lab safety procedures.
- use the scientific method to solve a problem.
- design and implement their own procedure.
- use kinematic equations to solve a projectile-motion problem.

Planning

Recommended time

1 lab period

Students should have their plan approved before the class begins.

Materials

[for each lab group]

- ✔ adhesive tape
- ✔ ball, 19 mm, steel or plastic
- ✔ 2 support stands with rings
- ✔ ball launcher, such as "Motion in Two Dimensions Apparatus"
- ✔ carbon paper
- ✔ cardboard box
- ✔ clay
- ✔ cloth towel
- ✔ large extension support ring with clamp
- ✔ lattice rod, 30 cm long
- ✔ masking tape
- ✔ meterstick
- ✔ metric ruler
- ✔ photogate timing system
- ✔ plumb bob and line
- ✔ protractor
- ✔ small extension support ring
- ✔ stiff card, 20 cm × 20 cm
- ✔ stopwatch
- ✔ white paper
- ✔ **Optional:** data analysis and graphing software

Materials Preparation

Make sure ball launchers are in working order and that they produce consistent results by launching at approximately the same speed every time.

Classroom Organization

- Lab groups should have at least two students and no more than four.
- Each group needs a level work surface and a work space of at least 2.0 m square.
- **Safety warnings:** Eye protection should be worn at all times. Projectiles can cause serious eye damage. Ball launchers should always be aimed away from people. Balls rolling on the floor present a safety hazard; use padded boxes to catch the balls.

Techniques to Demonstrate

Show students how to use the photogates to measure the speed of the ball. The photogate will record the time interval between when the ball triggers the photogate and when the ball clears the photogate. Dividing the diameter of the ball by this time interval will give the speed of the ball. However, the photogate will not trigger or clear exactly at the edge of the ball. To accurately measure the speed of the ball through the photogate, students should determine the diameter of the ball as measured by the photogate.

For each photogate and ball, perform the following calibration experiment. Place a meterstick on edge on the lab table. Use a piece of clay to adhere the ball to the top edge of the meterstick. Place the photogate so that it straddles the meterstick, with its beam at exactly the same height as the center of the ball. Slowly push the meterstick so that the ball moves through the photogate. When the gate triggers, place a metric ruler flat on the table next to the meterstick with the zero points aligned. Hold the metric ruler in place, and move the meterstick farther until the photogate just clears. Read the distance the meterstick has moved since the metric ruler was placed. This is the perceived diameter of the ball and should be used in place of the ball's actual diameter to calculate the ball's velocity from the time measured by the photogate. For sample data, a ball with 19 mm diameter was seen as having a 17 mm diameter by the photogate.

Throughout the lab, the photogate beam must be aligned with the center of the ball.

Pre-Lab Discussion

Ask students to challenge themselves as they prepare their plans. They should try to develop a plan that will work on the first try in the lab. Discuss the factors students will need to consider in their plans.

Tips for Evaluating the Pre-Lab Requirements

Students' plans should address both parts of the problem, launching to a horizontal net and to a net below the platform. Complete plans will include a materials list; diagrams showing the placement of the launcher, the net, and the ring; and a brief description of the procedure for each part. Plans should also explain how students will determine where to place each item. Plans should include a set of equations that will allow students to predict the maximum vertical displacement and the maximum horizontal displacement given the speed of the ball.

Proposed Procedure

Set up the ball launcher at a 20° angle. Use the photogate to measure the initial speed of the ball.

Perform several trials, and take the average. Use this value as the speed in all equations.

To find the values for the displacements, use the equations given in Chapter 3:

1. $\Delta y = v_i(\sin \theta) \Delta t - \frac{1}{2}g(\Delta t)^2$
2. $\Delta x = v_i(\cos \theta) \Delta t$

First, use the equation for the final velocity to find the time interval from launch to the highest point, where the vertical speed is zero.

$$v_{y,f} = 0 = v_i(\sin \theta) - g\Delta t$$
$$\Delta t = \frac{v_i(\sin \theta)}{g}$$

Solve for Δt using the measured values for the velocity and the angle. Use this value for Δt in the first equation above to find Δy, the highest point reached by the ball. This gives the position to place the ring.

For the first act, the net will be placed at the same level as the cannon. Multiply the value for Δt found above by 2. This is the time interval from the launcher to the net. Use this value for Δt to solve the second equation above for Δx. This gives the position to place the net.

For the second act, the net will be placed far below the cannon. Leaving the cannon in the same position, place the net and measure the vertical distance between them. Because the cannon is in the same position, the highest point will be the same as for the previous example. Because the speed in the vertical direction is zero at this point, we can use the equation for the horizontal motion of a projectile.

First, find the time interval using the following equation:
$$\Delta y = -\frac{1}{2}g(\Delta t)^2$$
where Δy is the vertical distance from the highest point to the net.
$$\Delta t = \sqrt{\frac{2\Delta y}{-g}}$$

Use this time interval to solve the equation for Δx:
$$\Delta x = v_x \Delta t = v_i(\cos \theta) \Delta t.$$

This value for Δx is the horizontal distance between the highest point and the net. Use this to determine where to place the net.

Repeat for different angles.

HOLT PHYSICS Laboratory Experiments Teacher's Edition continued

In the lab, set up the apparatus securely. Clamp the ball launcher to a support stand. Use the second support stand and the large extension support ring as the net. Cover the large support ring with the stiff card. Secure the card with tape. Cover the card with a small piece of white paper, and tape the paper in place. Tape a small piece of carbon paper, carbon side down, on top of the white paper. Secure the ring at the desired height for the landing pad. Place a padded cardboard box near the landing pad support stand to catch the ball when it bounces. Place the launcher at the correct angle, and place the net in the determined position for the first act. Securely clamp a support stand and ring so that the center of the ring is at the determined position.

When the area is clear of obstacles, launch the ball. The ball should go through the hoop, land on the paper, and bounce into the box.

Repeat for the second act setup. Adjust the position of the landing pad and clamp so that they are held securely in place.

Post-Lab

Tips for Evaluating Patent Application Lab Report

Student lab reports should include diagrams of the setups for both acts. Diagrams should be labeled and clearly drawn, and there should be a section describing each diagram. Reports should include a description of the method used to determine the positions of the net and the hoop and should analyze the results. If the results were significantly different from the predictions, the report should contain an analysis of the causes of the discrepancy.

Reports should contain an organized explanation of the equations used to find the horizontal and vertical displacements.

Additional Notes

HOLT PHYSICS *Laboratory Experiments Teacher's Edition*

Discovery Lab

Pre-Chapter Exploration 4

Discovering Newton's Laws

OBJECTIVES

Students will

- explore the factors that cause a change in the motion of an object.
- determine the effect of mass on an object's acceleration.
- investigate the acceleration of two objects acting on one another.

Planning

Recommended Time

1 lab period

Alternatively, each section of the lab could be performed separately on different days.

Materials

[for each lab group]

- ✔ 3 masses, 1 kg each
- ✔ beaker
- ✔ coin, such as a quarter
- ✔ cord
- ✔ dynamics cart
- ✔ dynamics cart with spring mechanism
- ✔ human-figure toy or doll
- ✔ index card
- ✔ paper towels
- ✔ rubber band
- ✔ set of masses, 20 g–100 g
- ✔ stopwatch
- ✔ air track or dynamics track with pulley and car
- ✔ water

Materials Preparation

For this activity, either an air track or a dynamics track will work well. If this lab will be performed in stations around the room, set up the apparatus before class.

Classroom Organization

- This lab may be performed in groups of two or more.
- The first two parts of the lab may be presented as demonstrations for the entire class.
- It may be easiest to give each group materials for the first, second, and fourth sections of the lab and to have the groups take turns at the air track or dynamics track for the third part of the lab.
- **Safety warnings:** Specify areas where students are permitted to work; this activity can damage furniture and walls. Do not allow students to drag the car across the air track when the air is off. Do not allow students to toss coins.

Techniques to Demonstrate

Demonstrate the proper way to use the air track or dynamics track.

Show students how to release the spring mechanism on the dynamics carts without affecting the motion of the carts.

Show students how to thread a pulley.

Checkpoints

Step 3: If the coin does not fall into the beaker, students may be pulling too slowly or at an angle.

HOLT PHYSICS Laboratory Experiments Teacher's Edition continued

Step 6: Remind students to exercise care and caution in the laboratory.

Step 10: If using an air track, make sure students hold the car securely in place until the air is turned on. Moving the car on the track can damage the surface of the track.

Step 11: The cord should be long enough for the mass to reach the floor before the car reaches the end of the track.

Steps 17–21: If students are working on lab tables, make sure the carts do not fall off the table. You may want to clamp wooden blocks to the ends of the tables to serve as bumpers to stop the carts.

Answers To
Analysis

A. The coin drops into the beaker of water.

B. Answers will vary. Some students will think that the coin should have moved with the card; others will expect it to fall; and some may expect it to fly off.

C. The coin remains on the card as the card is pulled away.

D. The doll moved forward and hit the wall.

E. The doll stayed in place in the cart.

F. The rubber band kept the doll in the cart. When the doll moved forward, the rubber band pulled the doll back.

G. The coin started at rest, and it stayed in the same horizontal position even when the card moved away. The unrestrained doll was initially moving, and it continued moving even when the cart stopped. Both objects continued doing what they were originally doing.

H. The falling mass and the cord pull the car.

I. Answers will vary. Students should be able to determine that the cart accelerated, because it was moving faster at the end of its motion.

J. The larger the falling mass, the greater the car's acceleration.

K. Both carts move; they move away from each other in opposite directions.

L. With equal masses, both carts accelerate from rest to move with the same velocity. When one cart has 1 kg mass added, the cart with the mass moves more slowly. When one cart has 2 kg mass added, the cart with the mass moves much more slowly. When one cart has 2 kg mass added and the other has 1 kg mass added, the cart with more mass moves more slowly.

M. The greater the mass, the smaller the acceleration.

HOLT PHYSICS *Laboratory Experiments Teacher's Edition*

Invention Lab

Post-Chapter Activity 4

Friction: Testing Materials

OBJECTIVES

Students will

- use appropriate lab safety procedures.
- design and implement their own procedure.
- determine the coefficients of static and kinetic friction for a variety of surfaces.
- classify materials according to coefficients of friction.
- compare the coefficients of static friction to the coefficients of kinetic friction.

Planning

Recommended Time

1 lab period

Students should have their plan approved before the class begins.

Materials

[for each class]

✔ large box of unidentified surface materials that may include carpet, sandpaper, plastic wrap, felt, wallpaper samples, paneling, rubber, mouse pads, fax paper, bricks, ball bearings, etc.

[for each lab group]

✔ 1 sheet corkboard
✔ 1 sheet linoleum
✔ 1 sheet sandpaper
✔ 2 force meters: spring scale, 2.5 N × 0.02 N spring scale, 5.0 N × 0.05 N
✔ balance
✔ masking tape
✔ set of slotted masses
✔ wooden friction block with hook

Materials Preparation

The testing procedure is fairly quick, so it is a good idea to provide a wide array of testing samples. Students should wipe all surfaces clean before taking measurements.

Classroom Organization

- This lab may be performed by students in groups of two or more.
- The box of materials should be located where all groups can access it easily.
- The box of materials should contain some duplicates; there should be enough samples for each group to have two or three at a time.
- **Safety warnings:** Remind students to attach spring scales securely and to make sure the blocks do not fall onto the floor.

Techniques to Demonstrate

Make sure students are familiar with the spring scales. Students should understand that the spring scale measures force.

Pre-Lab Discussion

You may provide some of the following leading questions for students to consider as they prepare their plans.

- Can the coefficient of friction be measured directly? If not, what measurements will you have to make to find the coefficient?
- How can you be sure you are finding the maximum coefficient of static friction? How will it affect your results if you do not record the maximum value?

CHAPTER 4 **T43**

- How will you know when to take the measurements? What conditions must be true for the data to be accurate?

Tips for Evaluating the Pre-Lab Requirements

Students' plans should present a clear explanation of the procedure. Students should realize that the coefficients of friction cannot be measured directly; they must be calculated from measurements for the normal force and the friction force between two objects.

Students must understand that the force of static friction must be measured as the maximum force under which the object does not move.

Students must also understand that the force of kinetic friction must be measured when the object is moving at a constant velocity.

Proposed Procedure

Use the block of wood as the standard, and make all measurements for the block being pulled across other surfaces. Use tape to secure the samples to the tabletop. Find the mass of the block. Use this to find the force of gravity acting on the block. Because the table is horizontal and the block is in equilibrium, the normal force will be equal to and opposite the force of gravity on the block. Use this value in all calculations.

Use the spring scale to pull the block horizontally across the various surfaces. Carefully watch the spring scale to find the maximum value at which the block remains at rest. When the block is moving, record the constant force at which the block moves with constant velocity. If necessary, use the slotted masses to increase the mass of the wooden block to bring the readings into a good range for the spring scale. Record the total mass of the block and masses for each trial.

Use the measured forces to calculate the coefficients of friction using the equations from Chapter 4.

$$\mu_{s,max} = \frac{F_{s,max}}{F_n}$$

$$\mu_k = \frac{F_k}{F_n}$$

Post-Lab

Tips for Evaluating Patent Application Lab Report

Student lab reports should include diagrams of the apparatus used to measure the forces. Diagrams should be labeled and clearly drawn, and there should be a section describing each diagram. Reports should include an analysis of the method used to measure the forces.

Reports should include all data analysis, including calculations. Calculations should be accurate, and results should have the appropriate number of significant figures. Students should realize that the coefficient of friction is a dimensionless value.

Students should classify the materials according to their coefficient of static friction and according to their coefficient of kinetic friction. If students tested the samples against more than one material, they should classify the results for each material separately. Although individual results will vary, class results on the whole should indicate that the order based on the coefficients of static friction is the same as the order based on coefficients of kinetic friction for most materials.

HOLT PHYSICS *Laboratory Experiments Teacher's Edition*

Discovery Lab

Pre-Chapter Exploration 5

Exploring Work and Energy

OBJECTIVES

Students will

- measure the force required to move a mass over a certain distance using different methods.
- compare the force required to move different masses over different time intervals.

Planning

Recommended Time

1 lab period

Materials

[for each lab group]

✔ clamps
✔ cord, 1.00 m
✔ 2 force meters: spring scale, 20 N × 0.5 N
   spring scale, 2.5 N × 0.1 N
✔ inclined plane
✔ masking tape
✔ meterstick
✔ set of hooked masses, including 1 kg and 0.2 kg masses
✔ stopwatch

Materials Preparation

It is essential to have two different spring sensors available. The 20 N spring sensor measures forces when moving the 1 kg mass. The 2.5 N spring sensor is essential to give believable data to the student while doing the second part of the lab.

Most supply stores provide 1.5 V–3.0 V battery-operated vehicles, but they can be expensive. Sometimes they can be bought at garage sales and tag sales. Students can also bring in battery-powered toy cars from home. Wind-up toy cars are acceptable, but they can give inconsistent results.

A path of paper towels taped to the surface of the table provides better traction and allows cars to lift more mass.

Classroom Organization

- Students can perform this lab by themselves or in groups of two or more.
- Because each section of this exercise builds on the previous section, it is more efficient to leave the apparatus in place throughout the lab unless directed to remove it.
- **Safety warnings:** Students should secure all masses and apparatus. Students should perform this experiment in a clear area, out of the way of traffic and emergency exits. Students should handle only one mass at a time to decrease the likelihood of dropping the mass.

Techniques to Demonstrate

Set up an inclined-plane apparatus for the students to use as an example.

Checkpoints

Step 9: A supervised student may step on a sturdy chair to raise the mass more easily to this height.

Step 13: Ideally, the base of the inclined plane should rest against a wall to ensure that the inclined plane does not fall.

Step 14: Make sure that students measure both the vertical distance and the distance along the inclined plane. Students should measure vertical distances to the top of the inclined plane.

HOLT PHYSICS Laboratory Experiments Teacher's Edition continued

Answers To

Analysis

A. No, the 1 kg required more force.

B. No, the same amount of force was constantly applied.

C. the force of friction

D. No, the 1 kg mass required more force

E. No, the same amount of force was constantly applied.

F. the force of gravity

G. The force required to lift the mass is much greater than the force required to drag the mass an equal distance across the table.

H. No, the 1 kg mass required more force.

I. No, the same force was constantly applied.

J. the forces of friction and gravity

K. The angle between the ramp and the floor was less than 90°, so less force was required to lift the mass using the inclined plane.

L. Use a longer ramp and decrease the angle between the ramp and the floor.

Additional Notes

Invention Lab

HOLT PHYSICS *Laboratory Experiments Teacher's Edition*

Post-Chapter Activity **5**

Bungee Jumping: Energy

OBJECTIVES

Students will

- use appropriate lab safety procedures.
- design and implement their own procedure.
- determine the spring constant of a single elastic band and elastic bands in series and in parallel configurations.
- determine the potential energy stored in a stretched elastic-band system.
- calculate gravitational potential energy.
- apply the law of conservation of energy to develop a cord design that will allow students to predict the free-fall distance.

Planning

Recommended Time

One lab period is necessary to test the bungee cord. Students can design and construct the bungee cord at home or use one more lab period to design and construct the bungee cord.

Materials

[for each lab group]

- ✔ braided cord, 1.5 m–2.0 m
- ✔ elastic bands (towing bands), 2 or 3
- ✔ Hooke's law apparatus
  hooked masses, 0.2 kg, 0.25 kg, or 0.5 kg
- ✔ meterstick
- ✔ set of slotted masses
- ✔ slotted mass holder
- ✔ suspension clamp

Materials

[for the launching platform]

- ✔ 2 stand rods, each 1.00 m long
- ✔ extension support ring, 7.5 cm diameter
- ✔ heavy cardboard, 10 cm × 10 cm
- ✔ markers
- ✔ masking tape
- ✔ meterstick
- ✔ parallel clamp
- ✔ pendulum cord
- ✔ poster board
- ✔ right-angle clamp
- ✔ sheet of foam rubber or several large cloths
- ✔ stepladder
- ✔ table clamp

Materials Preparation

Construct a platform that is 3.00 m high by using stand rods and clamps. Secure a stand rod in a table clamp. Secure the other stand rod to this stand rod by using the parallel clamp. At the top of the stand rods, securely clamp the extension support ring. Secure the heavy cardboard at the top to form a platform. Using a meterstick and masking tape, measure and mark off a landing area with a 3.00 m radius on the floor below the platform.

Place a large light-colored piece of poster board upright behind the dive-landing area, and mark prominent horizontal lines on it at 5 cm intervals above the floor. This will make it much easier to measure the lowest point of the mass's fall. Place sheets of foam rubber or several large cloths on the floor to cushion the impact of masses that "crash."

For safety reasons, it is best to use this platform apparatus to test all students' designs. You will securely attach the free end of the students' bungee cord to the platform. The other end of the bungee cord should be securely attached to a mass, and the mass should be completely covered with tape. The tape serves both to secure the mass to the cord and to protect the mass in case it strikes the floor. Attach a pendulum cord securely to the mass, and place the mass on the platform. Stand at least 3 m away from the apparatus, holding the free end of the pendulum cord. When you are ready, make sure no one is standing within 3 m of the apparatus and warn everyone that you are about to begin. Slowly pull the pendulum cord until the mass falls off the platform. Continue to hold onto the cord as the mass falls, and use the cord to control the random bounce after the mass reaches the bottom of the fall.

Classroom Organization

- Students working in groups of two or more can design the bungee cord.
- Provide only one launch site to lessen the likelihood that anyone will get hurt.
- **Safety warnings:** Students should wear eye protection and perform this experiment in a clear area. Attach the masses and cords very securely. Cover the mass entirely with tape. **Do not allow students to use the launching platform. A teacher must perform all launches.** Exercise caution when tying the cord to the dive platform. Be certain that no people or obstacles are within 3.00 m of the drop site. Make sure that students stand far from the landing area.

Techniques to Demonstrate

Follow the directions described in the Materials Preparation section to drop a safely assembled hooked-mass-bungee system from a height different from that which students will be using (or with a mass different from what students will be using). Be certain that all safety precautions have been addressed.

Pre-Lab Discussion

Discuss the measurements needed to calculate the spring's potential energy and the spring constant. Explain the effects of putting springs in series (end to end, as in a chain) or parallel (side by side) on the elastic constant of the elastic band system. (For example, as the bands are hooked together in series, the spring constant is diminished by a factor of the number of bands used. That is, three elastic bands in series have an effective constant of 7 N/m if each separately has a constant of 21 N/m.) Have students compare the effects of air resistance on a person in a real bungee jump and on a mass in a simulated one. Students should decide how to determine the length of cord needed to reach from the platform to the floor. They should realize that this sample calculation does not make allowance for either the height of the diver itself or for a target height above the floor where the diver should stop. As calculated, the end of the rubber band would just touch the floor. The height of the diver and the target height should both be subtracted from the length of cord calculated; the actual length used should be measured in place. As the bands stretch, the upward force on the mass increases, reaching a maximum at the point of greatest stretching, the bottom of the fall. If students know the minimum height their mass reached, they can calculate the length of the bands at that point.

Tips for Evaluating the Pre-Lab Requirements

Students' plans should include a materials list and a diagram illustrating the design of the bungee. A procedure should be described for measuring the elastic band constant. Students should properly apply the conservation of energy. The loss of gravitational potential energy of the falling hooked mass is equal to the elastic potential energy of the bungee cord and is written as follows:

$PE_g = PE_{elastic}$, which means

$mgh = \frac{1}{2}kx^2$

Students must determine the spring constant, k, using the equations above. The length of the bungee cord is determined by accounting for the length, stretch, and configuration of the elastic bands. In calculating the spring constant for *n* bands connected in series, they should not just divide the value for one band by *n* but should use the formula

$1/k = (1/k_1) + (1/k_2) + (1/k_3) + \ldots + (1/k_n)$.

Proposed Procedure

Students should use the Hooke's law apparatus to calibrate each of the two or three bands they will use, using the actual mass value planned for the dive. They should then calculate the total length needed for the cord. With careful work, the masses can be consistently brought to a halt 5 cm–10 cm above the floor. Students should not leave masses hanging from the bands for extended periods (greater than 1 h). Stretching in the bands and tightening of the knots can cause a previously well adjusted mass to crash. Do not allow students to use the tall launching platform. A teacher must perform all launches. Students should perform preliminary tests at their workstations using the Hooke's law apparatus or single support stands. When students have completed their testing and their designs are ready, you may test the designs using the procedure described in the Materials Preparation section. Clear the drop site of all people and obstacles.

Grading: Mount a meterstick 100 cm end down to a ring stand 10 cm above the floor and near the drop site. A design grade is the number on the meterstick to which the bottom of the mass falls.

Post-Lab

Tips for Evaluating Patent Application Lab Report

Student lab reports should include diagrams of the apparatus used to find the spring constant of the elastic bands and diagrams of the finished bungee cord and the launching apparatus. Diagrams should be labeled and clearly drawn, and there should be a section describing each diagram. Reports should include an analysis of the method used to measure the forces on the elastic bands.

Reports should include all data analysis and calculations. Calculations should be accurate, and results should have the appropriate number of significant figures. Students should realize that the spring constant is a dimensionless value.

Reports should describe how the spring constant of each band was used to determine the final design of the cord. Students should give a detailed report of the method and calculations used to predict the length of the fall. Students should also report the actual measurement for the distance between the floor and the mass at the lowest point in the jump. Any discrepancies between the prediction and the result should be examined.

Have students suggest improvements on the bungee-cord design. This might include cutting the elastic bands, using a braided cord to cut the fall short, or making the mass fall closer to the floor.

HOLT PHYSICS Laboratory Experiments Teacher's Edition

Discovery Lab

Pre-Chapter Exploration 7

Circular Motion

OBJECTIVES

Students will

- distinguish between forces required to hold a variety of masses in a horizontal circular path moving at several speeds.
- compare the circular movement of masses with the linear movement of masses.
- discover the relationship between mass, speed, and the force that maintains circular motion.

Planning

Recommended Time

1 lab period (includes time to assemble the cupsling)

Materials

[for each lab group]

- ✔ balance (portable electronic balance, 2000 g cap, or triple-beam balance with weight)
- ✔ 14 oz. plastic drinking cup with three equally spaced holes below the rim
- ✔ 8 rubber bands, ⅛ in. wide
- ✔ plastic bottle marked at the 150 mL level
- ✔ meterstick
- ✔ stopwatch

Materials Preparation

To prevent breakage accidents, use plastic bottles instead of glassware to carry water. Put three equally spaced holes in the rim of each plastic drinking cup by heating a large nail in flame and pressing the nail to the cup or by drilling a half-inch hole in the cup with an electric drill. Remember to handle the nail with a hot mitt while doing this. The class can assemble cupslings during the lab period, or you can assemble them beforehand by following steps 1–4 in the Chapter 7 Discovery Lab. Mark small recycled plastic soda bottles (with a non-water-soluble marker) to measure 150 mL and 300 mL of water so that students can measure outside. Use 2 L bottles or milk jugs to carry larger quantities of water to be measured for each part of the experiment.

Classroom Organization

- This lab should be performed in groups of three or more.
- Because water is used in the lab, it is recommended to go to grassy area outside to avoid a slippery, wet surface.
- **Safety warnings:** Students should wear eye protection and perform this experiment in a clear area away from electrical equipment or outlets. They should always be aware of the motion of the cups so that they can get out of the way if one is released. Warn students not to spin the cup too quickly or in any way other than the horizontal circular path. Replace the rubber bands at least once a year because rubber breaks down over time. If water drips or spills inside the classroom, clean it up immediately because this creates a safety hazard.

Techniques to Demonstrate

If the students assemble the cupslings, lead them through steps 1–4 of the Chapter 7 Discovery Lab to ensure that all cupslings are correctly assembled. Show students how the device works by spinning it yourself. Ask students what happens to the rubber band as you spin the cupsling. Let them see that the rubber band stretches as it exerts force on the cup to keep it on a circular path. Ask them where the cup would go if the band were released. You may want to release an empty cup and let them see that the cup will move in a straight line tangent to the circle in accordance with Newton's first law. Often students will think that the cup will follow a spiral or continue in a circle when released until they see this for themselves.

A good way to estimate the horizontal radius is to lay the meterstick on the floor pointing at the student swinging the cupsling at a measured distance from the student's feet. The observer can then stand at a distance and estimate the point on the meterstick vertically below the cup. A pencil held vertically at arm's length can provide a reference line.

Checkpoints

Step 4: Check to make sure all loops are tightly drawn and the cup is well secured to all bands.

Steps 7, 13, & 19: Make sure students warn nearby groups that they are about to begin their experiment. Students should slowly spin the cupsling, increasing speed only until they reach the slowest speed possible to maintain a horizontal circle. If students spin the cupsling too quickly or swing it into a figure 8, the rubber bands may break.

Steps 8–9, 14–15, & 20–21: Students should take measurements only when the cup is moving in a horizontal circle. One student spins the cupsling while another student times 10 cycles and another student measures the radius of the circle from below. At this point, it is critical that the moving cupsling does not collide with anything or move outside the horizontal circular path because it can cause injury. Check to be sure that students are measuring as accurately as possible. Typical results for the time required to make 10 rotations are: 150 g of water, 11.24 s; 300 g of water, 14.28 s.

Answers To

Analysis

A. Yes.

B. Yes. It is obvious that a force is exerted because the muscles in the arm and hand contract.

C. The student holds the rubber band, which causes the cupsling to change direction from its straight-line motion and move in a circular path.

D. Some students may realize that a change in direction is an acceleration.

E. The cup moves in a straight line tangential to the circle.

F. The rubber band gets longer as the force increases to spin the cupsling in a horizontal circle.

G. Answers will vary. Make sure that students use the appropriate SI units and the correct number of significant figures based on their measurements.

H. The rubber band stretched and became longer as the speed increased.

I. The force on the rubber band increased as the speed increased.

J. Answers will vary. Make sure that students use the appropriate SI units and the correct number of significant figures based on their measurements.

K. The rubber band stretched and became longer as the mass of the cup increased.

L. An increase in the cup's mass increased the force on the rubber band.

M. The inertia of a body moving in a straight line increases as its mass increases.

N. Students should realize that the same thing happens to a body in circular motion, which means that a larger mass has greater inertia.

O. Answers will vary. Make sure that students use the appropriate SI units and the correct number of significant figures based on their measurements.

Discovery Lab

Pre-Chapter Exploration 8

Torque and Center of Mass

OBJECTIVES

Students will

- discover what factors are important for an object to rotate when a force is applied.
- construct a model of the human arm and understand the role of forces and rotation in its function.
- locate the point about which an object that is free to rotate will pivot.

Planning

Recommended Time

One lab period if the model arm is already assembled beforehand and the class is set up in stations (see classroom setup). It will take an additional lab period if the students assemble the human-arm model.

Materials

[for each lab group]

✔ 0.5 m dowel rod with a 1.25 cm diameter
✔ 2 frozen-juice cans and lids
✔ 15 mm bolt, 5 cm long
✔ 15 mm nut
✔ metal washer, 15 mm inner diameter
✔ adjustable wrench or 15 mm socket wrench
✔ apple
✔ clay (enough to fill 1⅓ can)
✔ force meter: spring scale, 5.0 N × 0.5 N
✔ masking tape
✔ masses, 20 g, 50 g, and 100 g
✔ plastic cup with handle
✔ support stand with clamps
✔ table clamp
✔ cord, 1.00 m
✔ wooden plank, 5 cm × 10 cm × 15 cm with a 15 mm hole

Materials Preparation

Wear eye protection and follow appropriate safety procedures. Drill a hole in the wooden planks using the 15 mm drill bit and the electric drill. If this size is unavailable, any size will work as long as the nut, the bolt, and the inner diameter of the washer have the same measurements as the drill bit.

All wooden surfaces should be sanded smooth. Make sure the drilled hole is cleaned out; remove any rough pieces or edges. Use a dowel rod for the model arm because it has a small mass. A 0.5 m ruler can be used in place of the dowel rod. Use any type of clamp that freely rotates. If the station setup is used, some prior assembly of the human-arm model will be necessary (follow steps 6–11 in the Chapter 8 Discovery Lab).

Classroom Organization

- The most efficient and cost-effective setup is to have three stations with 2 to 4 devices at each station, corresponding to each part of the lab (for example, there would be 2 to 4 model arms at one station, and 2 to 4 wrench setups at another). Students can make their observations and then rotate to another station.
- Students should work in groups of two or more.
- **Safety warnings:** Students should attach masses securely because swinging or dropped masses can cause serious injury.

Techniques to Demonstrate

If the students assemble the model arm, lead them through steps 6–11 in the Chapter 8 Discovery Lab.

HOLT PHYSICS Laboratory Experiments Teacher's Edition continued

Checkpoints

Step 1: Make sure the wooden plank is secure in the table clamp and does not move. You may need to show some students how to adjust the wrench to fit snugly around the nut.

Steps 2,3: The terms *head* and *tail* of the wrench are defined in the diagram.

Steps 6–11: Students may need some assistance assembling the model arm.

Step 8: To secure the cord to the dowel, wrap tape securely around the cord and the dowel.

Step 11: Each time students add mass, they will need to move the clamp holding the spring scale up the rod until the dowel is horizontal. A correct value for the torque can only be obtained from measurements taken when the force is normal to the lever arm.

Step 17: You may wish to clamp the support stand to the tabletop to secure it in place so that it does not fall or tip over.

Answers To

Analysis

A. The force is perpendicular to both the wrench and the bolt, and tangent to the direction of motion of the wrench's tail. The student's diagram should show this.

B. no

C. The nut and the wrench move around the center of the bolt.

D. The wrench should be held in the plane 90 degrees from the plane of the bolt.

E. It is easier to loosen the nut with your hand near the tail of the wrench. It is easier to loosen the nut applying the force farther from the bolt.

F. Some students may realize that the rotational force of the nut and the bolt is equally opposed by the force of the wood on the bolt. Students should realize that friction between the wrench and the nut and between the nut and the bolt also causes the bolt to stop turning.

G. The bicep is represented by the force meter in the model.

H. The forearm is represented by the dowel rod in the model.

I. The elbow is represented by the clamp.

J. The rotation in the model occurs about the clamp in the model, which corresponds to the elbow in the human arm.

K. The mass stretches a spring on the force meter and it registers that a force is exerted.

L. Some students may realize that the dowel rod moves when the downward force of the mass on the dowel is greater than the upward force of the force meter.

M. Students should draw a downward arrow where the mass hangs from the dowel, indicating the direction of the force as it is applied on the dowel rod.

N. The force meter produces a force to balance the force due to a hanging mass and prevents the dowel from dropping downward. Students should draw an upward arrow where the force meter meets the dowel, indicating the direction of the force as it is applied on the dowel rod.

O. There is an upward force exerted by the force meter on one end of the dowel rod, and there is a downward force exerted by the mass on the opposite end of the dowel rod.

P. The two forces must be equal in magnitude and opposite in direction for the dowel rod not to move.

Q. no

R. No, for some objects the lines intersected at a point that was not the geometric center of the object.

Invention Lab

HOLT PHYSICS *Laboratory Experiments Teacher's Edition*

Post-Chapter Activity **8**

The Rotating Egg Drop

OBJECTIVES

Students will

- use appropriate lab safety procedures.
- use the scientific method to solve a problem.
- design and implement their procedure.
- identify dependent and independent variables in an experiment.

Planning

Recommended time

One lab period is necessary to test the egg-drop device. Students can design and construct the egg-drop device at home or use one more lab period to design and another lab period to construct the device.

Materials

[for each class]

✔ plastic tarp

[for each lab group]

✔ toothpicks
✔ uncooked egg
✔ glue or quick-drying cement

Materials Preparation

Specify whether students should use round toothpicks or flat toothpicks. Round toothpicks are considerably stronger, but flat toothpicks are easier to use in construction. Do not allow students to use superglue or hot glue. Select a location from which to drop the eggs. Secure the plastic tarp on the ground where the egg-drop devices will land.

Classroom Organization

- This lab may be performed by students working alone or in pairs.
- If weather permits, do this experiment outdoors. The egg-drop devices could be dropped from the top of a football stadium, for example. Check with your administration for specific issues relating to student movement around campus.
- **Safety warnings:** Students should perform this experiment in a clear area and remain at least 5 m away from the drop site during a drop. Do not walk or stand on the tarp.

Techniques to Demonstrate

You can make a sample design or sketch some design ideas on the board to inspire your students. The **Proposed Procedure** section provides some ideas.

Pre-Lab Discussion

Ask students to consider the following questions as they prepare their plans:

- According to the impulse-momentum theorem, what variables can be changed in the design for optimum results?
- How does the center of mass and the air resistance influence the rotational motion and velocity of the egg-drop device?
- How can the device be constructed to absorb the shock upon impact?
- How do different geometrical configurations of the toothpick frame influence the rotational motion of the free-falling egg-drop device?
- Where is the center of mass in the egg-drop device? (Unless more than 1400 toothpicks are used, the center of mass will be located in the egg.)

Tips for Evaluating the Pre-Lab Requirements

From the impulse-momentum theorem $(F\Delta t = \Delta p = m\Delta v)$, students should develop a device that minimizes the force and pressure on the egg. Because the mass is relatively constant, Δt could be large so that F is small or v could be reduced so that F is small. Students should use Newton's laws of motion to describe the free-fall, defining all variables and describing details of the design that influence the magnitude of the variables. They should provide a description of how rotational motion applies to their design. They should comment on the comparison of the egg-drop device to a weathervane and should recognize that the weathervane approach will work well. Plans should include a force diagram illustrating rotational forces and torque on the design of their egg-drop device.

Proposed Procedure

Remember that even if students incorporate good ideas in their design, the design may not work. This is a difficult project. Most devices will entirely enclose the egg to prevent it from breaking upon impact. The egg should be enclosed in a small container of toothpicks that will not break apart. All designs should avoid pointing toothpicks toward the egg because it is difficult to distribute the force evenly on all parts of the egg. Examples of designs are provided below.

Method 1: The center of mass (the egg) is in the center of the device with any symmetrical geometrical configuration. An example of this is putting the egg in the center of a cube or a triangle made of toothpicks. Students using this method should design the device to be well supported on all corners. Strengthen all joints in this design by coating the toothpicks with glue or by building staggered double or triple rows of toothpicks. This will help prevent the joints from breaking on impact.

Method 2: This method uses the principle of the weathervane to orient the device so that the egg lands on a cushion of toothpicks and glue. Build a strong crate around the egg using toothpicks in triangular configurations. The joints are the weakest point in this structure, so strengthen them as much as possible to protect the egg. Below the egg's crate, build a tower with tiers of toothpick frames. These frames should be strong, but the purpose of this tower as a whole is to act as a spring. When the egg lands on this structure, the toothpicks should absorb the force of the collision. The very bottom of the tower should be built with vertical toothpicks that will break when they hit the ground on their ends. Because the structure will rotate around the center of mass (the egg) as it falls and because the tower adds wind resistance and torque to the design, the egg will not land on the tower unless you build a weathervane-type tail on top of the egg. This tail must be rather long and thin, with a wide, flared top. This design is very effective at causing the entire tower to land vertically with the crumple tower hitting the ground first and protecting the egg.

Method 3: This design attempts to make the stopping time large so that the stopping force is small. To do this, pieces of the cage will either have to break apart or bend a great deal. Surrounding this cage should be an outer flimsy cage that will break apart or bend a great deal upon collision. This outer cage should not have toothpicks in triangular configurations because triangular structures are strong. They should incorporate flimsy single toothpick struts that form a cage or a porcupine-type ball. Any design that distorts and cushions the blow should receive some credit.

Method 4: In this design, students try to make a parachute of toothpicks and glue to stop the egg from free-falling. If the parachute works and the egg-drop device falls slowly, the egg can easily survive. The difficult part of this design is that students can use only glue and toothpicks to make the parachute and attach it to the egg drop device. Students can make the fabric of the parachute by drying thin sheets of glue. A fairly strong rope can be made by twisting cords of dried glue together. Students will have to plan ahead to let the glue dry.

HOLT PHYSICS Laboratory Experiments Teacher's Edition continued

Do not allow students to wrap the egg in a sheet of glue.

Because the device will rotate about its center of mass during the free-fall, the student should construct the device so that it will land on some type of cushion.

Post-Lab

Tips for Evaluating Patent Application Lab Report

Student lab reports should include clearly drawn and labeled diagrams of the egg-drop device following the format of a patent application. There should be a section describing each diagram and a complete explanation of why certain features of the design were chosen. Reports should include a materials list and a brief procedure of the drop. They should also indicate whether the design worked and give an analysis of why or why not, with suggestions for improvements in the design.

Additional Notes

Discovery Lab

Pre-Chapter Exploration 10

Temperature and Internal Energy

OBJECTIVES

Students will

- investigate the phenomenon of energy transfer by heat.

Planning

Recommended time

1 or 2 lab periods

Materials

[for each lab group]

- ✔ 600 g copper shot
- ✔ 4 large plastic-foam cups with lids
- ✔ balance
    portable electronic balance, 2000 g cap, or triple-beam balance with weight
- ✔ hot tap water, 700 mL
- ✔ 4 ice cubes of uniform size
- ✔ masking tape
- ✔ paper towels
- ✔ plastic container with a 100 mL mark
- ✔ sharpened pencil
- ✔ stopwatch
- ✔ thermometer
- ✔ weighing paper

Materials Preparation

This lab can be performed with a variety of metals, such as copper, aluminum, or zinc. New zinc pennies work well.

At the end of each trial, students should place wet copper shot in designated containers to be dried and used again. Between classes, dry the metal shot by placing it in a laboratory oven at low heat. Cool the samples before class begins. Metal samples should be placed in large beakers with spatulas for students to measure out.

Classroom Organization

- Students can work alone or in groups of two or more students.
- **Safety warnings:** Metal shot or ice that falls on the floor is a safety hazard. Keep plenty of paper towels on hand. Use a hot mitt and wear safety goggles when drying samples in the lab oven.

Techniques to Demonstrate

Show students how to correctly read a thermometer. Make sure students read the thermometer at eye level to avoid parallax.

You may want to have students use weighing paper to find the mass of the copper shot and the ice cube. Show students how to find the mass of the paper. Because the mass is so small, it is usually best to find the mass of 100 sheets and then divide by 100 to find the average mass of one sheet. Remind students to subtract the mass of the paper from the total to find the mass of the object.

Checkpoints

Steps 2, 5: Taping the set of cups together will ensure that they do not fly apart during shaking and will minimize heat loss.

Steps 6, 8: Taping the outer hole of the cup with masking tape will minimize heat loss.

Step 7: This step helps to ensure an accurate reading of the copper sample. Ideally, the bulb of the thermometer should touch the center of the sample. Instruct students not to force the thermometer into the metal.

HOLT PHYSICS Laboratory Experiments Teacher's Edition continued

Step 8: Using the pencil to block the hole in the inner cup will prevent copper shot from falling into the space betweeen the cups.

Step 9: This will take about 3 min. Before students shake the contents of the calorimeter, make sure the rims are well taped so that the calorimeter does not come apart during the shaking.

Step 14: Students must carefully insert the thermometer until the bulb just touches the copper. Do not allow students to force the thermometer into the copper.

Step 15: Hot tap water can scald. If hot tap water splashes on a student, quickly run cold water over the affected area until a cold compress or ice pack can be applied.

Step 19: Instruct students to drain as much water as possible from the copper shot.

Answers To

Analysis

A. The best way to hold the ice cube is with two fingertips or with two fingernails in order to minimize the energy transferred by heat from the hand to the ice.

B. Yes, the heat from the hand influenced how quickly the ice cube melted.

C. Answers will vary.

D. Answers will vary. Students should realize that the energy introduced to the system by shaking increased the internal energy and the temperature of the copper. Students exerted a force on the copper by shaking the calorimeter. Because the force was exerted on the copper and the copper was displaced from one cup to the other cup, work was done on the copper.

E. Answers will vary.

F. The temperature of the water decreased.

G. The temperature of the copper increased.

H. The final temperature was higher when there was more hot water in the calorimeter.

I. As the ice cube melted, the temperature did not change.

J. The final temperature was higher when there was more hot water in the calorimeter.

Additional Notes

HOLT PHYSICS *Laboratory Experiments Teacher's Edition*

Invention Lab

Post-Chapter Activity 10

Thermal Conduction

OBJECTIVES

Students will

- use appropriate lab safety procedures.
- design and implement their own procedure.
- test the thermal conduction properties of different materials.
- classify materials based on their thermal conduction properties.

Planning

Recommended time

1 or 2 lab periods

Students should have their plan approved before the class begins.

Materials

[for each lab group]

- ✔ 250 W bulb and socket
- ✔ aluminum can
- ✔ CBL system with 2 temperature probes or 2 fractional thermometers
- ✔ ceramic cup
- ✔ connecting wires and plug
- ✔ Erlenmeyer flask, 1000 mL
- ✔ glass jar
- ✔ graduated cylinder, 500 mL
- ✔ hot plate
- ✔ masking tape
- ✔ metal cup, painted black
- ✔ metal cup, painted white
- ✔ meterstick
- ✔ paper cup
- ✔ plastic food-storage containers
- ✔ steel can
- ✔ stopwatch
- ✔ thick soft-foam can holders
- ✔ TI graphing calculator

Materials Preparation

Each lab group should choose materials that are similar in size in order to compare results more directly. Provide additional materials, or have students bring materials to class. A halogen lamp may be substituted for the 250 W bulb, but students should be warned to keep their hands away from the halogen bulb because it may explode if any oil is deposited on it. Because students will need to perform several trials with water at the same initial temperature, it may be convenient to place large containers of water at stations around the classroom so that the water will start at room temperature. Because of the small temperature changes for some samples, it may be best to perform this activity using two temperature probes that give digital readouts, such as the probes used with the CBL system. If thermometers are used, fractional thermometers will give the best results.

Classroom Organization

- This lab may be performed by groups of two or more students.
- Net measurement time for one set of heating and cooling experiments is 25 min. To optimize time, all student groups should have two temperature probes or thermometers. This activity can be performed over two or more periods or it can be performed as a class activity, with each group testing 2–4 materials and comparing results.

CHAPTER 10 **T59**

- Each group needs a level work area that is near an electrical outlet and away from any sources of water.
- **Safety warnings:** Observe standard precautions for working with glass, electricity, and water. Remind students to report all spills and breakage immediately.

Pre-Lab Discussion

Discuss the importance of maintaining controls throughout the experiment. Before students submit their plans, they should realize that it is necessary to keep all materials the same distance from the heat source, to expose the materials to the heat source for the same amount of time, and to choose materials that are approximately the same size.

Tips for Evaluating the Pre-Lab Requirements

Students' plans should present a clear explanation of the procedure. Students should realize that the temperature of each sample will need to be taken at regular intervals and that each sample must be tested under exactly the same conditions.

Proposed Procedure

Choose several containers made from different materials. All containers should be approximately the same size; select cylindrical containers with the same diameter and volume.

Set up the bulb and socket. Place the light apparatus at the center of a half-circle with a radius of 0.3 m. Mark the circumference of the half-circle on the tabletop with tape.

Plug in the lamp.

Place two sample containers on the tape mark so that the containers are equidistant from the lamp.

Use the two thermometers to measure and record the initial temperature of the water in each container. Construct a holder for each thermometer by punching a hole in the center of a plastic disk, such as a margarine-container lid. Place the thermometer through the hole and position the thermometer so that the bulb will be in the center of the container when the plastic lid rests on the rim of the cylinder. Make sure you will be able to read the thermometer in this position. Tape the thermometer securely in place. Place the plastic lid on the sample container, and read the initial temperature.

Take temperature readings for each container at 30 s intervals for 5 min. Do not move the containers or remove the thermometers during this time.

Turn off the light. Fill each container with 400 mL of room-temperature water. Replace the thermometers in the containers. Measure and record the initial temperature of the water in the containers. Read and record the temperatures of the containers at 30 s intervals until they reach a constant temperature. Note that this may not happen at the same time for both containers.

Repeat the procedure for two more containers. Place the empty containers on the tape mark and turn on the light. Read and record the temperature every 30 s for 5 min.

For each container, plot a graph of the temperature change versus time for the empty container exposed to the light source. Plot a second graph of temperature change versus time for the containers filled with water.

Compare these graphs to determine which materials retain heat the most effectively and which materials radiate heat the most quickly.

Classify the materials according to the results.

Post-Lab

Tips for Evaluating Patent Application Lab Report

Student lab reports should include diagrams of the conditions under which each container was tested. Diagrams should be labeled and clearly drawn, and there should be a section describing each diagram. Reports should include an analysis of the method used in the lab. Students should explain the controls that were in place to make sure all samples were tested under the same conditions. They should also explore any factors that may have affected their results, such as air currents, differences in stirring, and placement of the thermometer.

Reports should include all data analysis, including calculations. Calculations should be accurate, and results should have the appropriate number of significant figures. Graphs should be clearly drawn and labeled and should accurately reflect the reported data.

Students should classify the materials according to their thermal-conduction properties. Reports should recommend a material to be used in making coolers and a different material to be used as a thawing plate.

Additional Notes

HOLT PHYSICS Laboratory Experiments Teacher's Edition

Discovery Lab

Pre-Chapter Exploration 12

Pendulums and Spring Waves

OBJECTIVES

Students will

- determine the factors that influence the time interval required for a pendulum to complete one full swing.
- investigate the nature of pendulum and wave motion.

Planning

Recommended time

1 lab period

Materials

[for each lab group]

✔ 5 metal washers
✔ cord, 1.00 m
✔ long, loosely coiled spring, 5m
✔ masking tape
✔ meterstick
✔ paper clip
✔ protractor
✔ support stand and clamp

Classroom Organization

- Students can work alone or in groups.
- It is more efficient to set up each lab station ahead of time and allow each group to rotate from station to station.
- **Safety warnings:** Make sure lab groups work sufficiently far apart because pendulums may swing in wide arcs. Do not hang more than 0.25 kg because it might break the cord. Make sure all work is done in an area away from obstructions or traffic.

Checkpoints

Step 3: Students should raise the washer so that the pendulum encounters no obstacles as it swings.

Step 13: Students should realize that it takes the shorter pendulum less time, so they will have to shorten the cord even more. The length of a pendulum with a period of 1.0 s is 0.25 m.

Steps 15, 18, 23: The spring should be straight but not taut.

Step 17: Students should do this step in less than 1.0 s to get good results.

Step 18: The diagram should resemble a spring with a wave that looks like a raised bump traveling away from the starting point on the floor.

Step 20: The diagram should resemble a spring with a wave that looks like a snake slithering on the ground traveling away from the starting point on the floor.

Step 23: The diagram should resemble a spring with a wave that has compressed coils in an area traveling away from the starting point on the floor.

Answers To

Analysis

A. Answers will vary but should be close to 1.4 s.

B. Answers will vary but should be close to 1.4 s.

C. The pendulum took the same time, regardless of the angle.

D. Answers will vary but should be between 0.9 s and 2.0 s.

E. The longer pendulum required more time to complete one full swing. The graph should show a straight diagonal line pointing up and to the right.

F. 0.25 m

G. No, the time required for one full swing was the same, regardless of the mass.

H. Lengthen the cord, because longer pendulums require a longer time to complete one full swing.

I. Answers will vary. Students should describe something similar to a raised bump traveling away from them.

J. Answers will vary. Students should describe something similar to a snakelike wave moving laterally away from them along the floor.

K. Answers will vary. Students should describe a wave of compressed coils traveling away from them.

Additional Notes

HOLT PHYSICS Laboratory Experiments Teacher's Edition

Invention Lab

Post-Chapter Activity **12**

Tensile Strength and Hooke's Law

OBJECTIVES

Students will

- test a spring to find the elongation of the spring due to applied masses.
- test a rubber band to find the elongation of the band due to applied masses.
- plot a force-versus-elongation curve for both the spring and for the rubber band.
- find the spring constant of the spring from the slope of the spring graph.

Planning

Recommended time

1 lab period

Students should have their plan approved before the class begins.

Materials

[for each lab group]

✔ 2 rubber bands
✔ 2 sets of masses (50 g–1000 g)
✔ extension clamp
✔ masking tape
✔ mass hanger
✔ meterstick
✔ pad
✔ ruler
✔ spring
✔ stopwatch
✔ support stand

Materials Preparation

The springs and rubber bands should be distributed by the teacher. Any spring will work. Particularly good springs are those included in the Hooke's law apparatus. Rubber bands may be of any size. If rubber bands are to be tested to failure, it is best to use small, thin rubber bands. Larger bands require loads of more than 1500 g to break them.

Classroom Organization

- Students may perform this lab in groups of two or more.
- Each group should have enough room to work so that students will not risk being hit by falling masses from nearby groups.
- If possible, apparatus should be set up so that masses will fall onto a padded table, not onto the floor.
- **Safety warnings:** Students must wear safety goggles and sturdy closed-toe shoes. When rubber bands break, masses will fall and pieces of the bands will become projectiles.

Techniques to Demonstrate

Demonstrate taping masses to the mass holder to prevent them from falling off.

Pre-Lab Discussion

You may provide some of the following leading questions for students to consider as they prepare their plans.

- Can the spring constant be measured directly? If not, what measurements will you have to make to find the constant?

- How will you compare the rubber band with the spring? What criteria will the rubber band have to meet to be a serviceable replacement for the spring?

Tips for Evaluating the Pre-Lab Requirements

Students' plans should present a clear explanation of the procedure. Students should realize that the spring constants cannot be measured directly; they must be calculated from measurements of the elongation of the spring under different forces.

Students should realize that the spring will have a constant value for the relationship between the displacement of the spring and the applied force. The rubber band will need to have a constant value in order to work as a substitute.

Proposed Procedure

Obtain the test spring, and hang it securely from an extension clamp secured to a support stand. Securely tape the meterstick to the support stand so that it is held vertically next to the spring.

Find and record the mass of the mass hanger. Attach the mass hanger to the spring. Measure the length of the spring and mass hanger by using a ruler to find the position of the bottom of the mass hanger against the meterstick.

Place a small mass on the hanger. Measure the length of the spring and mass hanger.

Add one mass at a time, and measure the length of the spring and mass hanger after each mass is added.

Add masses until the mass hanger hits the tabletop or the spring shows signs of stretching; do not overstretch the spring.

Calculate the force acting on the spring for each mass. Plot a graph of the force versus the elongation of the spring. The slope of this graph represents the spring constant of the spring.

Attach the rubber band to the support stand and clamp, and repeat the above procedure. Add one mass at a time; measure the length of the rubber band and mass hanger after each addition until the band breaks.

Plot a graph of the force versus the elongation of the rubber band.

Compare the two graphs.

If time permits, test additional rubber bands. One possibility is to use two rubber bands—or to double one band—to see if this gives a more linear response.

Post-Lab

Tips for Evaluating Patent Application Lab Report

Student lab reports should include diagrams of the apparatus used to find the spring constant of the spring and of the rubber band. Diagrams should be labeled and clearly drawn, and there should be a section describing each diagram. Reports should include an analysis of the method used to measure the elongation. Students should notice that the rubber bands exhibit "creep," that is, the extension of the band at a constant load continues to increase for a time after the load is applied. Typical bands may continue to lengthen for about 5 min, adding up to 1 cm to the length. In the drum-pedal application of this lab, force would only be applied for a short time, so students should measure the length immediately.

Some students will realize that they can perform data analysis using just the length, without calculating the difference between the original length and the stretched length. Reports should include all data analysis, including calculations. Calculations should be accurate, and results should have the appropriate number of significant figures. Students should realize that the spring constant has units of newtons per meter.

Students should recognize that the spring has a linear response; the graph will be linear, and it will be easy to find a constant value for the relationship between the displacement of the spring and the applied force. The rubber band will not give a linear graph. In addition to simply viewing the shape of the graph, students can perform the following test for linearity: Take the average value for the slope between each successive pair of plotted values, then find the slope of the line between the first and last plotted points. For an ideal straight line, these values are equal.

Students' reports should come to the conclusion that the rubber band is not a good substitute for the spring.

Additional Notes

HOLT PHYSICS *Laboratory Experiments Teacher's Edition*

Discovery Lab

Pre-Chapter Exploration **13**

Resonance and the Nature of Sound

OBJECTIVES

Students will

- explore the phenomenon of resonance in pendulums and determine what conditions are necessary for resonance to occur.
- explore the phenomenon of resonance with tuning forks and determine what conditions are necessary for resonance to occur.
- discover what variables affect the sound produced by an instrument.

Planning

Recommended time

1 lab period

Alternatively, each section could be performed during a part of class on three different days.

Materials

[for each lab group]

- ✔ masking tape
- ✔ narrow-mouthed glass bottle, 125 mL
- ✔ pendulum bobs
- ✔ pendulum cord
- ✔ polyethylene tubing, 1 cm I.D.
- ✔ protractor
- ✔ right-angle clamp
- ✔ rubber tuning-fork hammer
- ✔ support stand and base
- ✔ pairs of tuning forks with resonance boxes

Materials Preparation

Glass soda or juice bottles work well for the fundamental-frequency section of the lab. Each bottle should be accompanied by tubes of different lengths; the tubes should have a diameter slightly smaller than the mouth of the bottle. One end of each tube will be wrapped with masking tape to make a snug fit. For best results, the longest tube should be the same length as the bottle. The tubes may be made from sections of polyethylene tubing. The tubes should be cut to one fourth, one half, and one full bottle height. Both ends of the tube should be sanded smooth. All tubes should be cleaned thoroughly before each class.

Water should be available for this section of the lab. Students may need funnels to pour water into the bottles.

Classroom Organization

- This lab may be performed by students alone or in groups of two or more.
- It is more efficient to set up each lab station ahead of time and allow groups to move from station to station.
- **Safety warnings:** Remind students to clean up all spills immediately.

Techniques to Demonstrate

Show students how to strike a tuning fork with a rubber hammer. Tuning forks must never be struck against a hard object or surface.

HOLT PHYSICS Laboratory Experiments Teacher's Edition continued

Checkpoints

Step 1: Make sure all setups are secure.

Step 4: When the pendulums have different lengths, the first pendulum should swing but the second pendulum should remain at rest. If the second pendulum moves, check the apparatus to make sure there is enough space between the pendulums.

Step 8: Students should realize that the second pendulum is moving and that it has the same frequency as the first pendulum.

Step 9: Tuning forks should be labeled with their frequencies. Students may be confused by the use of the word *frequency* in this context; encourage them to discover what effect the frequency of the tuning forks has on the sounds produced throughout the lab.

Step 12: Make sure students set up the resonance boxes so that the hollow bases are lined up with each other.

Step 14: If students do not hear the second fork, have them move the boxes closer together and strike the first fork with more force. Some students may need to move to a quiet area or touch the fork to feel the vibrations.

Answers To

Analysis

A. With pendulums of different lengths, the first pendulum swung but the second pendulum remained at rest.

B. With pendulums of the same length, the second pendulum began swinging while the first pendulum was swinging.

C. The second pendulum swung at the same frequency as the first pendulum.

D. When the forks had different frequencies, the first tuning fork produced a sound when struck. The second fork produced no sound.

E. When the forks had the same frequency, the second fork began to produce a sound after the first fork was struck.

F. The sound became lower as longer tubes were added.

G. The sound became higher as more water was added.

H. Adding tubes to the top of the bottle increased the total length of the apparatus.

I. Adding water to the bottle decreased the total length of the apparatus.

J. The longer the apparatus was, the lower the sound was. The shorter the apparatus was, the higher the sound was.

Additional Notes

Invention Lab

Post-Chapter Activity **13**

Building a Musical Instrument

OBJECTIVES

Students will

- use appropriate lab safety procedures.
- design and implement their own procedure.
- apply physics principles to the design of a musical instrument.
- describe the instrument using the concepts of frequency, pitch, and resonance.

Planning

Recommended time

2 lab periods

Students should have their plan approved before the class begins.

This activity is well suited for use as a long-term project or homework assignment.

Materials

[for each lab group]

✔ adhesive tape
✔ bottles
✔ cans
✔ cardboard
✔ cord
✔ drinking glasses
✔ funnel
✔ glue
✔ pipes of various lengths
✔ pipe adapters and fittings
✔ plastic combs
✔ plastic containers
✔ pots and pans
✔ rubber bands
✔ silverware/flatware
✔ stones
✔ tape
✔ wire
✔ wood blocks

Materials Preparation

The materials list provides enough types of materials for students to construct many different types of instruments; however, you may want to provide more materials or allow students to collect their own materials.

Classroom Organization

- This activity may be performed by students working alone or in groups of two or more.
- The amount of time required for this project will be determined by the complexity of the completed instruments.
- **Safety warnings:** Students should never work unsupervised, especially with sharp objects or tools. Emphasize the importance of wearing appropriate protective gear.

Techniques to Demonstrate

To help the students get started, you may want to demonstrate several simple musical principles and explain them using the physics concepts presented in Chapter 13.

A 4 ft long cardboard tube held over a lighted burner will produce a very loud low-frequency sound. A longer tube will produce a higher pitched sound.

Hold a 30 cm ruler against a table so that the end of the ruler is over the edge of the table. Pluck the free end of the ruler. Move the ruler so that a shorter segment is over the edge. Pluck the free end of the ruler again; it will produce a higher-pitched sound.

Pre-Lab Discussion

Ask students who play musical instruments to bring them to class and play different notes for the class. Have students determine what physical properties determine the sound produced by the instruments.

Tips for Evaluating the Pre-Lab Requirements

Students' plans should include a description of the instrument they intend to build and an analysis of the physics principles involved. Students should explain how the instrument will produce a complete octave.

Proposed Procedure

Construct a musical instrument using household materials. Use physics principles to design an instrument capable of producing an entire octave.

Some possible instrument designs are listed below:

1. Use a set of eight soda bottles or drinking glasses to make a percussion instrument. Fill the glasses with varying amounts of water to regulate the length of the tube. Strike the glasses gently with a mallet or rub a wet finger along the rim of thin glasses to produce music.

2. Use a box or a piece of wood to make a stringed instrument. Use different-sized rubber bands, light wire, or strong nylon thread as the strings. To produce an octave, strings should be different lengths.

3. A set of small rectangular boxes (such as those for candy, raisins, or gum) may be used to construct a wind instrument.

4. A "brass" instrument similar to a trombone can be made from copper water pipe and pipe fittings. The body and slide are made from pieces of copper pipe about 35 cm long. Use two $\frac{1}{2}$ in. tubes for the slide and two $\frac{3}{4}$ in. tubes for the body. Use four copper elbow fittings to make the bend at the end of the slide. Wrap the free ends of the slide tubes with masking tape until they fit smoothly inside the $\frac{3}{4}$ in. tubes of the body. Use wooden blocks as spacers to hold the body tubes parallel so the slide fits properly.

The mouthpiece (a threaded pipe adapter with a fender washer pushed inside) and the bell (a kitchen funnel with a wide stem) are attached to the free ends of the body pipes using 45° elbow fittings.

For all instruments, tuning will be performed mostly by trial and error, but students should recognize general requirements for producing higher and lower notes.

Post-Lab

Tips for Evaluating Patent Application Lab Report

Student lab reports should include diagrams of the instrument. Diagrams should be labeled and clearly drawn. Student reports should explain the physics principles related to the sound produced by the instrument and should describe in terms of resonance, frequency, and pitch how different pitches are attained.

Students should also demonstrate that the instrument can produce an entire octave. Some students may wish to perform a piece of music for the class, either solo or as an ensemble.

Additional Notes

HOLT PHYSICS *Laboratory Experiments Teacher's Edition*

Discovery Lab

Pre-Chapter Exploration **14**

Light and Mirrors

OBJECTIVES

Students will

- form a variety of images using several techniques.
- locate images using different methods.

Planning

Recommended time

1 lab period

Materials

[for each lab group]

✔ 2 mirror supports

✔ curved mirror, combined concave and convex

✔ eye chart, normal

✔ eye chart, reverse (optional)

✔ masking tape

✔ meterstick

✔ pencil with unused eraser

✔ protractor

✔ ruler or straightedge

✔ small flat mirror, 10 cm × 15 cm or smaller

✔ T-pin

✔ white paper

Materials Preparation

If a reverse eye chart is unavailable, use the normal eye chart for both parts of the activity. Any small object can substitute for the T-pin and pencil eraser. Mount all mirrors in cardboard to protect students from sharp edges. Use a craft knife to cut cardboard squares to make a frame for each mirror, and tape the mirror securely into the frame.

Classroom Organization

- Students can work alone or in groups of two or more.
- It is more efficient to set up the lab in stations so that groups can rotate from station to station.
- **Safety warnings:** Secure mirrors to the wall with strong tape and to the table with clamps. The mirror taped to the wall should be lightweight and no larger than 10 cm × 15 cm.

Techniques to Demonstrate

Show students how to properly secure mirrors to the table using mirror supports and to the wall using strong tape.

Checkpoints

Step 3: For the bench test of this lab, line 11 became unreadable at a distance of 3.6 m.

Step 4: Make sure that the mirror is small and lightweight. A mirror that is too heavy will fall and break. Tape all sides of the mirror to the wall.

Step 6: For the bench test, line 11 became unreadable at 1.75 m.

Step 8: Secure mounted mirrors to the table using clamps to prevent any broken-glass hazard.

Step 9: The pencil's eraser should be new and not worn. The purpose of putting the eraser on the tip of the pin is to protect the student's eye. Make sure that students wear safety goggles. It is possible to substitute another small object, such as an eraser or the cap of a pen, for the T-pin.

HOLT PHYSICS Laboratory Experiments Teacher's Edition continued

Step 13: The angle between the incoming beam and the nearest perpendicular line should be approximately equal to the angle between the outgoing beam and the nearest perpendicular line.

Step 18: At close range (20 cm), objects appear enlarged and upright; at middle range (30 cm), objects appear greatly enlarged and upright; at long range (65 cm), objects appear reduced and inverted.

Step 21: At close range (20 cm), objects appear enlarged and upright; at middle range (30 cm), objects appear reduced and upright; at long range (65 cm), objects appear greatly reduced and upright.

Answers To

Analysis

A. The image of the reverse eye chart seen in the mirror is identical to the appearance of the normal eye chart viewed directly.

B. Answers will vary.

C. Answers will vary.

D. The distance from the chart to the mirror is approximately one-half the distance from the student to the chart. Some students may realize that the distance between the image and the eye is actually the same in both cases.

E. The angles are equal.

F. Diagrams should show that the incoming and outgoing angles are equal in each trial.

G. When an object is close to a convex mirror, its image appears upright and larger than the object. When the object is far from the mirror, the image appears inverted and smaller than the object.

H. When an object is close to a concave mirror, its image appears upright and reduced.

I. When an object is far away from a concave mirror, its image appears upright and much smaller than the object.

Additional Notes

HOLT PHYSICS *Laboratory Experiments Teacher's Edition*

Invention Lab

Post-Chapter Activity **14**

Designing a Device to Trace Drawings

OBJECTIVES

Students will

- use appropriate lab safety procedures.
- design and implement their own procedure.
- use mirrors to produce an image of an object.

Planning

Recommended time

1 lab period

Students should have their plan approved before the class begins.

Materials

[for each lab group]

- ✔ adhesive tape
- ✔ cardboard
- ✔ converging lens, focal length =100 cm
- ✔ diverging lens
- ✔ drinking straw
- ✔ glass
- ✔ knife
- ✔ light source
- ✔ 2 mirrors, 10 cm × 15 cm
- ✔ see-through mirror or one-way mirror, 10 cm × 10 cm
- ✔ support stands and clamps
- ✔ top from a sports drink bottle
- ✔ various hollow cylinders

Materials Preparation

See-through mirrors are available from most glass dealers. An alternative to using a see-through mirror is to apply window-tinting foil to an ordinary glass plate. The foil is available at most hardware stores. Carefully apply the adhesive foil to one side of an ordinary glass plate; smooth the foil as you work to prevent bubbles from forming under the surface. This works best with glass that is about $\frac{1}{6}$ cm thick.

The regular mirror pieces should not be larger than 10 cm × 15 cm.

All mirrors should be mounted in cardboard to protect students from sharp edges. Use a craft knife to cut cardboard squares to make a frame for each mirror, and tape the mirror securely into the frame.

You may wish to make a toy periscope available for students to look at.

Classroom Organization

- This activity may be performed by students working in groups of two or more.
- **Safety warnings:** Students should never work unsupervised, especially with sharp objects or tools. Remind students to report all broken glass immediately.

Pre-Lab Discussion

Discuss the diagram of the periscope. Students should be able to analyze the path of the light to explain how the image forms. Ask students to consider how they would change the device to produce an image in a different location.

Tips for Evaluating the Pre-Lab Requirements

Students' plans should include a description of the device they intend to build and an analysis of the physics principles involved. Students should explain how they will determine where the image appears.

Proposed Procedure

Use one mounted mirror and one mounted see-through mirror. Hold the mirror securely on a support stand with a clamp. Securely clamp the see-through mirror onto a second support stand. Arrange the pieces so that the mirrors are held parallel to each other and at about a 45° angle to the tabletop. The regular mirror should have its reflective side facing the tabletop. Make an eyepiece by mounting a clear cylinder in a cardboard frame. Tape it securely in place.

Securely clamp the eyepiece frame into position above the see-through mirror. The eyepiece frame should be parallel to the tabletop and should make a 45° angle with the see-through mirror frame.

Place a drawing on the table under the regular mirror. Look through the eyepiece and adjust the device until it is possible to trace the drawing.

Note: If the see-through mirror is placed glass-side up, it will produce double images that are impossible to trace. Turning the see-through mirror reflective-side up should solve this problem.

Depending on the level of lighting in the room and on the ratio of transmission to reflection in the see-through mirror, it may be hard to see the tracing pen and the drawing through the mirror. This can be overcome by using a light to illuminate the tracing page, increasing the brightness of its image relative to the image of the manuscript. However, because this device is designed to handle manuscript that is light-sensitive, a barrier such as a piece of cardboard should be placed between the manuscript and the tracing.

Adjust the alignment of the mirrors to produce the best image. The final image should be oriented square to the paper, and the image of the manuscript sheet should appear parallel to the plane of the table, not tilted.

Post-Lab

Tips for Evaluating Patent Application Lab Report

Student lab reports should include diagrams of the instrument. Diagrams should be labeled and clearly drawn. Diagrams should include ray drawings showing how the image is formed.

Student reports should include a written description of the device.

For flat mirrors, the image always forms as far behind the mirror as the object is in front of the mirror. Therefore, the second image will be as far behind the see-through mirror as the first image is from the see-through mirror. The traceable image will always appear below the surface of the table and will be smaller than the object. Students should be able to explain why the image is always smaller. Students should also recognize that the eyepiece is necessary to limit the viewing angle so that the lines do not move as their head moves. Some students may build enclosed instruments to solve this problem.

Additional Notes

HOLT PHYSICS *Laboratory Experiments Teacher's Edition*

Discovery Lab

Pre-Chapter Exploration **15**

Refraction and Lenses

OBJECTIVES

Students will

- observe how light behaves as it passes from one substance to another.
- observe images formed by different lenses.

Planning

Recommended time

1 lab period

Materials

[for each lab group]

- ✔ coin
- ✔ converging lens
- ✔ diverging lens
- ✔ drinking straw
- ✔ electrical tape
- ✔ flashlight
- ✔ medicine dropper
- ✔ milk, dropperful
- ✔ modeling clay
- ✔ opaque bowl
- ✔ paper
- ✔ paper towels
- ✔ pencil
- ✔ plastic electrical tape
- ✔ protractor
- ✔ ruler
- ✔ small, clear, rectangular container, such as the rectangular cells sold for optics experiments
- ✔ 2 used chalkboard erasers

Materials Preparation

Place a small container of milk (about 250 mL) in a central location where students can fill their droppers.

A clear bowl can be used in place of the opaque bowl, but an opaque bowl makes the demonstration more dramatic.

Classroom Organization

- Students can work alone or in groups of two or more.
- It is more efficient to set up the lab in stations so that groups can rotate from station to station.
- **Safety warnings:** Spilled water presents a safety hazard. Clean up all spills immediately.

Checkpoints

Step 3: Milk scatters the light, making the beam more visible.

Step 4: For best results, the flashlight should be flat on the table. Modeling clay can be used to ensure that the flashlight remains in position.

Step 6: Chalk dust scatters the light, making the beam more visible. Make sure that students do not create too much chalk dust. You may choose to have students call you when they are ready so that you can tap the erasers for each lab group. Too much dust in an enclosed area presents a safety hazard. Open windows in the classroom to promote circulation of fresh air if weather permits.

Step 8: Students should observe this from above, with the lights dimmed or turned off.

Answers To

Analysis

A. The diagram should include all parts of the setup as viewed from above. The light beam should travel in straight paths, except at the container wall, where the light bends. The light beam should bend toward the perpendicular line in the water and away from the perpendicular line as it enters the air.

B. No, the straws do not lie in a straight line.

C. As the light traveled in air before reaching the container, it traveled in a straight path.

D. The light bent as it traveled into the container.

E. The light traveled through the milky water in a straight path.

F. The light bent as it traveled from the container to the air.

G. The light traveled in a straight line in the air after leaving the container.

H. Diagrams should include the bowl, the coin, the water, and the eye. The light beam should travel in straight paths, except at the surface of the water, where the light bends. An arrow should indicate that the light beam travels into the eye.

I. As the light traveled in air before reaching the surface of the water, it traveled in a straight path.

J. The light bent as it traveled into the bowl of water.

K. The light traveled through the water in a straight path.

L. The light bent as it traveled from the bowl of water to the air.

M. The light traveled through the air to the student's eye in a straight path.

N. Answers will vary. Students should recognize that the line the light beam traveled in water was not the same as the line it traveled in air.

O. When the object was far away from the diverging lens, the image appeared small and upside-down.

P. When the object was close to the converging lens, the image appeared enlarged and upright.

Q. When the object was in front of the converging lens, the image appeared small and upright.

R. Answers will vary. Students should recognize that light reflects off mirrors and passes through lenses. Both mirrors and lenses can create images with different sizes and orientations as the original objects.

Additional Notes

HOLT PHYSICS *Laboratory Experiments Teacher's Edition*

Invention Lab

Post-Chapter Activity **15**

Camera Design

OBJECTIVES

Students will

- use appropriate lab safety procedures.
- design and implement their own procedure.
- investigate the design of a nonfocusing disposable camera.
- design an apparatus to find the focal length of various lenses.

Planning

Recommended time

1 lab period

Students should have their plan approved before the class begins.

Materials

[for each lab group]

- ✔ black construction paper, 1 sheet
- ✔ black electrical tape
- ✔ black paint (water-based), 1 pint
- ✔ cardboard box
- ✔ craft knife
- ✔ disposable camera
- ✔ double-sided tape
- ✔ foamboard or mounting board, 1 sheet
- ✔ 4 lens and screen supports
- ✔ magnifier
- ✔ masking tape
- ✔ matte acetate, 3 mL–5 mL, 1 sheet
- ✔ medium-sized paint brush
- ✔ 2 metersticks
- ✔ 4 meterstick supports
- ✔ support stand
- ✔ symmetrical clamp
- ✔ tracing paper, 1 sheet
- ✔ unfrosted bulb and socket

Materials Preparation

Many film developers are willing to donate used cameras. Contact them at least one month in advance of the lab so they will have time to collect the cameras.

If you are using cameras with flash units, do not allow students to open the cameras to remove the lenses. You should open them yourself while wearing rubber gloves. Holding the plastic or wooden handle of a screw driver, place the metal shaft across the leads of the large capacitor to discharge it, then remove the battery from the camera.

To measure the distance between the film and the lens and to form images, it is necessary to disable the camera's shutter mechanism, which normally obscures the lens. In most cameras, this can be achieved by removing the small activating spring located close to the lens.

Classroom Organization

- This activity may be performed by students working in groups of two or more.
- **Safety warnings:** Remind students to report all broken glass immediately.

Pre-Lab Discussion

Ask students to think about a photographer taking a picture. Have students identify the placement of the light source, object, lens, and image.

Tips for Evaluating the Pre-Lab Requirements

Students' plans should include a description of the method they will use to find the focal length of the

CHAPTER 15 **T77**

lens. Plans should also include a diagram of the apparatus to test the lenses. Students should present a convincing physical argument that the lens will work. Students should recognize that the focal length can be found by finding the image distance of a distant object.

Proposed Procedure

Obtain a used disposable camera that has been opened. Make sure the shutter mechanism is disabled. Leave the lens in place on the camera. Tape a screen made from a small piece of tracing paper or designer's appliqué film to the back of the camera, where the film goes. Securely clamp the camera to the support stand. Choose a distant object or use a light source positioned about 8 m away from the lens, and point the mounted camera toward the object. Carefully move the support stand until the object's image is observed on the screen.

Continue to move the stand until the image is as distinct as possible. Look at the image using a magnifying glass to determine whether the image is in focus. Record the distance between the lens and the image screen. Move the lens to another position, and repeat the procedure using a different distant object. Average the two results for the distance between the lens and the screen. Record this average image distance as the *focal length* of the lens.

Use the light bulb as the object to determine the distance between the lens and the film as well as the minimum distance between the lens and the object.

Finally, use a shoe box or meterstick apparatus to design a device that will allow you to find the focal length of different lenses. Most methods of designing the box have several essential things in common. Carefully cut a 2 cm hole in the center of one end of the box. The lenses will rest over this hole and allow light into the box. A U-shaped lens holder is built around this hole to hold the lenses in place. A simple, adaptable lens holder can be made by rolling a piece of card into a U-shape and attaching small blocks of foam board to the inner curve to hold the lenses. These lens holders can be "nested" to allow for different lens diameters. Use foam board to make a holder for the screen. The screen will be made of matte acetate, mounted between two foam-board frames, and taped securely in place. The foam-board frames will be notched to fit into a sled set on runners placed inside the box. This way, the screen can be moved easily inside the box to adjust the distance between the lens and the screen. Attach a rigid pull tab to the screen mechanism. The pull tab should be about 30 cm long and 3 cm wide, and there should be a horizontal exit slit cut at the end of the box below the lens hole. The pull tab should be divided by centimeter gradations to enable students to measure the distance between the lens and the screen. An index mark should be fitted outside the box to indicate where the scale should be read, and millimeter divisions can be added to the index mark, instead of marking the entire pull tab in millimeters. Everything inside the box except the screen should be painted black. The lid should be sealed onto the box with black tape to prevent light leakage. Cut a large rectangular hole in the back of the box opposite the lens. Use black construction paper to construct a viewing hood. Test several lenses using the same procedure.

Post-Lab

Tips for Evaluating Patent Application Lab Report

Student lab reports should include diagrams of each part of the experiment. Diagrams should be labeled and clearly drawn. Diagrams should include ray drawings showing how the image is formed. Diagrams should include dimensions of each part of the apparatus.

Student reports should include a written description of the device.

Reports should include all data and calculations. Students should classify the lenses in terms of the focal length and the minimum distance between the lens and the object. Students should identify which lenses will work for nonfocusing cameras and which will not. Reports should contain an explanation of the criteria used to determine which lenses will be suitable.

HOLT PHYSICS *Laboratory Experiments Teacher's Edition*

Discovery Lab

Pre-Chapter Exploration **17**

Electrostatics

OBJECTIVES

Students will

- discover the electrical properties of metallic and nonmetallic objects.
- construct an electroscope and investigate how it works.
- observe forces between charged and uncharged objects.

Planning

Recommended time

1 lab period

Materials

[for each lab group]

✔ 2 drinking cups, large clear-plastic
✔ 2 plastic-foam cups
✔ balloon
✔ felt cloth, small piece
✔ flannel cloth, small piece
✔ glue
✔ hairdryer (optional)
✔ aluminum pie pan, large
✔ paper clip
✔ ruler
✔ aluminum foil, 1 sheet
✔ silk cloth, small piece
✔ aluminum pie pan, small

Materials Preparation

Electrostatic experiments should be done on days with very low humidity. If you have problems charging materials, a hairdryer can also be used to dry materials to help them hold their charge.

Thick plastic cups should be used for the electroscope. Thin plastic cups do not work well because they hold charge. Narrow clear glass water glasses or jars can be substituted but will work only on days with low humidity. Blow-dry the glasses on days with higher humidity.

Do not substitute beakers for jars or drinking glasses because students can blow air under an upside-down beaker. Students can ground the aluminum if they do not remove their fingers from the aluminum at the appropriate time, causing the charge to leave the pan.

Classroom Organization

- Students can work alone or in groups of two or more.
- **Safety warnings:** Electrostatic work can produce sparking, so remove all flammable liquids and gases near the work area. Students should not wear long-sleeved shirts during this lab because the sleeves may become charged.

Techniques to Demonstrate

Show students how the electroscope works to detect charge. You may wish to construct an electroscope before the lab so that students have a model to work from. Demonstrate using a dry plastic cup so students can see that the cup may carry charge. Wash and dry the cup to show how this removes built-up charges.

Checkpoints

Step 1: Make sure students punch carefully so that the two holes are neatly formed. Do not use tape to attach the paper clip to the aluminum pan because the tape may insulate the paper clip from the pan.

CHAPTER 17 **T79**

Step 6: A clear glass, a jar, or some other insulating container can be substituted for the plastic cup. If you use glass, be sure to review the safety precautions for handling glass. Glass will work well only on days with low humidity. It is advisable to wash and gently dry the plastic cups, because they usually carry a charge when dry. During the experiment it may be necessary to wash the cup to eliminate built-up charges.

Step 7: Some students may need assistance tying the knot of the balloon. You may want to blow up balloons before class.

Step 8: Students should spend some time convincing themselves that the presence of the charged balloon causes the strips to move. They should try to make sure the strips are not responding to any other influence, such as air currents, a force exerted by the paper clip, or any other cause.

Step 12: The devices created in this step can be saved for use in the Chapter 17 Invention Lab. The aluminum pie pan glued to a plastic-foam cup acts as an electrophorus.

Step 13: Students may have to rub the pie pan vigorously before they will be able to observe a significant movement of the foil strips on the electroscope.

Step 14: It is possible to build up a large charge on the balloon, so students may see more dramatic effects using the balloon to charge the electrophorus.

Step 17: Students will probably not observe a qualitative difference between the effects of the large pan and the small pan.

Answers To

Analysis

A. Students should not have seen a spark as they touched the aluminum pan.

B. After the balloon was rubbed with flannel, the foil strips on the electroscope moved as the balloon was moved near the electroscope.

C. After students touched the balloon with one finger, nothing happened to the foil strips as the balloon was moved near the electroscope.

D. A force acted on the foil strips to move them apart from one another. Nothing was in contact with the foil strips to move them, so a field force acted on the foil strips.

E. As the aluminum pan was first moved toward the electroscope, the foil strips did not move.

F. As the pan that had been rubbed with silk was moved, the foil strips did not move.

G. As the pan that had been touched by the student's finger was moved toward the electroscope, the foil strips did not move.

H. As the pan that had been rubbed with flannel was moved toward the electroscope, the foil strips moved.

I. After students touched the pan with one finger, nothing happened to the foil strips on the electroscope as the pan was moved near the electroscope.

J. As the pans were moved close to one another, students heard a crackling noise.

K. As the ink mark on the pan was moved toward the electroscope, the foil strips moved apart from one another.

L. After the large aluminum pan was rotated so that the side of the pan with the ink mark was far from the electroscope, the foil strips on the electroscope moved.

M. A force acted on the foil strips to move them apart from one another.

N. Nothing was physically in contact with the foil strips to move them, so a field force must have acted on the foil strips of the electroscope.

O. The foil strips of the electroscope never moved as students touched the pan.

P. The plastic-foam cup acted as an insulating handle so the pie pan would not be discharged when students handled it.

HOLT PHYSICS Laboratory Experiments Teacher's Edition continued

Additional Notes

HOLT PHYSICS *Laboratory Experiments Teacher's Edition*

Invention Lab

Post-Chapter Activity 17

Levitating Toys

OBJECTIVES

Students will

- use appropriate lab safety procedures.
- design and implement their own procedure.
- manipulate electrostatic field forces to cause objects to levitate.

Planning

Recommended time

1 lab period

Students should have their plans approved before class begins.

Materials

[for each lab group]

- ✔ plastic-foam plate or polystyrene board
- ✔ plastic-foam cup
- ✔ aluminum pie pan
- ✔ fur or wool cloth, small piece
- ✔ space blanket, small piece
- ✔ coat hanger
- ✔ polyester thread, 1 m
- ✔ rubber cement
- ✔ meterstick
- ✔ craft knife
- ✔ cardboard or poster board, small piece

Materials Preparation

If students have completed the Chapter 17 Discovery Lab, they may use the electrophorus apparatus constructed in that lab.

Space blankets are a very good source of thin conducting material. Students should be very careful when cutting the blanket. They should cut on a cutting board or a piece of cardboard or poster board. Metallized mylar film may also be used. It is often sold as gift wrap.

Thick polystyrene foam works better than a plastic-foam plate to charge the electrophorus. Polystyrene foam pieces are used to pack many consumer electronic items. If the foam is unavailable, performance can be substantially improved by stacking several plastic-foam plates.

Classroom Organization

- This lab may be performed by groups of two or more students.
- This activity will work best in low-humidity conditions.
- This activity will work best away from air currents and drafts.
- **Safety warnings:** Students should never work with sharp objects unsupervised.

Techniques to Demonstrate

Show students how important it is for the hoop to be constructed with very smooth edges. Corners and jagged edges can collect charge and make it difficult to manipulate the toy.

Pre-Lab Discussion

Discuss field forces and the attractive and repellent characteristics of charge. Before they make their plan, students should realize that the electrophorus and the levitating toys will need to have the same charge.

HOLT PHYSICS Laboratory Experiments Teacher's Edition continued

Tips for Evaluating the Pre-Lab Requirements

Students' plans should be complete and safe. Plans should include designs for the hoop and for the figure and should describe how the toys and the electrophorus will be charged to make the toys levitate.

Proposed Procedure

A hoop can be made by cutting a 35 cm × 0.7 cm strip of space blanket. Use rubber cement to tape the ends of the strip to create a closed loop. The hoop should be cut in an even width and should have a mass of 0.03 g or less.

Charge the electrophorus by rubbing it with fur or wool and then touching it with your finger.

Hold the electrophorus by the plastic-foam handle so that the bottom of the pie pan is facing up, parallel to the ceiling.

Drop the hoop onto the pan.

The hoop will touch the pan, become charged, and hover above the pan. Typically, the hoop will fly 20 cm–30 cm above the pan.

To make a portal for the hoop to fly through, use a 130 cm × 3 cm strip of posterboard or other non-conductive material. Adhere the ends together with rubber cement to make a closed loop. Because this may accumulate charges and make it hard to fly the hoop through the portal, use damp paper towels to make the portal slightly damp. Hold the portal securely in place with a clamp or suspend it from a secure stand with polyester thread.

Post-Lab

Tips for Evaluating Patent Application Lab Report

Student lab reports should include diagrams of the hoop, the figure, the ring, and the electrophorus. Diagrams should be labeled and clearly drawn, and there should be a section describing each diagram. Reports should include an analysis of the method used in the lab to charge the electrophorus, the hoop, and the figure.

Students should describe the best design for the various parts and should explain how to solve any problems they may have had in the lab.

Additional Notes

Discovery Lab

HOLT PHYSICS Laboratory Experiments Teacher's Edition

Pre-Chapter Exploration 19

Resistors and Current

OBJECTIVES

Students will

- measure current, resistance, and potential difference across resistors.
- graph the relationships between the potential difference and current for different resistors.
- interpret graphs of potential difference versus current for different resistors.

Planning

Recommended time

1 lab period

Materials

[for each lab group]

- ✔ 6 battery holders for D-cells
- ✔ 6 D-cell batteries
- ✔ 6 V light bulb and socket
- ✔ 2 multimeters or 1 dc ammeter, 1 ohmmeter, and 1 voltmeter
- ✔ insulated connecting wires
- ✔ momentary contact switch
- ✔ 1.0 kΩ–2.0 kΩ resistor
- ✔ 400 Ω–600 Ω resistor

Materials Preparation

See page T21 for instructions on using multimeters to measure current, potential difference, and resistance.

All batteries should be fresh. Remind students to conserve batteries by leaving circuits connected only long enough to make their observations.

Classroom Organization

- This activity may be performed by students in groups of two or more.
- If desired, each section of the lab may be performed during a short part of class on different days.
- **Safety warnings:** Follow all safety precautions for working with electricity. Make sure all work surfaces are dry. Remind students to report all breakage immediately.

Techniques to Demonstrate

If students will be required to cut and strip connecting wires, show them how to use the wire cutters and strippers. Wear eye protection at all times.

Checkpoints

Step 1: If students touch any metal parts while taking the resistance measurement, they will affect the readings. Make sure students touch only the plastic parts of the meter and leads.

Step 2: Have students trace the circuit with their finger. Start at the positive pole of the battery, and follow the circuit to the negative pole. Make sure the circuit is connected properly.

Step 4: Make sure all circuits are connected correctly, with the voltage meter connected in parallel and the current meter connected in series with the resistor.

Step 7: Make sure students have correctly added another battery in series with the first battery without changing the rest of the circuit.

HOLT PHYSICS Laboratory Experiments Teacher's Edition *continued*

Step 16: Make sure all circuits are connected correctly, with the voltage meter connected in parallel and the current meter connected in series with the resistor.

Answers To

Analysis

A. The potential difference increased.

B. The current increased.

C. The ratio should be approximately equal to the value of the resistor.

D. Students should realize that the ratio is equal to the value for the resistor.

E. Graphs should show a straight diagonal line pointing up and to the right.

F. The slope should be approximately equal to the value for the resistor.

G. The values are the same.

H. The values are the same.

I. The potential difference increased.

J. The current increased.

K. The ratio should be approximately equal to the measured value of the resistance of the light bulb.

L. The ratio is equal to the value for the resistance.

M. The graph will show a straight diagonal line pointing up and to the right.

N. yes

O. The slope of the graph should be equal to the value measured for the resistance.

P. The slope is equal to the value for the resistance.

Q. The slope is equal to the ratio between the potential difference and the current.

Additional Notes

HOLT PHYSICS *Laboratory Experiments Teacher's Edition*

Invention Lab

Post-Chapter Activity **19**

Battery-Operated Portable Heater

OBJECTIVES

Students will

- use appropriate lab safety procedures.
- use the scientific method to solve a problem.
- design and implement their own procedure.
- use the relationship between current and the resistance and length of a wire to cause a wire to reach a certain temperature when there is current in the wire.

Planning

Recommended time

1 lab period

Students should have their plan approved before the class begins.

Materials

[for each lab group]

- ✔ 2.5 m Nichrome™ wire, 24 AWG
- ✔ 1.5 m insulated connecting wire
- ✔ battery holder for 2 D-cell batteries
- ✔ 6 D-cell batteries
- ✔ 2 pieces of felt, 20 cm × 60 cm
- ✔ masking tape
- ✔ 2 connectors for wire
- ✔ multimeter or dc ammeter with connecting leads
- ✔ thermometer or CBL system with temperature probe
- ✔ liquid crystal thermometer strip (optional)
- ✔ cardboard box
- ✔ 1.0 m bare copper wire, 18 AWG
- ✔ 2 wire leads with alligator clips
- ✔ plastic-foam sheet for insulation
- ✔ stopwatch
- ✔ needle and thread (optional)

[for each class]

- ✔ 2 crimping tools
- ✔ 2 wire cutters

Materials Preparation

See page T21 for instructions on using multimeters to measure current, potential difference, and resistance.

Batteries will be exhausted quickly in this experiment. Each student group should start with six new D-cell batteries.

The crimping tool will be used to join the Nichrome wire to the insulated connecting wire. Connectors can also be used to crimp the wire together.

Liquid crystal thermometers, available at many pet stores, easily determine the temperature of the wire, but a CBL system with temperature probe or regular classroom thermometers may also be used.

Classroom Organization

- This activity may be performed by students working alone or in groups of two or more.
- All work should be performed away from sources of water. All work areas must be kept dry at all times.
- **Safety warnings:** Warn students not to touch uninsulated wire with their fingers or to allow the wire to cross or contact itself. Students should be supervised when working with sharp objects. Eye protection should be worn at all times.

Techniques to Demonstrate

Discuss the best method of finding the right length of wire. Students should start with a long piece of wire and gradually cut off small pieces until they find the correct length to produce the desired temperature. This technique will prevent many safety hazards and will also preserve the batteries. Warn students not to produce current in a short segment of wire. The wire will become very hot and may burn.

Show students how to use the battery holders. Tell students to place batteries in the battery holder only when it is in use. Use only connecting wires with alligator clips to connect the circuit. The batteries should be the last elements connected and the first elements disconnected.

Pre-Lab Discussion

You may provide some of the following leading questions for students to consider as they prepare their plans.

- Do you expect a longer or a shorter wire to reach a higher temperature when a current is in the wire?
- How will you measure the temperature of the wire when current is present?
- How can the temperature change of the wire be regulated? Consider the final temperature you want in relation to the temperature of the air in cool weather. Think about whether you will need to use insulation to maintain the desired temperature.
- How will you implement the heating device in a pet-carrier design? What precautions should be taken to make the device safe?

Tips for Evaluating the Pre-Lab Requirements

Students' plans should present a clear explanation of the procedure. Plans should be safe and complete and should include a description of how and when the temperature measurements should be taken.

Students should include a diagram or description of how the heater will be incorporated into the design of a pet carrier.

Proposed Procedure

With the 2.5 m piece of Nichrome wire, make a loose coil in the center of the wire, and carefully place a thermometer bulb inside the coil. The diameter of the coil should be 1.0 cm or less. Make sure the wire does not cross or touch at any point. Use a piece of plastic foam or cardboard to hold the thermometer in a readable position.

Carefully cut two pieces of insulated connecting wire about 80 cm long. Use clips or connectors to carefully connect the ends of the insulated wire to the ends of the Nichrome wire. Place two fresh D-cell batteries in a battery holder, and connect the connecting wires with the leads on the battery holder.

Watch the thermometer. When the temperature reaches a constant level or rises above the desired range, immediately disconnect the battery holder.

If the temperature reached by the wire was too high, replace the Nichrome wire with a longer piece of wire. If the temperature reached by the wire was too low, wait for the Nichrome wire to cool. When it is cool, carefully use the wire cutters to cut approximately 10 cm from one end of the Nichrome wire.

Reconnect the battery holder. Repeat this procedure until you find the length of wire at which the desired temperature is attained. As you get close to the desired temperature, cut smaller pieces of wire until you find the correct length. (For sample data, the correct length of wire is about 34.5 cm of 24 AWG wire.)

Replace the batteries as needed.

To construct the pet-carrier heater:

Cut two pieces of felt to fit into the bottom of the cardboard box. For a typical shoe box, this will be two pieces approximately 18 cm × 31 cm each.

Use the length of Nichrome wire that produced the desired temperature. Bend the Nichrome wire into an oval loop so that it will lie flat on one piece of felt. The wire should be arranged so that it will heat all parts of the felt. Position the wire loop so that the wire does not cross or touch anywhere.

Use the crimping tool to crimp the ends of the insulated wire to the ends of the Nichrome wire.

Lay the wire loop flat on one piece of felt. Make sure the wire does not cross or touch at any point. Use masking tape to firmly tape the wire to the felt.

CHAPTER 19 **T87**

Smooth the tape so that it is entirely in contact with the felt. Place the second piece of felt on top of the wire, and align the edges of the pieces of felt. Tape or sew the two pieces of felt together securely to make a heating pad, with the two insulated wires extending out of the pad.

Connect the ends of the insulated wires with the battery holder containing two fresh D-cell batteries. Mount the battery holder securely to the outside of the pet carrier or box, and place the heating pad on the bottom of the box. Use tape to adhere the connecting wires securely to the side of the box.

As an alternative design, use two pieces of 18 AWG bare copper wire, 50 cm each. Connect each wire at one end to about 20 cm of insulated wire using crimp connectors. Wrap the free ends of the bare wire with tape for 2 cm–3 cm to insulate them. Bend the copper wires to form two halves of a rectangular frame around the outside edge of the felt. Tape the taped ends of wire together securely, making sure they do not connect electrically. Cut several pieces of Nichrome wire into lengths 10 cm longer than the width of the frame. Place the wires across the width of the frame, and attach the ends by wrapping them four or five times tightly around the copper wire and twisting the free end around the wire. The final frame will resemble the defroster found in the rear window of many cars. Tape the frame to a piece of felt, and place the remaining piece of felt over the first to cover the wires and frame. Close the pad by taping or sewing the felt pieces together.

Post-Lab

Tips for Evaluating Patent Application Lab Report

Student lab reports should include diagrams of the setup used to find the correct length of wire and of the finished heating pad. Diagrams should be labeled and clearly drawn, and there should be a section describing each diagram.

Reports should include a detailed description of the principles behind the heating pad. Students should realize that high-resistance wires must be relatively short, while low-resistance wires must be relatively long to achieve the same temperature range.

Additional Notes

HOLT PHYSICS *Laboratory Experiments Teacher's Edition*

Discovery Lab

Pre-Chapter Exploration **20**

Exploring Circuit Elements

OBJECTIVES

Students will

- construct circuits using different combinations of bulbs, batteries, and wires.
- observe the effects of an electrical current.
- compare observations from different trials to discover how relationships are affected by changing one or more variables.
- classify and analyze observations.

Planning

Recommended time

1 lab period

Materials

[for each lab group]

- ✔ 1.5 V flashlight batteries, 2 or 3
- ✔ 5 miniature light bulbs
- ✔ 5 miniature light sockets
- ✔ 20 connecting wires
- ✔ capacitor
- ✔ rubber bands or tape

Materials Preparation

All batteries should be fresh. Remind students to conserve batteries by leaving circuits connected only long enough to make their observations.

Classroom Organization

- This activity may be performed by students working alone or in groups of two.
- If desired, each section of the lab may be performed during a short part of class on different days.

- **Safety warnings:** Follow all safety precautions for working with electricity. Make sure all work surfaces are dry.

Techniques to Demonstrate

If students will be required to cut and strip connecting wires, show them how to use the wire cutters and strippers. Wear eye protection at all times.

Before step 13, show students how to connect the capacitor in a circuit, or set up a sample apparatus.

Checkpoints

Step 1: Some students will be able to produce light immediately, but it may take other students more time. If students are working in groups, make sure both students are able to produce light.

Step 4: Make sure all circuits are connected with three bulbs in series.

Step 7: Make sure students wear gloves or use hot mitts and exercise care when removing bulbs from the sockets. The bulbs may be hot or may have exposed metal parts.

Step 8: Make sure all circuits are connected with three bulbs in parallel.

Step 13: Make sure the capacitor is set up correctly and that it is wired in series with the bulb.

Step 14: The light bulb should light and should gradually dim until it goes out. If this does not happen, check the connections in the circuit.

HOLT PHYSICS Laboratory Experiments Teacher's Edition continued

Answers To

Analysis

A. Answers will vary. Students should describe the light as bright or should compare the light with other lights.

B. Answers will vary. Some systems include comparing the bulb with another light, such as a candle, or comparing the intensity of the lights at some distance from the source.

C. Answers will vary and may include a temperature change of the wire or the bulb. Light is the primary effect.

D. In this circuit, the light is the best indication of current.

E. The lights have the same brightness, and they are dimmer than the bulb in the one-bulb system.

F. When any bulb was removed, all bulbs went out. It did not matter which bulb was removed because the current must be present in all of the bulbs at once.

G. If two bulbs were added to the circuit, all bulbs would be the same brightness but would be dimmer than the bulbs in the three-bulb system.

H. Students should realize that the current is the same in each bulb because the brightness is the same.

I. Using more than one bulb increases the resistance and decreases the total current.

J. The bulbs all have the same brightness, and they are just as bright as the bulb in a one-bulb system.

K. When any bulb was removed, the other two bulbs remained lit because the circuit was still closed.

L. If two bulbs were added to the circuit, all bulbs would have the same brightness. If the bulbs were different wattages, the brightness of each bulb would depend on its wattage.

M. The current is the same in each bulb, but the bulbs would have different currents if they provided different amounts of resistance.

N. The total resistance is lower. The total current is higher.

O. When the bulb and capacitor were connected to the battery, the bulb was bright and gradually faded until it went out because there was no current.

P. When the battery was removed, the light lit again and then went out.

Q. The current was not constant because the brightness of the light was not constant.

R. When the battery was removed, the current in the circuit caused the bulb to light until there was no potential difference and the current ceased.

Additional Notes

Invention Lab

HOLT PHYSICS *Laboratory Experiments Teacher's Edition*

Post-Chapter Activity **20**

Building a Dimmer Switch

OBJECTIVES

Students will

- use appropriate lab safety procedures.
- use the scientific method to solve a problem.
- design and implement their own procedure.
- construct a dimmer switch circuit containing a capacitor and a resistor.

Planning

Recommended time

1 lab period

Students should have their plans approved before class begins.

Materials

[for each lab group]

✔ adhesive tape
✔ metal paper clips
✔ rubber bands
✔ 1.5 V flashlight battery and battery holder
✔ 6.0 V lantern battery
✔ capacitor—1 F
✔ resistor—390 kΩ
✔ resistor—180 kΩ
✔ 2 resistors—10 Ω
✔ 3 miniature light bulbs, 1.5 V
✔ 3 miniature light sockets
✔ miniature light bulb, 2.5 V
✔ miniature light bulb, 6.3 V
✔ connecting wires with alligator clips
✔ 2 switches, single-throw and double-throw

Materials Preparation

Students will have the best results with one 1 F capacitor, two 10 Ω resistors, and one each of the light bulbs.

Classroom Organization

- Students may perform this activity in groups of two or more.
- **Safety warnings:** Warn students not to touch uninsulated wire with their fingers or to allow the wire to cross or contact itself. Students should be supervised when working with sharp objects. Eye protection should be worn at all times.

Techniques to Demonstrate

One of the requirements of the design is for the light to "shine at three different brightness levels." You may want to construct a covered circuit that accomplishes this to show the students what you are looking for in their designs. Communicate to students whether you want the designs to include low, medium, and high light levels or whether the device can include off, low, and high levels. Both designs are possible.

Pre-Lab Discussion

Discuss the differences and similarities between the three designs described. Before making their plans, students should realize that they will use switches to incorporate different elements into the circuit.

Tips for Evaluating the Pre-Lab Requirements

Students' plans should be complete and safe. Plans should include circuit diagrams and should

CHAPTER 20 **T91**

demonstrate that students understand the basic criteria for each circuit. The first circuit should contain methods for controlling the amount of potential difference supplied by the batteries. The second circuit should allow students to use switches to add resistance to the circuit. The third circuit should contain a capacitor in series with the light bulb.

Proposed Procedure

I. Construct a circuit that will vary the brightness of the light depending on the potential difference supplied to the circuit.

Method I (to achieve off, dim, and bright levels): Wire two 1.5 V batteries in holders in series with one 2.5 V light bulb in socket. Use a switch to wire the circuit so that it can include only one battery or both batteries. When the switch is open, the light is off. When the switch is closed to include only one battery, the light is dim; when the switch is closed to include both batteries, the light is bright.

Method II (to achieve off, dim, medium, and bright levels): Wire three 1.5 V batteries in holders with one 6.3 V light bulb in socket. Use two switches to wire the circuit so that it can include one, two, or all three batteries. When the switches are open, the light is off. When one switch is closed so that the circuit includes one battery, the light is dim. When the circuit includes two batteries, the light is medium, and when the circuit includes three batteries, the light is bright.

II. Construct a circuit that will vary the brightness of the light depending on the resistance in the circuit.

Method I (to achieve off, dim, and bright levels): Wire one 6 V (or three 1.5 V) battery in series with a 6.3 V light bulb and one 10 Ω resistor. Use a switch to wire the circuit to include the battery and light bulb only, or the battery, light bulb, and resistor. When the switch is open, the light is off. When the switch is closed to include the resistor, the light is dim. When the switch is closed to exclude the resistor, the light is bright.

Method II (to achieve off, dim, medium, and bright levels): Wire one 6 V (or three 1.5 V) battery in series with a 6.3 V light bulb. Use switches to wire two 10 Ω resistors in series in the circuit so that the circuit can include zero, one, or two resistors. When the switch is open, the light is off. When the circuit includes both resistors, the light is dim. When the circuit includes one resistor, the light is medium. When the circuit includes no resistors, the light is bright.

III: Construct a circuit with a light that stays on for a short amount of time, gradually growing dimmer until it goes out.

Method I (for a light that turns on and dims while charging): Wire one 6 V (or three 1.5 V) battery in series with one 1 F capacitor, one 6.3 V light bulb, and a switch. When the switch is closed, the bulb will light, dim, and turn off.

Method II (for a light that turns on and dims while charging and discharging): Wire one 1 F capacitor in series with a 6.3 V light bulb. Use a switch to connect one 6 V battery to the circuit so that the circuit can include all three components or only the bulb and capacitor. When the switch is closed to include all three componets, the bulb will light, dim, and turn off. When the switch is then closed to include only the capacitor and the bulb, the light will again light, dim, and turn off.

Post-Lab

Tips for Evaluating Patent Application Lab Report

Student lab reports should include circuit diagrams of all three devices constructed in the lab. Diagrams should be labeled and clearly drawn, and there should be a section describing each diagram.

Reports should include a detailed description of the operation of each design as well as an explanation of the physics principles involved. Students should be able to explain that increasing the potential difference in the current increases the current and makes the light brighter, while increasing the resistance decreases the current and makes the light dimmer.

Students should also be able to explain that the capacitor stores charge, gradually decreasing the potential difference until there is no current. When the charged capacitor is connected to the light bulb, the capacitor discharges through the bulb until there is no current.

Additional Notes

Discovery Lab

Pre-Chapter Exploration 21

Magnetism

OBJECTIVES

Students will

- investigate the properties of the field surrounding a magnet.
- explore the relationship between the distance from a magnet and the strength of the magnetic field.

Planning

Recommended time

1 lab period

Materials

[for each lab group]

- ✔ 2 steel bar magnets with labeled poles
- ✔ 4 large, rectangular erasers
- ✔ aluminum foil, 10 cm × 10 cm, cut into thin strips
- ✔ cardboard sheet, 25 cm × 25 cm
- ✔ compass, 1.8 cm diameter
- ✔ graph paper
- ✔ iron filings in a shaker
- ✔ paper
- ✔ 15 paper clips
- ✔ plastic pen
- ✔ plastic cup
- ✔ rubber band
- ✔ metric ruler
- ✔ scissors
- ✔ 20 metal staples

Materials Preparation

All magnets should be labeled with *N* and *S* to mark the north and south poles. If your magnets are unlabeled, use masking tape to label one pole of each magnet. To determine the poles of the magnet, hold a small compass next to the end of the magnet. The needle points toward the south pole of the magnet.

The erasers are used to stabilize the apparatus. Small pieces of wood or any nonmetallic, nonmagnetic object will work as well.

Classroom Organization

- This activity may be performed by students working alone or in groups of two.
- If desired, each section of the lab may be performed during a short part of class on different days.
- **Safety warnings:** Students should wear closed-toe shoes; falling objects can cause serious injury.

Checkpoints

Step 5: Students should try to distinguish between the reactions that occur at different points on the side of the magnet. Encourage students to pay attention to subtle differences.

Step 9: Make sure all students have a work area away from other magnets, metal objects, and electrical appliances in use. If desks are metal, students may perform this section on the floor.

Step 13: Make sure students correctly identify which direction the compass is pointing.

HOLT PHYSICS Laboratory Experiments Teacher's Edition continued

Step 17: Some students may think they are causing the filings to move by applying a contact force to the cardboard. In fact, the field force of the magnetic field determines how the filings will land.

Answers To

Analysis

A. no

B. The interaction was stronger between the magnets held end-to-end.

C. The ends marked *N* repelled the ends marked *N*; the ends marked *S* repelled the ends marked *S*.

D. *N* attracted *S*; *S* attracted *N*.

E. All the metallic objects except the aluminum foil were attracted to the magnet. The other objects were not attracted to the magnet.

F. no

G. No, sometimes the needle points toward the magnet, and sometimes it points away from the magnet.

H. The compass needle points toward the pole marked *S* and away from the pole marked *N*.

I. a field force

J. The iron filings lined up in a pattern similar to the pattern made by the direction of the compass needle.

K. A field force was required to cause the filings to move into position.

L. The force is strong at points *A* and *G*, less strong at *B*, *C*, *E*, and *F*, and weakest at *D*.

M. a field force

Additional Notes

CHAPTER 21 **T95**

HOLT PHYSICS *Laboratory Experiments Teacher's Edition*

Invention Lab

Post-Chapter Activity **21**

Designing a Magnetic Spring

Objectives

Students will

- use appropriate lab safety procedures.
- use the scientific method to solve a problem.
- investigate magnetic repulsive forces for different combinations of magnets.
- construct a magnetic spring to meet given performance criteria.

Planning

Recommended time

2 lab periods, one for design and construction and one for testing. Alternatively, students may construct the device before entering the lab.

Students should have their plan approved before class begins.

Materials

[for each lab group]

- ✔ 6 bar magnets
- ✔ 8 ceramic-ring magnets
- ✔ clay, 150 g
- ✔ cord, 5 m
- ✔ craft knife
- ✔ glue or hot glue and glue gun
- ✔ heavy plastic cup, 14 oz
- ✔ 2 lids for 12 oz plastic-foam cups
- ✔ meterstick
- ✔ plastic drinking straw
- ✔ 15 cm plastic water pipe $\frac{1}{2}$ in diam.
- ✔ plastic-foam cup, 12 oz
- ✔ plumber's Teflon™ tape or PVC electrical tape
- ✔ rare-earth magnet
- ✔ self-adhesive plastic tape
- ✔ slotted masses, 10 g–500 g
- ✔ 2 steel screws

[for each class]

- ✔ electronic balance, 400 g × 0.1 g capacity

Materials Preparation

Ring magnets are usually available in sets. They should be large enough to easily support a 500 g mass when eight magnets are used. Magnets with a diameter of 50 mm diameter are common and work well. Plastic pipe is available at hardware stores. The outer diameter of the pipe should fit inside the hole in the magnets so that the magnets slide easily but do not wobble. For magnets with a diameter of 50 mm, use water pipe with a diameter of $\frac{1}{2}$ in. Have the pipe cut to 15 cm lengths. Provide one very strong rare-earth "button" magnet for use as the retrieval device. Most small conventional magnets will not lift 120 g reliably, but a rare-earth magnet will easily lift a probe fitted with an ordinary steel screw.

Hot glue gives the best results, but other glue types designed for plastic materials may also be used. Students should not use hot-glue guns without supervision.

Classroom Organization

- Students may perform this activity in groups of two or more.
- **Safety warnings:** Students should never work unsupervised, especially with sharp objects or tools. Emphasize the importance of wearing goggles, aprons, gloves, and other protective gear.

HOLT PHYSICS Laboratory Experiments Teacher's Edition continued

Techniques to Demonstrate

Show students how to stack magnets in different combinations to yield springs of different strengths. For example, use a piece of pipe and eight ring magnets to levitate five single magnets, four double magnets, two triple magnets, and two quadruple magnets. Demonstrate that two repelling magnets will not "float" in a stable position without mechanical guidance.

Pre-Lab Discussion

Discuss and develop criteria for testing the springs. Suggest that students measure the springs' height for a series of loads, and have them graph the result, simulating a Hooke's law experiment. Encourage students to determine how the force characteristics of a magnetic spring differ from those of a conventional metal spring.

Discuss how the probe would move differently in water than in it does air.

Tips for Evaluating the Pre-Lab Requirements

Students' plans should present a clear and complete explanation of the probe design and of the procedure they will use to test the design. Make sure students' designs use only waterproof materials and that they allow for adequate mechanical constraint of the magnets.

Proposed Procedure

Construct a model probe as described on pages 93 and 94 of the student lab. Carefully cut three slits in the sides of a plastic-foam drinking cup. The slots should be evenly spaced at 120° intervals around the cup. Hold the cup securely on the tabletop while cutting the slits. Carefully poke a hole in the center of the bottom of the cup and in the center of the lid. The holes should be only large enough to allow the probe to slide freely down the anchor line without wobbling. Add three identical clay strips to the inside of the probe. Adjust the amount of clay until the total mass of the probe is 120 g.

For the retrieval device, use tape or glue to secure a strong magnet to the lid of the probe near the hole for the anchor line. Securely tape a small bar magnet to a 5 cm piece of plastic drinking straw. Tie 2.5 m of the thin retrieval line firmly to the magnet and straw. Wrap tape around the knot to secure the line to the magnet and straw.

To use the retrieval line to retrieve the probe, thread the anchor line through the straw and allow the straw to slide down to the probe. The strong magnet will capture the bar magnet, and the probe can be raised up the anchor line. If the magnets repel each other, correct polarity has not been observed in the design, and one of the magnets must be reversed.

To construct the magnetic spring, wrap one ring magnet with Teflon tape until it fits firmly on the end of the plastic tube. Cut a hole in the bottom of the rigid plastic cup. The hold should be at least 5 mm larger than the plastic tube, but make sure a ring magnet can fit squarely on the bottom of the cup. Glue a ring magnet in place on the bottom of the cup.

Make a hole in the center of the second plastic lid just large enough for the anchor line to pass through freely. Glue the lid in place on the heavy plastic cup. Make sure that the polarity of the top magnet and the bottom magnet is correct for the magnets to repel one another. Fit the rigid cup onto the plastic pipe.

The spring is now ready for testing. Add magnets to the taped magnet on the plastic tube by removing the cup and slipping the magnets on before replacing the cup. Be sure to check the polarity of the magnets as you add them. For some combinations, it will be necessary to remove the taped magnet and reverse it.

Test the spring with various combinations of magnets before attaching the anchor line. Slotted masses can be added to the lid of the cup. Add masses, and measure the final height of the top of the cup. For each combination of magnets, find the total mass required to compress the spring until all the magnets are touching and the spring is totally compressed.

This gives a measure of the maximum implosive force the spring can sustain without allowing the probe to hit the bottom.

For the bench-tested model, triple and quadruple combinations of magnets work better because the multiple magnets give a longer bearing to keep the spring sliding smoothly on the tube. These springs are also stiffer, and they resist bottoming, although they do not result in as great a final height as that given by single- or double-magnet combinations.

After completing all tests, put the chosen combination of magnets in place and thread the anchor line through the hard plastic cup. Attach the line firmly to the top of the plastic tube with glue or tape. Reassemble the spring for testing with the probe.

The anchor line must be held vertically during the tests. Thread the probe onto the anchor line, and release the probe so that it falls down the anchor line and hits the hard plastic cup at the top of the spring. The design is successful if the probe is brought to a stop after falling down the anchor line from a height of 2.0 m without the spring bottoming and without the clay being dislodged from the model probe. The probe should come to rest with the bottom of its slots no less than 20 cm above the floor.

Use the retrieval device to pull the probe back up the anchor line.

Post-Lab

Tips for Evaluating Patent Application Lab Report

Student lab reports should include diagrams of the final design of the apparatus. Diagrams should be labeled and clearly drawn, and there should be a section describing each diagram.

Reports should include an analysis of the data. Students should describe the procedure they used to test the springs and the criteria they used to determine which combination of magnets would provide the best solution. Students should recognize that the force versus displacement curve for the magnetic spring is nonlinear, in contrast to the result expected for metal springs that conform to Hooke's law.

Students should include a description of how the device will function in water. They should support their explanation with descriptions of the probe's performance in air and the differences between air and water.

Additional Notes

HOLT PHYSICS *Laboratory Experiments Teacher's Edition*

Discovery Lab

Pre-Chapter Exploration **22**

Electricity and Magnetism

OBJECTIVES

Students will

- observe the effects of a current in a wire.
- discover how the core of an electromagnet affects the magnet's strength.
- construct a simple speaker.

Planning

Recommended time

1 lab period

Materials

[for each lab group]

- ✔ $\frac{1}{8}$ in. headphone plug
- ✔ 2 D-cell batteries
- ✔ 3 in. × $\frac{1}{4}$ in. brass screw or bolt
- ✔ 3 in. × $\frac{1}{4}$ in. steel screw or bolt
- ✔ $\frac{1}{4}$ in. brass nut
- ✔ $\frac{1}{4}$ in. steel nut
- ✔ battery holder for 2 D-cell batteries
- ✔ 10 ceramic disk magnets (2.5 cm diameter)
- ✔ cylindrical plastic pen
- ✔ black electrical tape
- ✔ film canister with a hole in the bottom
- ✔ magnet wire, 26 AWG
- ✔ solid core insulated wire, 20 or 22 AWG
- ✔ insulated connecting wires with alligator clips
- ✔ masking tape
- ✔ meterstick
- ✔ 10 paper clips
- ✔ portable battery-powered radio
- ✔ metric ruler
- ✔ small compass
- ✔ wire cutters

Materials Preparation

Wear eye protection and safety gloves. Use a craft knife to carefully cut a hole in the bottom of each film canister. The hole should be about the size of a quarter. Many film canisters have a circle on the bottom that is approximately this size; simply cut along the circle, and discard the small plastic circle.

The bolts should have the same diameter as the plastic pen and can be of any length.

Classroom Organization

- This activity may be performed by students working alone or in groups of two.
- If desired, each section of the lab may be performed during a short part of class on different days.
- **Safety warnings:** Students should wear closed-toe shoes; falling objects can cause serious injury.

Techniques to Demonstrate

If students will have to use the wire cutters to strip the ends of the wire, show them how to do this safely. Students should wear eye protection at all times.

HOLT PHYSICS Laboratory Experiments Teacher's Edition

Checkpoints

Step 1: Students should leave a 20 cm tail of wire before they begin wrapping; the finished coil should have 20 cm left on each end.

Step 4: All batteries should be fresh. If students have trouble with this section of the lab, replace the batteries with new batteries and try again.

Step 18: Students often have problems wrapping the wire for the speakers. They need to tape the wire down as they progress. Small pieces of tape will work to hold the wire down.

Step 22: Make sure students wire the headphone plug correctly.

Step 25: If a speaker does not work, check the headphone plug connection. Open the headphone plug, restrip the wires, and reconnect them. The speakers can work with any kind of magnet, but if the magnet is very small or oddly shaped, the volume will be very low. Students may need to listen to the speakers in a quiet place.

Answers To

Analysis

A. The needle is perpendicular to the wire, and it points in opposite directions above the wire and below the wire, switching directions as it moves.

B. The magnetic field was stronger with the steel bolt inside the coil.

C. The paper clips were attracted to the bolt.

D. The coil with the steel bolt was much stronger than the coil with the brass bolt.

E. The batteries in the portable radio power the electromagnet.

F. The magnetic fields of the coiled wire and the ceramic magnets interact as the current in the wire changes.

G. Adding more ceramic magnets or increasing the number of wire coils would increase the strength of the magnetic fields and increase the volume of the speaker.

Additional Notes

Invention Lab

HOLT PHYSICS *Laboratory Experiments Teacher's Edition*

Post-Chapter Activity **22**

Building a Circuit Breaker

OBJECTIVES

Students will

- use appropriate lab safety procedures.
- use the scientific method to solve a problem.
- design a circuit breaker using a solenoid.

Planning

Recommended time

1 lab period if students wrap solenoids prior to class

Students should have their plan approved before class begins.

Materials

[for each lab group]

- ✔ box of large metal paper clips
- ✔ roll of magnet wire, 22 AWG
- ✔ plastic drinking straw
- ✔ cardboard
- ✔ battery pack for 2 D-cells
- ✔ 2 D-cell batteries
- ✔ lamp board with 5 miniature sockets
- ✔ 5 miniature bulbs (3 V)
- ✔ craft knife
- ✔ electrical tape
- ✔ scissors
- ✔ aluminum foil
- ✔ modeling clay
- ✔ 3 connecting leads with alligator clips
- ✔ switch
- ✔ 70 cm bare copper wire, 18 AWG

Materials Preparation

You may want to make multimeters or dc ammeters and voltmeters available to students during this lab. See page T21 for instructions on using multimeters, to measure current, potential difference, and resistance.

All batteries should be new.

Classroom Organization

- Students may perform this activity alone or in groups of two or more.
- All work should be performed away from sources of water. All work areas must be kept dry at all times.
- **Safety warnings:** Warn students not to touch uninsulated wire with their fingers or to allow the wire to cross or contact itself. Students should be supervised when working with sharp objects. Eye protection should be worn at all times.

Techniques to Demonstrate

You may want to prepare a solenoid from the directions given in the lab for students to use as an example.

Remind students that wire coils may heat rapidly during this activity. Students should close the switch only long enough to make their observations.

Pre-Lab Discussion

Remind students to concentrate on safety throughout this experiment. Ask students to think about what role a circuit breaker plays in safety and how circuit breakers can be used to prevent hazards.

CHAPTER 22 **T101**

HOLT PHYSICS Laboratory Experiments Teacher's Edition continued

Ask students to make sure their plans include a complete description of the current in the circuit, both when the circuit is functioning under normal conditions and when the current in the solenoid is high enough to create a magnetic field that can move the plunger.

Tips for Evaluating the Pre-Lab Requirements

Students' plans should be complete and safe. Students should describe the procedure they will use to build the circuit breaker, and they should explain why they think the circuit breaker will work.

Plans should include circuit diagrams and a written explanation of how different parts of the circuit work together to act as a circuit breaker when there is too much current. Students should realize that the lamps must be wired in parallel so that the current will increase as more bulbs are added to the circuit.

Proposed Procedure

Construct a solenoid coil following the directions given in the lab notes. Measure and mark 6 cm from the end of a plastic drinking straw. Measure a 10 cm tail at the end of a magnet wire, and bend the wire 90°. Tape the tail to the long part of the straw so that the bend is at the 6 cm mark. Wind the wire around the straw in tight, even coils from the bend to the free end of the straw. Make sure the coils touch each other, with no space between them. Count the coils as you wrap. Tape the coils down at regular intervals. When you reach the end of the straw, place a layer of tape over the first layer of coils, and begin wrapping in the opposite direction. Continue wrapping back and forth down the length of the straw until you have 200 coils. Leave a 5 cm tail of wire when you finish. Make sure the coil is taped securely so it will hold its shape. Unbend the outer leg of a large paper clip to make a plunger to use with the solenoid. Construct a circuit that includes a switch, the solenoid, and the batteries. Place the paper clip so that the straight leg is partially inside the solenoid, and connect the batteries to start the current. The magnetic field of the solenoid should cause the plunger to move when current is applied.

Cut two 5 cm pieces from a normal-sized plastic drinking straw. Cover each straw neatly and securely with aluminum foil. After wrapping the straw, leave about 5 cm of aluminum foil unwrapped to connect a wire to. Glue these two straws parallel to each other on a piece of cardboard. The paper clip will rest on top of the straws and will close the circuit between them.

Use connecting wires to connect the positive post of the battery with the first contact foil. Connect the second contact foil in series with the solenoid, the lampboard, the switch, and the negative post of the battery.

Wire the lamps on the lampboard in parallel using the bare copper wire. Start the test with one bulb screwed in and the rest loosely in place.

Close the switch so that there is current in the circuit. The light bulb should light. If the light bulb does not light because the plunger does not make good contact with both straws, wrap the plunger tightly with aluminum foil or use modeling clay on top of the plunger to weigh down the plunger.

Screw the second bulb in, and close the switch. Continue adding bulbs until the circuit breaker trips. (Usually the circuit breaker will trip when three or four bulbs are screwed in.)

When too much current is in the circuit, the plunger should be pulled partway into the solenoid. This will pull the plunger out of contact with the straws and cause the current to stop.

Post-Lab

Tips for Evaluating Patent Application Lab Report

Student lab reports should include diagrams of the circuit and the circuit breaker. Diagrams should be labeled and clearly drawn. Student reports should explain how the solenoid causes the plunger to move when there is too much current. Some students will realize that they can control the number of lamps it takes to trip the breaker by varying the amount of clay added to weigh down the armature.

HOLT PHYSICS Laboratory Experiments Teacher's Edition continued

Additional Notes

HOLT PHYSICS

LABORATORY EXPERIMENTS

HOLT, RINEHART AND WINSTON

A Harcourt Classroom Education Company

Austin • New York • Orlando • Atlanta • San Francisco • Boston • Dallas • Toronto • London

Holt Physics
Laboratory Experiments

Lab Authors

Douglas W. Biedenweg, Ph.D.
Chadwick School
Palos Verdes, CA

Kaye M. Elsner-McCall
Physics Teacher
Riverwood High School
Fulton County Schools
Atlanta, GA

Anthony L. Komon
Physics Teacher
Science Department
Niskayuna High School
Schenectady, NY

Sean P. Lally
Chairman of Science
Sewickley Academy
Sewickley, PA

Safety Reviewer

Gregory Puskar
Laboratory Manager
Physics Department
West Virginia University
Morgantown, WV

Laboratory Reviewers

Lee Sennholtz
Central Scientific Company
Franklin Park, IL

Martin Taylor
Central Scientific Company
Franklin Park, IL

Cover Photo: © Lawrence Manning/CORBIS

Cover Design: Jason Wilson

Illustrations: All art is contributed by *Holt, Rinehart and Winston* and David Kelley.

Copyright © by Holt, Rinehart and Winston

All rights reserved. No part of this publication may be reproduced or transmitted in any form or by any means, electronic or mechanical, including photocopy, recording, or any information storage and retrieval system, without permission in writing from the publisher.

Teachers using HOLT PHYSICS may photocopy blackline masters in complete pages in sufficient quantities for classroom use only and not for resale.

Printed in the United States of America

ISBN 0-03-057358-0

1 2 3 4 5 6 095 04 03 02 01 00

Contents

Holt Physics Laboratory Experiments Booklet v
Sample Patent Application Lab Report vii
Laboratory Safety ix

Chapter 1
Discovery Lab The Circumference-Diameter Ratio of a Circle 1
Invention Lab Bubble Solutions 4

Chapter 2
Discovery Lab Motion 7
Invention Lab Race Car Construction 10

Chapter 3
Discovery Lab Vector Treasure Hunt 13
Invention Lab The Path of a Human Cannonball 16

Chapter 4
Discovery Lab Discovering Newton's Laws 19
Invention Lab Friction: Testing Materials 22

Chapter 5
Discovery Lab Exploring Work and Energy 25
Invention Lab Bungee Jumping: Energy 28

Chapter 7
Discovery Lab Circular Motion 31

Chapter 8
Discovery Lab Torque and Center of Mass 35
Invention Lab The Rotating Egg Drop 38

Chapter 10
Discovery Lab Temperature and Internal Energy 41
Invention Lab Thermal Conduction 44

Chapter 12
Discovery Lab Pendulums and Spring Waves 47
Invention Lab Tensile Strength and Hooke's Law 50

Chapter 13
Discovery Lab Resonance and the Nature of Sound 53
Invention Lab Building a Musical Instrument 56

Chapter 14
Discovery Lab Light and Mirrors **59**
Invention Lab Designing a Device to Trace Drawings **62**

Chapter 15
Discovery Lab Refraction and Lenses **65**
Invention Lab Camera Design **68**

Chapter 17
Discovery Lab Charges and Electrostatics **71**
Invention Lab Levitating Toys **74**

Chapter 19
Discovery Lab Resistors and Current **77**
Invention Lab Battery-operated Portable Heater **80**

Chapter 20
Discovery Lab Exploring Circuit Elements **83**
Invention Lab Designing a Dimmer Switch **86**

Chapter 21
Discovery Lab Magnetism **89**
Invention Lab Designing a Magnetic Spring **92**

Chapter 22
Discovery Lab Electricity and Magnetism **95**
Invention Lab Building a Circuit Breaker **98**

HOLT PHYSICS Laboratory Program Overview

Using the labs in this book

Taking different approaches to the challenge of physics

The *Holt Physics Laboratory Experiments* booklet contains 33 all-new laboratory experiments. The two types of labs in this booklet are designed to help you learn physics from the beginning of each chapter to the end. You will probably find that the labs in this booklet are organized differently from those in the textbook and from any laboratory experiments you have done before. The first type of lab, called a *Discovery Lab*, guides you through new lessons with a step-by-step, hands-on approach that gives you real-world experience with the physics concepts you will study in each chapter. The second type of lab is called an *Invention Lab*, and it gives you the opportunity to use your physics knowledge by developing an invention or process to solve a real problem.

As you work on both of these types of labs, you will develop a solid understanding of how the concepts presented in the textbook relate to everyday physical phenomena, and you will use your understanding of physics to solve problems like those faced by physicists and engineers every day.

Discovery Labs

The Discovery Labs are divided up into small sections, each presenting a basic physics concept. Each section provides step-by-step procedures for you to follow, encouraging you to make careful observations and interpretations as you perform each step of the lab. After each section, there is a series of questions designed to help you make sense of your observations and data and relate them to the physics concepts you will study in the chapter.

What you should do before a Discovery Lab

Preparation will help you work safely and efficiently. Before a lab, be sure to do the following:

- **Read the lab procedure** to make sure you understand what you will do in each step.
- **Read the safety information** that begins on page ix, as well as the special safety instructions provided in the lab procedure. Plan to wear appropriate shoes, clothing, and protective safety equipment while you work in the lab.
- **Write down any questions** you have in your lab notebook and ask them before the lab begins.
- **Prepare all necessary data tables** so that you will be able to concentrate on your work when you are in the lab.

What you should do after a Discovery Lab

Most teachers require a written lab report as a way of making sure that you understood what you were doing in the lab. Your teacher will give you specific details about how to organize your written work for the Discovery Labs, but most lab reports will include the following:

- **the title** of the lab
- **data tables and observations** that are organized, complete, and easy to understand
- **answers** to the items and questions that appear after each section of the procedure

Invention Labs

The Invention Labs may seem unusual to you because they do not provide you with step-by-step instructions. The Invention Labs present problems in the context of assignments for an engineering and research company. These labs refer to you as an employee of the company, and your teacher has the role of a supervisor. Lab situations are given for real-life problems. The Invention Labs require you to develop your own procedure to solve a problem presented to your company by a client. As part of the research and development team working for the client, you must choose equipment and a procedure to solve the problem. Each lab is designed to use physics concepts that you have studied in the previous chapters, and each lab contains hints and useful information about how to solve the problem.

HOLT PHYSICS Laboratory Program Overview continued

What you should do before an Invention Lab

Before you will be allowed to work on the lab, you must turn in an initial plan. Your teacher will tell you exactly how to write an initial plan, but most plans must include a detailed description of the procedure you plan to use, the measurements and observations you will take, and a list of equipment you will use to complete the lab. Your teacher, acting as your supervisor, must approve your plan before you are allowed to proceed. Before you begin writing an initial plan, complete the following steps:

- **Read the Invention Lab thoroughly** to make sure you understand the problem. Read carefully, and pay attention to the hints and guidelines that are presented in the lab.
- **Jot down notes** in your lab notebook as you find clues and begin to develop a plan.
- **Consider how to use physics concepts** to solve the problem. Think about the measurements and observations you will have to make to find a solution.
- **Imagine working through a procedure,** keeping track of each step and the equipment you will need. Pay special attention to safety issues.
- **Carefully consider** ways to improve your approach, in terms of logic, safety, and efficiency.
- **Read the safety information** that begins on page ix, as well as the special safety instructions provided in the lab. Plan to wear appropriate shoes, clothing, and protective safety equipment while working in the lab.

What you should do after an Invention Lab

When you have completed the lab, you will present your results in the form of a Patent Application. Your teacher may have additional requirements for your report. A sample Patent Application lab report can be found on page vii.

The format for the Patent Application lab report is based on the real requirements for patent applications in the United States. For the Invention Lab reports, a Patent Application must include the following eight sections.

1. **Date, Title, and Inventor:** The date and title of the invention and the name of the principal inventor, followed by the names of any team members or joint inventors. If your team is preparing a single application, all members may be listed jointly.

2. **Background—Field of Invention:** A sentence that states both the general and specific field relating to your invention. For example, "This invention relates to direct current circuits, specifically to decorative lighting."

3. **Drawings:** Include as many types of drawings from as many perspectives as you need to present the mechanics of your invention. Each part of your invention should be labeled with a number or letter in the drawing for easy reference.

4. **Description of Drawings:** A brief description of each drawing, specifying the type of view being presented (cross-section, top view, side view, schematic, exploded, etc.).

5. **List of Reference Numerals:** This is a list of the numbers you used in your drawings, with a description of what each number refers to.

6. **Description of Invention:** This is a detailed description of all the parts of the invention. Refer to your diagrams. Describe the individual parts and how they are connected.

7. **Operation of Invention:** Describe the actual operation of your invention. Include a discussion of the theory of how it operates. Include any equations, proportions, or formulas necessary for an understanding of how your invention works. Also include the physical values you measured in the lab. (Hint: It is always helpful to proceed with the description in an orderly fashion—for example, when describing an electrical circuit, you may want to begin at the negative post of the battery and "follow" the current through the circuit.)

8. **Conclusion, Ramifications, and Scope of Invention:** One sentence restates the purpose and operation of the invention. The rest of this section is a discussion of possible variations of the design and can include ideas for other possible applications of the device or process.

HOLT PHYSICS Sample Invention Lab Report

Sample Patent Application Lab Report

This sample lab report is provided to give you a model to follow. Your patent applications will not be exactly like this one, but they should contain the same basic parts, as described above.

1. **Date:** May 18, 1999
   Title: Doormat Lighting System
   Inventor: Antonia Briggs
                 Sinh Ngyuen

2. **Background—Field of Invention:** This invention relates to resistors in direct current circuits, specifically to security lighting.

3. **Drawings:**

   Drawing A

   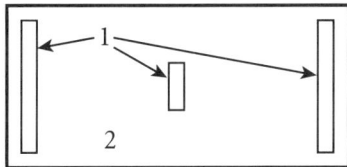

   Drawing B

   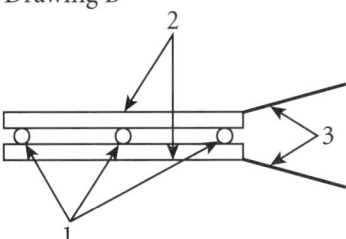

   Drawing C

   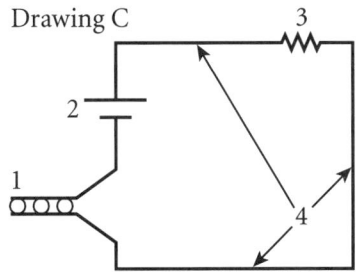

4. **Description of Drawings** and
5. **List of Reference Numerals:**

   Drawing A Top view of the bottom of the doormat
   1. plastic drinking straws, two on ends are 8 cm long, one in center is 4 cm long
   2. flat pieces of cardboard, 20 cm × 10 cm, covered with heavy-duty aluminum foil

   Drawing B Side view of the doormat
   1. side view of three plastic drinking straws (see Drawing A: 1)
   2. side view of two pieces of cardboard, 20 cm × 10 cm, both covered with aluminum foil
   3. connecting wires, connected to top side of aluminum foil

   Drawing C Circuit diagram
   1. Doormat (see Drawing B: 1, 2, and 3)
   2. dc battery
   3. light bulb
   4. insulated connecting wires

6. **Description of Invention:** The Doormat Lighting System consists of a doormat wired in a series circuit with a dc battery and a light bulb. The doormat is constructed by taking two pieces of cardboard or other firm material and covering them with aluminum foil. The aluminum foil is glued or taped securely to the cardboard. On one piece of cardboard, drinking straws are glued securely at each end and in the middle of the cardboard. The straws on the ends should be almost the same length as the end of the cardboard, and the straw in the middle should be about half that length. All straws should be centered lengthwise on the cardboard, so there is equal distance from the end of the straw to the edge of the cardboard on both sides. See Drawing A.

   The second foil-covered piece of cardboard is placed on top of the straws and glued securely. The cardboard pieces should be stacked so that the edges line up exactly, and the straws should prevent them from touching. Insulated connecting wires are attached to the top and bottom of the foil-covered pieces. See Drawing B for a side view.

   The insulated connecting wires are used to wire the doormat in series with a dc battery and a light bulb, as shown in Drawing C.

7. **Operation of Invention:** The Doormat Lighting System will light a lightbulb when weight is applied to the doormat. The purpose of this invention is to allow a person to step on the doormat and turn on the light. The dc battery connected in

series with the light bulb and the doormat provides a potential difference to the circuit. The doormat acts as a switch in this circuit. When the two surfaces of the doormat are not touching, as when no weight is applied to the doormat, the switch is open and there is no current in the circuit. When weight is applied to the doormat and the two foil-covered surfaces touch, the switch is closed and there is current in the circuit according to the potential difference and the resistance present in the circuit. This relationship is given by the following equation:

$$I = \frac{\Delta V}{R}$$

We developed our circuit using a 9 V dc battery and a 6.3 V, 115 mA light bulb.

When there is current in the circuit, the light bulb, which acts as a resistor in the circuit, will light.

When the weight is removed from the doormat, the plates of the doormat will separate, opening the switch, and there will be no current in the circuit. The light bulb will no longer be lighted.

8. Conclusion, Ramifications, and Scope of Invention: The Doormat Lighting System is a security lighting device that uses a resistor in a dc circuit with a battery. The doormat itself operates as a switch in this circuit, and a light bulb operates as a resistor. When the doormat is stepped on, the switch is closed and the light bulb lights. When the weight is removed from the doormat, the switch is opened and the light stops.

In this design, pieces of plastic drinking straws are used to separate the two conducting parts of the doormat. Other items, such as springs, may be used in place of the drinking straws. Any material used for this purpose must be flexible, so that it will compress when weight is applied and will return to its original position when the weight is removed, and it must not conduct electricity. In fact, another type of separator may be better, because the drinking straws become flattened with use and will need to be replaced often to maintain the required distance between the two pieces.

The dimensions of all the parts of this system, from the size of the doormat to the length of the wires, depends upon the desired use. This system may be used to place a doormat outside the door of a house and light a lamp above the door, or it may be used to light a lamp placed inside the house or at another location. The battery and light bulb must be selected so that the battery provides enough potential difference to light the selected bulb but not enough to cause a fire or short circuit.

Another possible use of the design would be to use a resistor other than a light bulb. For example, the circuit could contain a buzzer or some other device. In this way, the circuit could operate as an alarm system or a doorbell. In addition, the switch in the circuit could be designed for use in any device that required a pressure-sensitive switch. The switch could be placed in the bottom of a mailbox and wired to a light or buzzer inside the house; this system would notify someone inside the house that the mail had been delivered.

Because aluminum foil conducts electricity, it would be necessary to cover the entire switch in insulating material before using this device.

HOLT PHYSICS Safety in the Physics Laboratory

Safety in the Physics Laboratory

Lab work is the key to progress in science. Therefore, systematic, careful lab work is an essential part of any science program. In this class, you will practice some of the same fundamental laboratory procedures and techniques that experimental physicists use to pursue new knowledge.

The equipment and apparatus you will use involve various safety hazards, just as they do for working physicists. You must be aware of these hazards. Your teacher will guide you in properly using the equipment and carrying out the experiments, but you must also take responsibility for your part in this process. With the active involvement of you and your teacher, these risks can be minimized so that working in the physics laboratory can be a safe, enjoyable process of discovery.

These safety rules always apply in the lab

1. **Always wear a lab apron and safety goggles.**
   Wear these safety devices whenever you are in the lab, not just when you are working on an experiment.

2. **No contact lenses in the lab.**
   Contact lenses should not be worn during any investigations using chemicals (even if you are wearing goggles). In the event of an accident, chemicals can get behind contact lenses and cause serious damage before the lenses can be removed. If your doctor requires that you wear contact lenses instead of glasses, you should wear eye-cup safety goggles in the lab. Ask your doctor or your teacher how to use this important eye protection.

3. **Personal apparel should be appropriate for laboratory work.**
   On lab days avoid wearing long necklaces, dangling bracelets, bulky jewelry, and bulky or loose-fitting clothing. Long hair should be tied back. Loose, dangling items may get caught in moving parts, accidentally contact electrical connections, or interfere with the investigation in a potentially hazardous manner. In addition, chemical fumes may react with some jewelry, such as pearls, and ruin them. Cotton clothing is preferable to wool, nylon, or polyester. Wear shoes that will protect your feet from chemical spills and falling objects—open-toed shoes or sandals, and shoes with woven leather straps are not allowed in the laboratory.

4. **NEVER work alone in the laboratory.**
   Work in the lab only while under the supervision of your teacher. Do not leave equipment unattended while it is in operation.

5. **Only books and notebooks needed for the experiment should be in the lab.**
   Only the lab notebook and the textbook should be used. Keep other books, backpacks, purses, and similar items in your desk, locker, or designated storage area.

6. **Read the entire experiment before entering the lab.**
   Your teacher will review applicable safety precautions before the lab. If you are not sure of something, ask your teacher about it.

7. **Always heed safety symbols and cautions written in the experimental investigations and handouts, posted in the room, and given verbally by your teacher.**
   They are provided for your safety.

8. **Know the proper fire drill procedures and the location of fire exits and emergency equipment.**
   Make sure you know the procedures to follow in case of a fire or an emergency.

9. **If your clothing catches on fire, do not run; WALK to the safety shower, stand under it, and turn it on.**
   Call to your teacher while you do this.

10. **Report all accidents to the teacher immediately, no matter how minor.**
    In addition, if you get a headache, feel sick to your stomach, or feel dizzy, tell your teacher immediately.

11. **Report all spills to your teacher immediately.**
    Call your teacher rather than trying to clean up a spill yourself. Your teacher will tell you if it is safe for you to clean up the spill; if not, your teacher will know how the spill should be cleaned up safely.

HOLT PHYSICS Safety in the Physics Laboratory continued

12. **Student-designed inquiry investigations, such as the Invention Labs in the Laboratory Experiments manual, must be approved by the teacher before being attempted by the student.**

13. **DO NOT perform unauthorized experiments or use materials and equipment in a manner for which they were not intended.**
    Use only materials and equipment listed in the activity equipment list or authorized by your teacher. Steps in a procedure should only be performed as described in the textbook or lab manual or approved by your teacher.

14. **Stay alert in the lab, and proceed with caution.**
    Be aware of others near you or your equipment when you are performing an experiment. If you are not sure of how to proceed, ask.

15. **Horseplay in the lab is very dangerous.**
    Laboratory equipment and apparatus are not toys; never play in the lab or use lab time or equipment for anything other than their intended purpose.

16. **Food, beverages, chewing gum, and tobacco products are NEVER permitted in the laboratory.**

17. **NEVER taste chemicals. Do not touch chemicals or allow them to contact areas of bare skin.**

18. **Use extreme CAUTION when working with hot plates or other heating devices.**
    Keep your head, hands, hair, and clothing away from the flame or heating area, and turn heating devices off when they are not in use. Remember that metal surfaces connected to the heated area will become hot by conduction. Gas burners should be lit only with a spark lighter. Make sure all heating devices and gas valves are turned off before leaving the laboratory. Never leave a hot plate or other heating device unattended when it is in use. Remember that many metal, ceramic, and glass items do not always look hot when they are hot. Allow all items to cool before storing.

19. **Exercise caution when working with electrical equipment.**
    Do not use electrical equipment with frayed or twisted wires. Be sure your hands are dry before using electrical equipment. Do not let electrical cords dangle from work stations; dangling cords can cause electrical shocks and other injuries.

20. **Keep work areas and apparatus clean and neat.**
    Always clean up any clutter made during lab work, rearrange apparatus in an orderly manner, and report any damaged or missing items.

21. **Always thoroughly wash your hands with soap and water at the conclusion of each investigation.**

Safety Symbols

The following safety symbols will appear in the laboratory experiments to emphasize additional important areas of caution. Learn what they represent so you can take the appropriate precautions. Remember that the safety symbols represent hazards that apply to a specific activity, but the numbered rules given on the previous pages apply to all laboratory work.

 Waste Disposal

- Never put broken glass or ceramics in a regular waste container. Use a dustpan, a brush, and heavy gloves to carefully pick up broken pieces, and dispose of them in a container specifically provided for this purpose.

- Dispose of chemicals as instructed by your teacher. Never pour hazardous chemicals into a regular waste container. Never pour radioactive materials down the drain.

 Heating Safety

- When using a burner or hot plate, always wear goggles and an apron to protect your eyes and clothing. Tie back long hair, secure loose clothing and remove loose jewelry.

- Never leave a hot plate unattended while it is turned on.

- Wire coils may heat up rapidly during this experiment. If heating occurs, open the switch immediately and handle the equipment with a hot mitt.

HOLT PHYSICS Safety in the Physics Laboratory continued

- Allow all equipment to cool before storing it.
- If your clothing catches on fire, walk to the emergency lab shower and use the shower to put out the fire.

Hand Safety

- Perform this experiment in a clear area. Attach masses securely. Falling, dropped, or swinging objects can cause serious injury.
- Use a hot mitt to handle resistors, light sources, and other equipment that may be hot. Allow all equipment to cool before storing it.

Glassware Safety

- If a thermometer breaks, notify the teacher **immediately.**
- Do not heat glassware that is broken, chipped, or cracked. Use tongs or a hot mitt to handle heated glassware and other equipment that may be hot. Allow all equipment to cool before storing it.
- If a bulb breaks, notify your teacher immediately. Do not remove broken bulbs from sockets.

Electrical Safety

- Never close a circuit until it has been approved by your teacher. Never rewire or adjust any element of a closed circuit.
- Never work with electricity near water. Be sure the floor and all work surfaces are dry.
- If the pointer on any kind of meter moves off scale, open the circuit immediately by opening the switch.

- Do not work with any batteries, electrical devices, or magnets other than those provided by your teacher.

Chemical Safety

- Do not eat or drink anything in the laboratory. Never taste chemicals or touch them with your bare hands.
- Do not allow radioactive materials to come into contact with your skin, hair, clothing, or personal belongings. Although the materials used in this lab are not hazardous when used properly, radioactive materials can cause serious illness.

Clothing Protection

- Tie back long hair, secure loose clothing, and remove loose jewelry to prevent their getting caught in moving or rotating parts or coming into contact with hazardous chemicals.

Eye Protection

- Wear eye protection, and perform this experiment in a clear area. Swinging objects can cause serious injury.
- Avoid looking directly at a light source. Looking directly at a light source may cause permanent eye damage.

Pre-Chapter Exploration 1

HOLT PHYSICS
Discovery Lab

The Circumference-Diameter Ratio of a Circle

SAFETY

- Review lab safety guidelines. Always follow correct procedures in the lab.

MATERIALS

- ✔ cord
- ✔ masking tape
- ✔ metric rulers
- ✔ pencil
- ✔ several cylindrical objects of varying size
- ✔ white paper

OBJECTIVES

- Develop techniques for measuring the circumference and diameter of a cylinder.
- Use data to construct a graph.
- Determine the slope of a graph.
- Analyze error in an experiment.

Measurements of a cylinder

Procedure

1. Select one of the cylinders. Examine the cylinder to determine how many different measurements would be necessary to give a complete description of the cylinder. In this lab, you will use a cylinder's measurements to identify one cylinder from a group of cylinders, so make sure your measurements enable you to distinguish the cylinder from similar cylinders.

2. Determine at least two different methods of making the measurements. Be sure you include ways to measure the circumference of the cylinder in each method. Keep in mind that you must measure each quantity directly; no values can be found through calculations.

3. Take all the measurements for the cylinder using the first method you developed. Record all measurements in your notebook using the appropriate SI units. Make sure to include all measured digits plus one estimated digit.

4. Place the cylinder into a container with a group of other cylinders. Trade measurements with another group. Use your method of measurement to find the cylinder that matches the measurements you were given.

Analysis

A. What measurements did you make?

B. What was your method of measuring the cylinder? Describe your method in detail.

C. Did you find the cylinder that matched the measurements you were given? If not, why not?

D. Did the other group correctly identify the cylinder you measured? If not, why not?

E. Compare your measurements with the other group's measurements for the same cylinder. Are the measurements the same? Explain any differences in your methods or measurements.

Comparing methods of measurement

Procedure

5. Using the same method you used to measure the first cylinder, measure the length, diameter, and circumference of several more cylinders. Label each cylinder with an identifying name written on masking tape. Record your measurements in your notebook using the appropriate SI units.

6. Perform another trial, using a different method to take the measurements. Repeat the measurements for the length, diameter, and circumference of all cylinders. Record your measurements in your notebook using the appropriate SI units.

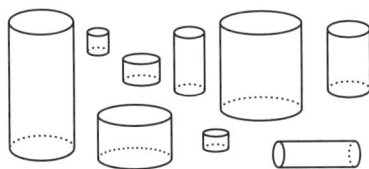

Analysis

F. Compare the results you obtained using two different methods of measurement. Did you get the same measurements for each cylinder regardless of which method you used? If not, explain what you think caused the difference.

G. Which method do you think was best for measuring the cylinders? What were some problems with the other methods you tried?

H. How could you determine which method of measuring the cylinders gave the best results?

Data analysis

Procedure

7. Use the data you collected to decide which method of measuring the cylinders gave the best results. For each cylinder, select the measurements taken with this method.

8. Use the data you selected in step 7. For each cylinder, find the value for the circumference of the cylinder divided by the diameter of the cylinder.

Analysis

I. Is the relationship between the circumference and the diameter the same for all cylinders, or is it different for each one?

J. Based on your results, what measurements do you think are necessary to give a complete description of a cylinder?

Graphing data

Procedure

9. Using the data you selected, make a graph of the circumference of the cylinders versus the diameter of the cylinders. For each cylinder, plot a point on the graph that represents the cylinder's circumference and diameter.

10. Draw the line or curve that best fits the points on the graph. Not all the points on the graph will actually fall directly on the line, but the line should follow the shape made by most of the points. The line should not connect each point directly to the next one. Instead, it should be drawn as a smooth line or curve connecting most of the points.

11. Select two points on the line, one at the beginning and one at the end. Make sure the points selected are points on the best fit line but are not data points. Use the scales on the axes of the graph to determine the circumference and diameter of the cylinders that would be represented by these points on the line.

12. Label the points that you selected A and B. Find the difference between the values for the circumference at these points, and use this as the *rise*. In other words, subtract the value for the circumference at A from the value for the circumference at B. Find the difference between the values for the diameter at these points, and use this as the *run*. Subtract the value for the diameter at A from the value for the diameter at B.

13. Find the slope of the line, using the equation $slope = \frac{rise}{run}$.

Analysis

K. On your graph, which quantity is the independent variable?

L. On your graph, which quantity is the dependent variable?

M. Describe the shape of the curve in your graph.

N. What is the value that you calculated for the slope of the curve in your graph? Compare this to the relationship between the circumference and the diameter that you calculated in step 8.

O. Based on your data and your graph, do you think it is better to find the relationship between the circumference and the diameter by using the slope of the graph or by calculating individual values? Explain your answer.

HOLT PHYSICS Invention Lab

Post-Chapter Activity 1

Bubble Solutions

TANTRUM TOYS, INC.
TROY, NEW YORK

August 15, 1999

Ms. Elaine Taylor
Product Development Department
1% Inspiration Laboratories
14557 West Post Road
Tempe, Arizona 85289

Dear Ms. Taylor:

At Tantrum Toys, we always try to stay one step ahead of the market. That's why we are looking into new formulations for our famous bubble solution. We have developed a new formula that we believe will help our bubble solution make bigger, longer-lasting bubbles.

We would like you to test our new bubble solution against several other commercially available solutions, including the solution currently marketed by Tantrum Toys. In order to cut down on human error or bias in the laboratory, we are sending the solutions to you in identical packaging, marked only with a letter. We would like you to test all solutions to find out which produces the biggest bubbles.

Please perform two tests: the dome test and the free-floating bubble test. For the dome test, use a straw to blow a domed bubble in a pan of solution. Measure the height and diameter of each dome. For the free-floating bubble test, construct a bubble maker to make large free-floating bubbles. Measure the diameter of each bubble.

When you have finished your tests, put together a report describing how you performed the tests, showing the equipment you used, and detailing your results. Please have the report and all unused solutions delivered to my office by September 8.

Good luck,
Stewart Clydesdale
Stewart Clydesdale

A description of a bubble maker is on page 6.

1% Inspiration Laboratories

MEMORANDUM

Date: August 19, 1999
To: Product Testing Team
From: Elaine Taylor

I think the best way to get all these tests done in time is to have several people work on them at once. Hopefully, one solution will be obviously better than the others and all our results will be the same. Before you go into the lab, prepare a plan for each of the tests described in the letter. Be sure to include your plan for measuring the width, height, and diameter of the bubbles in the lab. This will be a tricky procedure, because we have to find a way to get good measurements without actually touching the bubbles. Consistency and accuracy will also be very important, especially since we will have to work quickly and carefully to make our measurements before the bubbles pop.

Present your plan to me for approval before you start work in the lab. For each test, your plan should include a list of materials needed, a diagram, and a one- or two-sentence explanation of the procedure you will use. I have included a list of the equipment we have available. If you need something that you can't find on the list, be sure to ask about it; there may be more equipment available.

For the second test, you will need to construct a bubble maker using the materials on the list. The background information Mr. Clydesdale sent me on one type of bubble wand is attached to this memo, but I will be interested to see what you can come up with. Be sure to include your design when you submit your plan for approval.

When you have all your results, write a report using the format of a patent application. Remember to document all your testing and development procedures in your lab notebook.

14557 West Post Road • Tempe, Arizona 852

continued

MATERIALS

ITEM	QTY.
✔ adhesive tape	1 roll
✔ aluminum pans	
✔ bubble solutions	
✔ cord	100 cm
✔ meterstick	1
✔ metric ruler	1
✔ paper towels	
✔ plastic drinking straws	6
✔ rubber bands	4

SAFETY

- Do not eat or drink anything in the laboratory. Never taste chemicals or touch them with your bare hands.

- Dispose of chemicals as instructed by your teacher. Never pour hazardous chemicals into a regular waste container.

- Tie back long hair, secure loose clothing, and remove loose jewelry to prevent their coming into contact with hazardous chemicals.

- Wear eye protection. Keep chemicals away from eyes.

When it comes to bubbles, the bigger the better

It may not seem like a museum piece to some people, but to the children who visit The Discovery Science Museum in Birmingham, a simple contraption made of plastic drinking straws and string is among the best things the museum has to offer.

This device allows students to make soap bubbles bigger than any they've seen before. This magic wand was invented right here at the Discovery Science Museum, but it can be recreated by children everywhere because the materials are readily available.

All you need is a piece of thread about 1 meter long and two plastic drinking straws. Thread the string through both straws, and tie the two ends of the string into a knot. Pull the string around until the knot is safely hidden away inside one of the straws. Use both hands to pull the straws apart, so that they are parallel to each other, with the strings relaxed between them. Dip the two string sides into bubble solution—either a commercial brand, like the favorite from Tantrum Toys, or a solution made with ordinary dish soap.

To make a long bubble, pull the frame through the air or blow gently. This activity will delight children immediately, but we bet it won't take adults long to admit that it is a great work of art!

Pre-Chapter Exploration 2

HOLT PHYSICS
Discovery Lab

Motion

SAFETY

- Tie back long hair, secure loose clothing, and remove loose jewelry to prevent their being caught in moving or rotating parts.
- Perform this experiment in a clear area. Moving masses can cause serious injury.

MATERIALS

- ✔ battery-operated toy car
- ✔ block, book, or clay
- ✔ graph paper
- ✔ masking tape
- ✔ metal ball
- ✔ meterstick
- ✔ stopwatch
- ✔ track
- ✔ wooden block

OBJECTIVES

- Observe objects moving at a constant speed and objects moving with changing speed.
- Graph the relationships between distance and time for moving objects.
- Interpret graphs relating distance and time for moving objects.

Moving at a constant speed

Procedure

1. Find a clear, flat surface a few meters long to perform your experiment. Make sure the area is free of obstacles and traffic. Choose a starting point for your car. Mark this point with masking tape, and label it "starting point."

2. Start the car, and place it on the starting point. Release the car (your lab partner should start the stopwatch at the same time). Let the car move in a straight line for 2.0 s. Notice where the car is after 2.0 s. Repeat for several trials, until you find the point that the car consistently crosses after 2.0 s. Mark this point with masking tape, and label it "0.00 m." Throughout this lab, you will start the car at the original starting point, but you will begin to measure the distance and time of the car's motion when the car crosses the 0.00 m mark.

3. Start the car, and place it on the floor at the starting point. Observe the car as it moves. Be sure to start the stopwatch as the car crosses the 0.00 m mark.

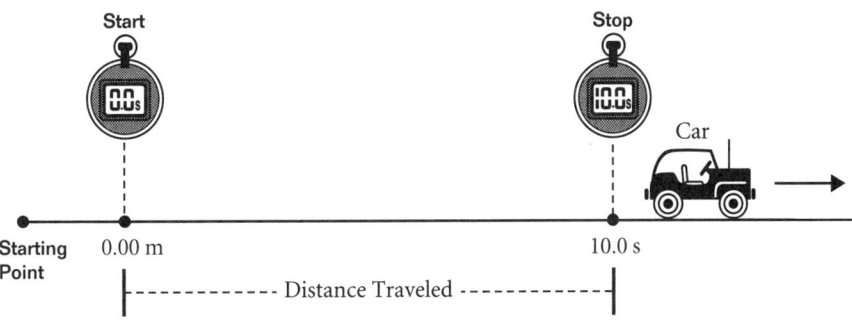

CHAPTER 2 **7**

4. After 10.0 s, mark the position of the car with the masking tape. Label this mark "10.0 s."

5. Repeat steps 3 and 4 for 9.0 s, 8.0 s, 7.0 s, 6.0 s, 5.0 s, 4.0 s, 3.0 s, and 2.0 s. Be sure to label each point according to how much time it took for the car to get to that point from the 0.00 m mark.

6. Use the meterstick to measure the exact distance from the 0.00 m mark to each timed position mark. (Do not measure the distance from the starting point.)

7. For each position marked with tape, record the position and time in your notebook, using the appropriate SI units. Make sure to record all measured digits plus one estimated digit.

8. If your car has a multiple speed switch, set the car at a new speed and repeat steps 3–7.

Analysis

A. Did the car speed up or slow down as it traveled, or did it maintain the same speed? How can you tell?

B. Make a graph of your data with time on the *x*-axis and position on the *y*-axis. Label each axis with the appropriate SI units. This graph tells you the position of the car at any time. Describe the shape of the graph.

C. How far did the car travel in each 1.0 s time interval (2.0–3.0 s, 3.0–4.0 s, 4.0–5.0 s, etc.)? For example, to find the distance traveled in the 2.0–3.0 s time interval, subtract the car's position at 2.0 s from the car's position at 3.0 s, and record this value in your notebook. Repeat to find the change in position for each time interval.

D. Predict the position of the car at 12.0 s. Explain your prediction.

E. Use your answers from C to make a graph with time on the *x*-axis and change in position on the *y*-axis. Label each axis with the appropriate SI units. This graph tells you the distance traveled by the car in each time interval. Describe the shape of this graph.

F. Compare the graphs you made in parts B and E. What similarities are there between these two graphs?

Moving at an increasing speed

Procedure

9. Support one end of the track 2 cm–3 cm above the floor with clay as shown. Secure the track so that it does not move. The base of the track should rest on the floor. Place a block of wood on the floor against the base of the ramp. Mark a point near the top of the track with masking tape, and label it "starting point."

10. Place the ball at the starting point. Hold the ball in place with a ruler.

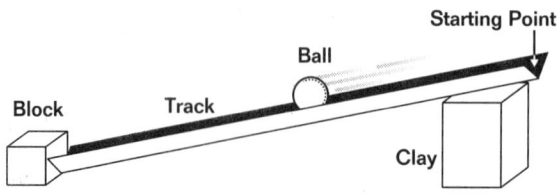

11. To release the ball, rapidly swing the ruler out of the way. Start the stopwatch the instant the ball is released. The ball will roll down the track.
12. Stop the stopwatch when the ball reaches the base of the track.
13. Repeat steps 10–12. Adjust the angle of the track for each trial until you find a position at which it takes the ball slightly longer than 5.0 s to travel from the starting point to the bottom of the track.
14. When the track is secured in position at the determined angle, place the ball at the starting point. Hold the ball in place with a ruler. To release the ball, rapidly swing the ruler out of the way. Start the stopwatch the instant the ball is released.
15. After 4.0 s, mark the position of the ball with masking tape. Label it "4.0 s."
16. Repeat step 14, but mark the position of the ball after 3.0 s of travel. Label the tape "3.0 s."
17. Repeat step 14, but mark the position of the ball after 2.0 s of travel. Label the tape "2.0 s."
18. Measure the exact distance from the starting point to each position marked with tape.
19. For each position, record the distance and time in your notebook, using the appropriate SI units. Make sure to record all measured digits plus one estimated digit.

Analysis

G. Did the ball speed up or slow down as it traveled, or did it maintain the same speed? How can you tell?

H. Make a graph of your data with time on the x-axis and position on the y-axis. Label each axis with the appropriate SI units. This graph tells you the position of the ball at any time. What shape does the graph have?

I. How far did the ball travel in each 1.0 s time interval (2.0–3.0 s, 3.0–4.0 s, 4.0–5.0 s, etc.)? To answer this, find the distance that the ball traveled in each 1.0 s time interval. For example, to find the distance traveled in the 2.0–3.0 s time interval, subtract the ball's position at 2.0 s from the ball's position at 3.0 s, and record this value in your notebook. Repeat to find the change in position for each time interval.

J. Predict the position of the ball at 12.0 s. Explain your prediction.

K. Use your answers from I to make a graph with "time" on the x-axis and "change in position" on the y-axis. Label each axis with the appropriate SI units.

L. Compare the shape of the graphs you made in parts H and B. What differences are there between the graphs?

Post-Chapter Activity 2
HOLT PHYSICS Invention Lab

Race-Car Construction

U.S. RACING ASSOCIATION
LYNCHBURG, SOUTH CAROLINA

September 27, 1999

Mr. Steve Thorpe
1% Inspiration Laboratories
14557 West Post Road
Tempe, Arizona 85289

Dear Mr. Thorpe:

To celebrate our 25th anniversary, we are promoting auto racing this season by having a contest to develop an inexpensive race car. Cash awards and free tickets to the U.S. Racing Association Silver Cup race are going to be awarded in each category to the fastest car that meets the criteria.

The contest will include judging in two categories: cars with motors and motorless cars (cars that move by the force of gravity). The cars that include motors should be powered only by batteries (no fuel) and should travel a displacement of 5.0 m. Motorless cars will need to accelerate to top speed using only a ramp or a similar physical structure and should travel a displacement of 3.0 m. The car may not be pushed, launched, or pulled. If you enter this category, you should also include a complete description of the device used to accelerate the car.

All cars should be composed of scrap materials found around the home. The appearance of the car will not be judged, but contestants should pay careful attention to physical design elements that affect the ability of the car to travel in a straight line at high speeds. Each contest entry should include an analysis of the car's speed, using appropriate SI units accurate to three significant digits. The analysis should average the speeds over three trials, traveling a horizontal distance on a smooth surface, such as tile or a similar surface. The speed must be calculated only on the horizontal path of the car's travel. Each contest entry should use the format of a patent application and include the name of the car. Good luck in the design of your contest entry.

Sincerely,

Billy Joe Greenfield

Billy Joe Greenfield

More information about the design is on page 12.

1% Inspiration Laboratories

MEMORANDUM

Date: September 28, 1999
To: Development Team
From: Steve Thorpe

This project reminds me of some of the soapbox derbies I entered when I was a kid. This really sounds like fun! The U.S. Racing Association car design contest could result in some great prizes, so we will need to do careful planning.

Before you go into the lab, prepare a plan for the design of the car. Your plan should include a list of materials needed and a diagram of the car. Remember to include all of your testing and development procedures. I have included a newspaper clipping with this memo that may be helpful to your design and setup. Your plan should also include a design of a car that will move in a straight path.

- An easy way to do this is to make sure that the car is stable and that it does not pull to either side. Your design should take into account the size and shape of the car.
- For the car without a motor, take into consideration that the car will begin to slow down at some point along its horizontal path.
- Determine the average velocity your car will travel over three trials, and show your calculations.

I will approve your plan before you start work on your project, so turn it in to me soon. When your car is ready, prepare your report using the format of a patent application. Be sure your report includes all parts of the application, and pay close attention to the number of significant figures throughout the lab. Good luck!

14557 West Post Road • Tempe, Arizona 852_

See next page for safety requirements, materials list, and more hints.

continued

MATERIALS

ITEM	QTY.
✔ 1.5 V–3.0 V dc motor	1
✔ 15 cm insulated wire	1
✔ AA batteries	2
✔ aluminum sheet	
✔ bamboo skewers	2
✔ drinking straws	2
✔ glue	
✔ large rubber bands	2
✔ masking tape	
✔ meterstick	
✔ plastic film-canister lid	3
✔ scissors	1
✔ small rubber bands	4
✔ stopwatch	1
✔ support stand and clamps	2
✔ table clamp	
✔ tongue depressors	5
✔ inclined plane	1

SAFETY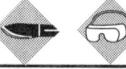

- Wear eye protection and perform this experiment in a clear area.
- Cut carefully, and be aware of those around you. When working with a knife, do not draw it toward you. After using a sharp tool, cover it with its protective sheath and return it to a safe place. Sharp objects can cause serious injury.

Coaster cars gravitate to a winning speed

In an event that combines elements of automobile racing and downhill sledding, coaster cars zip down a hill under the pull of gravity to pick up speed for the timed run on the flat surface of the track. Cars that win tend to be heavy, narrow, and low to the ground.

Races will be held today at Coaster Lanes. The track measures 50 meters from the starting line at the bottom of the hill to the finish line. The slope of the hill is 20 degrees.

Manuel Sanchez, last year's winner, explains that there are many tricks to building a successful coaster car. "Wheel alignment is important in making sure that the car will move in a straight path," he says, "Also, knowing how to distribute the mass is critical to building a winning car. You have to make sure the car does not slow itself down."

Pre-Chapter Exploration 3

HOLT PHYSICS
Discovery Lab

Vector Treasure Hunt

SAFETY

- Review the lab safety guidelines. Always follow correct procedures in the lab.

MATERIALS

- ✔ meterstick or trundle wheel
- ✔ index cards

OBJECTIVES

- Create a series of directions that lead to a specific object.
- Follow directions to locate a specific object.
- Develop a standard notation for writing direction symbols.
- Generate a scale map.

Giving directions

Procedure

1. In this lab, you will select a large, fixed object at your school and use standard physics notation to direct other students to the object. Your teacher will define the starting point and the physical boundaries for this activity. Select an object within the boundaries; the object you choose should be large and obvious, and it should be fixed in place so that other students will be able to find it by following your directions.

2. Plot out a course from the starting point to the chosen object. Remember to work quietly and to avoid disrupting classes and school traffic. Use a meterstick or trundle wheel to measure the distances along the course. Alternatively, you may measure your pace in meters and use your pace to count out the distance for each part of the course. Convert your pace to meters before recording the values for each distance.

3. You will break up the course into 15 different segments, and you will write each separate segment as a distance and a direction on an index card. Each card must contain a complete description of that segment, including the magnitude of the distance in meters and the direction. The direction must be specified using only these terms: north, south, east, west, up, and down. Your teacher will tell you where north is located for the purposes of this lab.

4. Keep in mind that the cards may be used to describe the most direct path from the starting point to the object, broken up into 15 segments, or they may describe a complicated path with many changes of direction.

5. When you have completed 15 cards that give an accurate description of a path between the starting point and the chosen object, write your name on an index card, and place the card on top of the 15 cards. On a separate piece of paper,

write your name and a description of the object you chose, including a description of its location. Give this paper and your deck of direction cards to your teacher. Your teacher will keep the paper with the name of the object until the end of the lab.

Analysis

A. Do your cards describe the straight-line path to the object divided into 15 parts, or do they describe a winding path to the object?

B. Is the path described by your cards the same length or longer than the straight-line path to the object? Can your cards be used to determine the straight-line path? Explain.

C. What was the most difficult part of plotting the path to the object?

D. Are you confident that another group will be able to find the object using your direction cards? Explain why or why not.

E. Would another group be able to find the object using your direction cards if your cards were placed out of order? Explain your answer.

Following directions

Procedure

6. When you turn in your cards, your teacher will shuffle them well and give the shuffled cards to another lab group. You will receive a shuffled deck of direction cards made by another group.

7. Devise a plan to use the directions on the cards you have been given to find the object chosen by the other group, then attempt to find the object.

8. When you find the object, go back through the cards to make sure you have correctly identified the object selected by the other group.

9. When you are sure that you have found the correct object, report your results to your teacher. Your teacher will confirm whether you have correctly identified the object. If not, review the cards and try again.

Analysis

F. Did shuffling the deck make it more difficult for you to locate the object? Explain why or why not.

G. Would you be able to place the cards in their original order? Explain why or why not.

H. Did you find the object described by the other group's cards? If not, explain what happened.

I. Explain the method you used to find the object, and include any tricks you discovered while you were working.

J. Was the other group able to correctly identify the object described by your direction cards?

Mapping the course

Procedure

10. In this section of the exercise, you will use the directions on a set of 15 cards to draw a map of the path from the starting point to the object. You will generate a map of the complete set of directions you used to find the object.

11. You will make the map by drawing each direction indicated on a card as an arrow. The arrow will be drawn to scale to represent the length in meters and it will point in the direction specified on the card. In a scale drawing such as this, it is important for all the objects in the drawing to have the same size relationship as the actual objects. For example, the arrow representing 2.0 m will be drawn twice as long as an arrow representing 1.0 m.

12. Draw the first arrow so that its tail is at the starting point, the point of the arrow is pointing in the direction specified on the card, and the length of the arrow represents the distance on the card.

13. Draw the second arrow on your map so that its tail starts at the point of the first arrow. The second arrow should also point in the direction specified by the card, and its length should represent the distance on the card.

14. Continue through the entire set of 15 cards. Draw the arrows tip-to-tail so that each arrow begins where the preceding one ends.

15. Make sure that the map is very neat. Include a legend, or key, that gives the directions and defines the scale of the map. You may wish to indicate specific landmarks, such as rooms or doors.

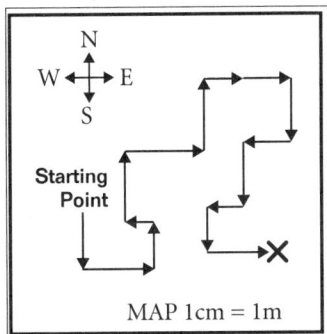

Analysis

K. Does the map accurately reflect the path you took to find the object? If not, explain any differences.

L. Explain how shuffling the cards affected the way you represented the directions from the starting point to the object. Use examples from your map to support your answer.

M. Based on this exercise, describe the most efficient method of using the set of direction cards to locate the object. Would this work for any set of directions? Explain why or why not.

Post-Chapter Activity 3
HOLT PHYSICS Invention Lab

The Path of a Human Cannonball

The Amazing Laslo Circus
Kittanning, PA

October 11, 1999

Dr. Wes Graham
1% Inspiration Laboratories
14557 West Post Road
Tempe, Arizona 85289

Dear Dr. Graham:

I spoke with you recently regarding our new "Human Cannonball" act, in which our daredevil, Clem, will be launched from a cannon into a net.

Our obvious problem is, how can we predict where to place the net? Using a portable radar gun, we've measured Clem's speed as he leaves the cannon. The net is strong enough to withstand the force of Clem's impact. In the first act, we plan to launch Clem so that he lands at the same horizontal level from which he was launched. For extra thrills, we will eventually mount a flaming ring at the highest point of his path so he can fly through the ring. Later in the show, Clem will be launched from a high platform and will land on a net placed far below the platform. For both acts, Clem's launch speed will be known, and we will determine the initial angle of launch and the placement of the net and ring based on your report.

Clem wears a special nylon suit and helmet that reduce air resistance significantly, so this should not be a problem. Also, I'm not sure if it matters, but Clem is 1.7 m tall, and he weighs 175 pounds.

Our tour starts in three months, so time is a critical factor here. On the other hand, a man's life is at stake, so accuracy is more important. Thank you very much for your time.

Respectfully,

John Lerner

John Lerner

Diagrams of the human cannonball act are on page 18.

16 HOLT PHYSICS Laboratory Experiments

1% Inspiration Laboratories

MEMORANDUM

Date: October 15, 1999
To: Research and Development Team
From: Wes Graham

You probably remember that I mentioned this contract at the last departmental meeting. Attached are copies of the letter and basic design specs, along with a list of relevant materials in stock. Start working up a plan so you can go into the lab as soon as possible. Work in SI, and keep track of significant figures. Present your plan to me before you start work. Make sure your plan includes the equipment you'll need and the measurements you are planning to take. You should also figure out what equations you'll need to determine where the net and ring should be placed for each part of the act.

As far as I can tell, this looks like a simple projectile-motion problem. Develop the equations and models to predict the maximum vertical and horizontal displacements at different angles. That will allow us to make recommendations based on our tests. Let's perform tests for launching at 20°, 40°, and 60°. For each angle, we need to recommend the placement of the ring and of the net.

For each part of the act, I think we should provide a set of equations and a working model of the act. We want to make sure that the equations will give the correct placement of the net for any angle they start with, given the initial speed. Pay special attention to answering the following questions:

- Exactly where should the net be placed?
- Where should the center of the flaming hoop be placed?

As I said at the meeting, it has been a great year at this company thanks to all of you.

14557 West Post Road • Tempe, Arizona 852—

See next page for safety requirements, materials list, and more hints.

continued

MATERIALS

ITEM	QTY.
✔ adhesive tape	1 roll
✔ ball launcher and ball	1
✔ carbon paper	1 sheet
✔ cardboard box	1
✔ clamps	3
✔ clay	200 g
✔ cloth towel	1
✔ lattice rod	1
✔ meterstick	1
✔ metric ruler	1
✔ photogate timing system	1
✔ plumb bob and line	1
✔ protractor	1
✔ support stand and ring	2
✔ white paper	1 sheet

SAFETY

- Wear eye protection, and perform this experiment in a clear area. Falling or dropped masses can cause serious injury.

Act 1

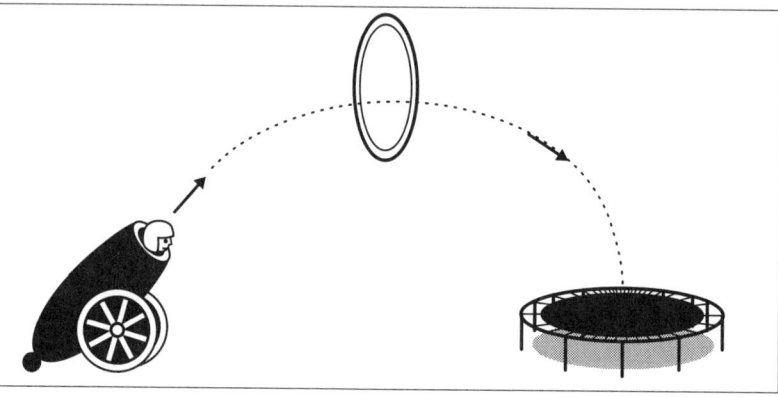

Act 2

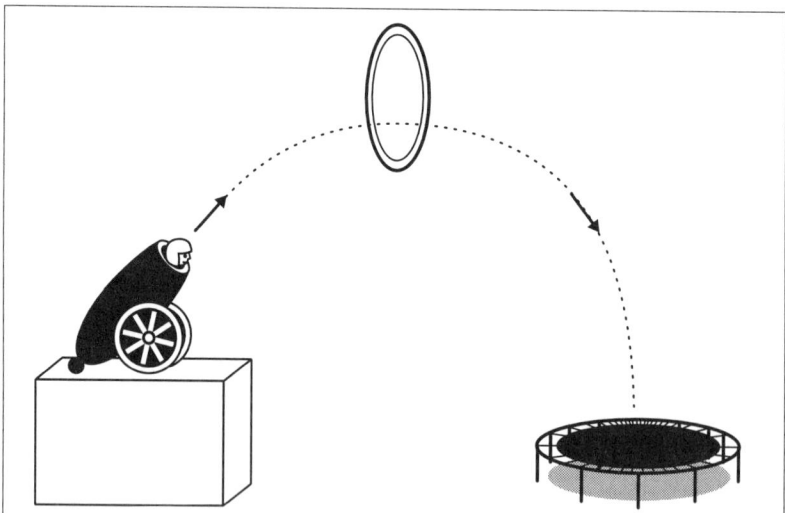

18 HOLT PHYSICS Laboratory Experiments

HOLT PHYSICS Discovery Lab

Pre-Chapter Exploration 4

Discovering Newton's Laws

SAFETY

- Perform this experiment in a clear area. Falling or dropped masses can cause serious injury.
- Tie back long hair, secure loose clothing, and remove loose jewelry to prevent their getting caught in moving or rotating parts.

MATERIALS

- ✔ 3 masses, 1 kg each
- ✔ beaker
- ✔ coin, such as a quarter
- ✔ cord
- ✔ dynamics cart
- ✔ dynamics cart with spring mechanism
- ✔ human-figure toy or doll
- ✔ index card
- ✔ paper towels
- ✔ rubber band
- ✔ set of masses, 20 g–100 g
- ✔ stopwatch
- ✔ track with pulley and car
- ✔ water

OBJECTIVES

- Explore the factors that cause a change in motion of an object.
- Determine the effect of mass on an object's acceleration.
- Investigate the acceleration of two objects acting on one another.

An object at rest

Procedure

1. Carefully fill the beaker about half-full with water. Wipe the lip and the outside of the beaker with a paper towel.
2. Place an index card on top of the beaker so that the card covers the opening of the beaker. Place the quarter on top of the card.
3. Remove the index card by pulling it quickly away. Make sure you pull the card perfectly horizontally.

Analysis

A. What happened to the coin when the card was pulled out from underneath?

B. Is this what you expected to happen? Explain why or why not.

C. What would happen to the coin if the card were pulled out very slowly? Try it, and compare your results.

CHAPTER 4

An object in motion

Procedure

4. Choose a location where you can push a dynamics cart so that it rolls for a distance without hitting any obstacles or obstructing traffic and then hits a wall or other hard surface.

5. Place the toy or doll on the cart, and place the cart about 0.5 m away from the wall.

6. Push the cart and doll forward so that they run into the wall. Observe what happens to the doll when the cart hits the wall.

7. Place the cart at the same starting place, about 0.5 m away from the wall. Return the doll to the cart, and use a rubber band to hold the doll securely in the cart.

8. Push the cart and doll forward so that they run into the wall. Observe what happens to the doll when the cart hits the wall.

9. When you are finished, return the cart to the table or storage place. Do not leave the cart on the floor.

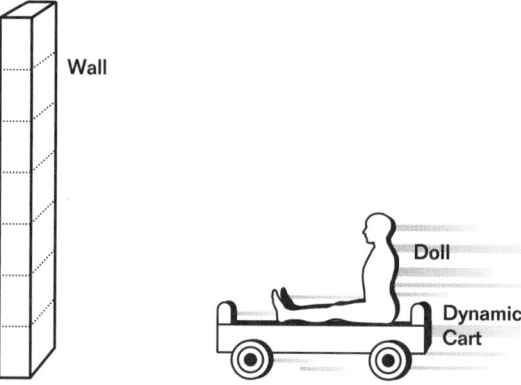

Analysis

D. What happened to the unsecured doll when the cart hit the wall?

E. What happened to the doll secured with the rubber band when the cart hit the wall?

F. How did the rubber band change the result of the experiment? Explain why this happened.

G. Compare the experiment with the doll and cart with the experiment with the card and coin. Explain how the results of the two are similar.

Newton's second law

Procedure

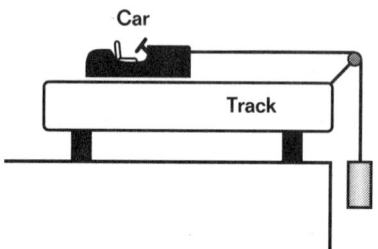

10. Perform this part of the lab using an air track and car or a dynamics track and car. Place the car on one end of the track with the pulley securely clamped to the other end of the track.

11. Securely attach one end of a cord to the car and the other end to a small mass. Thread the cord through and over the pulley wheel at the end of the air track or dynamics track. The car should be held securely in place at the opposite end of the track.

12. Make sure that the mass will be able to fall about 1 m without hitting any obstacles. If you are using the air track, turn on the air track and release the car at the same moment. If you are using the dynamics track, release the car. The mass will fall straight down, and the car will move along the track. Be ready to catch the car when it reaches the end of the track.

13. While the car is moving, make careful observations. Try to determine whether the car moves with constant velocity or whether it accelerates.

14. Replace the mass with another mass, and repeat steps 10–13. Carefully observe the motion of the car.

15. Repeat several times using different masses. Do not exceed 300 g. As you change the mass, watch the motion of the car for observable patterns.

Analysis

H. What caused the car to start moving?

I. Did the car move with a constant velocity, or was it accelerating?

J. How did the size of the falling mass affect the motion of the car? Explain.

Newton's third law

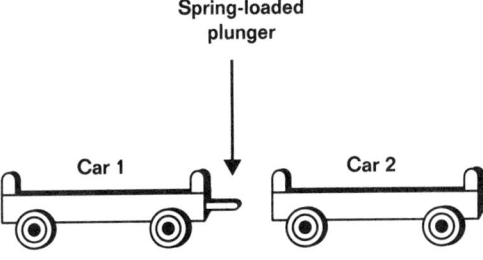

Procedure

16. Set up two dynamics carts as shown. Choose a location where each cart will be able to move at least 1.0 m on a smooth horizontal surface away from obstacles and traffic. Compress the spring mechanism and place the carts so that they are touching, as shown.

17. Quickly release the spring, and observe the two carts. If you are working on a lab table, do not allow the carts to fall off the table.

18. Return the carts to the original position, and compress the spring mechanism. Add a 1 kg mass to the cart with the spring.

19. Quickly release the spring, and observe the two carts.

20. Return the carts to the original position, and compress the spring mechanism. Add another 1 kg mass to the cart with the spring. Release the spring, and observe the two carts.

21. Return the carts to the original position, and compress the spring. Add a 1 kg mass to the second cart so that the mass on the first cart is twice the mass on the second cart. Release the spring, and observe the two carts.

Analysis

K. What happened to the two carts when the spring was released?

L. Compare the motion of the carts for each trial. Describe the motion in terms of the carts' acceleration from rest when the carts have equal mass (no masses added), one cart has 1 kg mass added, one cart has 2 kg mass added, and when one cart has 2 kg mass added and the other cart has 1 kg mass added.

M. What is the relationship between the mass of a cart and its acceleration when the spring is released?

Post-Chapter Activity 4
HOLT PHYSICS Invention Lab

Friction: Testing Materials

1% Inspiration Laboratories

MEMORANDUM

To: Dr. Jan Ingensen, Research and Development
From: L. Morales, Inventory Manager
Date: November 11, 1999

In order to comply with the new labeling regulations, we have been going through the materials supply room and replacing labels that no longer meet the required specifications. A recent inventory of the materials supply room has revealed a large surplus of untested materials. Many of these are surface-coating materials used to reduce friction between surfaces, or in some cases, to increase it.

In order to update the labels on these products, we need to ascertain their functions. With our new inventory system, we will be labeling these items based on the coefficient of friction. I have included a list of the untested materials in the storeroom. Please test each of these materials, and let me know the results by the end of next week. Be sure to give me all the documentation.

That's all for now. Thanks a lot.

14557 West Post Road • Tempe, Arizona 85289

The list of materials to be tested is on page 24.

1% Inspiration Laboratories

MEMORANDUM

Date: November 12, 1999
To: Research and Development Team
From: Jan Ingensen

I've looked over the list sent down from Inventory. With the recent hiring boom in the company, I think we have enough people to get these results in time to make the deadline for the new labels. We may even have freedom to do extra tests on these for future reference.

Look over the list I've included with this memo. It gives all the materials that need testing, and I've added the equipment we have available for performing the tests. Some of these materials have been used in the manufacture of nonslip feet (for appliances, bathtubs, etc.), while others have been used to reduce friction to aid in pushing large objects. Come up with a plan to analyze these materials for their relative value to reduce or increase friction. Remember to get my approval for your plan before you go into the lab to begin testing.

I think we should test each material against the same material so that we can compare the coefficients of friction. Make sure to perform the same tests on all the items on the list. Find the coefficients of static and kinetic friction to two significant figures. When you have your results, rank them in order of the coefficients of friction for each test, and be sure to distinguish between static and kinetic friction. Give me a full report detailing the tests you performed and your results. I would also be interested to see whether the rank according to the coefficients of kinetic friction is the same as the rank according to static friction.

14557 West Post Road • Tempe, Arizona 8528

See next page for safety requirements, materials list, and more hints.

continued

MATERIALS

ITEM	QTY.
✔ balance	1
✔ cork board	1 sheet
✔ force meters	2
✔ linoleum	1 sheet
✔ masking tape	1 roll
✔ sandpaper	1 sheet
✔ set of masses	1
✔ unidentified materials	1 box
✔ wooden friction block with hook	1

SAFETY

- Perform this experiment in a clear area. Falling or dropped masses can cause serious injury.
- Tie back long hair, secure loose clothing, and remove loose jewelry to prevent their getting caught in moving or rotating parts.

Keep in mind that the coefficient of friction describes a relationship between two surfaces. Your reports should include a complete description of both surfaces in each test. If there is time, perform all the tests against a second material to see if the ranking according to the coefficients of friction is the same regardless of what material you test against.

Make sure that you keep records of all data and measurements used to find the coefficient of friction. Because the coefficient of friction is a ratio of measured or calculated forces, it is important that you carefully document all your measurements.

Pre-Chapter Exploration 5

HOLT PHYSICS
Discovery Lab

Exploring Work and Energy

SAFETY

- Set up the apparatus, and attach all masses securely. Perform this experiment in a clear area. Swinging or dropped masses can cause serious injury.
- Tie back long hair, secure loose clothing, and remove loose jewelry to prevent their being caught in moving or rotating parts.

MATERIALS
- ✔ clamps
- ✔ cord, 1.00 m
- ✔ force meter
- ✔ inclined plane
- ✔ masking tape
- ✔ meterstick
- ✔ set of hooked masses
- ✔ stopwatch

OBJECTIVES

- Measure the force required to move a mass over a certain distance using different methods.
- Compare the force required to move different masses over different time intervals.

Pulling masses

Procedure

1. At one edge of the tabletop, place a tape mark to represent a starting point. From this mark, measure exactly 0.50 m and 1.00 m. Place a tape mark at each measured distance.

2. Securely attach the 1 kg mass to one end of the cord and the force meter to the other end. The force meter will measure the force required to move the mass through different displacements.

3. Place the mass on the table at the starting point. Hold the force meter parallel to the tabletop so that the cord is taut between the force meter and the mass. Carefully pull the mass at a constant speed along the surface of the table to the 0.50 m mark (this may require some practice). As you pull, observe the force measured on the force meter.

4. Record the force and distance in your notebook using the appropriate SI units.

5. Repeat steps 3 and 4 for a distance of 1.00 m.

6. Repeat steps 3, 4, and 5 with a 0.2 kg mass.

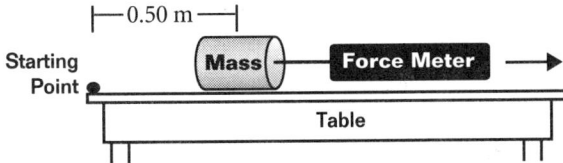

CHAPTER 5 **25**

Analysis

A. Did you exert the same force on the 1 kg mass as you did on the 0.2 kg mass to move them an equal distance?

B. Did it require more force to move the mass 1.00 m than to move the same mass 0.50 m?

C. What force did you pull against?

Lifting masses

Procedure

7. Using masking tape, secure a meterstick vertically against the wall with the 0.00 m end on the floor.

8. Securely attach the 1 kg mass to one end of the cord and the force meter to the other end.

9. Place the mass on the floor beside the meterstick. Hold the force meter parallel to the wall so that the cord is taut between the force meter and the mass. Carefully lift the mass vertically at a constant speed to the 0.50 m mark on the meterstick. Be sure that the mass does not touch the wall during any part of the process. As you lift, observe the force measured on the force meter. Be careful not to drop the mass.

10. Record the force and distance in your notebook using the appropriate SI units.

11. Repeat steps 9 and 10 for a vertical distance of 0.25 m.

12. Replace the 1 kg mass with the 0.2 kg mass, and repeat steps 9, 10, and 11.

Analysis

D. Did you exert the same force on the 1 kg mass as you did on the 0.2 kg mass to move them an equal distance?

E. Did it require more force to lift the mass 0.50 m than was required to lift the same mass 0.25 m?

F. What force did you lift against?

G. Did it require a different force to *lift* a mass than it did to *pull* the same mass across the table an equal distance?

Displacing masses using an inclined plane

Procedure

13. Carefully clamp an inclined plane to the tabletop so that the base of the inclined plane rests on the floor. Make sure the inclined plane is in a location where it will not obstruct traffic or block aisles or exits.

14. Measure vertical distances of 0.25 m and 0.50 m above the level of the floor. Use masking tape to mark each level on the inclined plane. Also measure the distance along the inclined plane to each mark. Record all distances in your notebook using the appropriate SI units. Be sure to label the vertical distance and the distance along the inclined plane.

15. Attach the 1 kg mass to the lower end of the cord and the force meter to the other end.

16. Place the mass at the base of the inclined plane. Hold the force meter parallel to the inclined plane so that the cord is taut between the force meter and the mass. Carefully pull the force meter at a constant speed parallel to the surface of the inclined plane until the mass has reached the vertical 0.50 m mark on the inclined plane. As you pull, observe the force measured on the force meter.

17. Using the appropriate SI units, record the force and distance in your notebook.

18. Repeat steps 16 and 17 for a vertical distance of 0.25 m.

19. Repeat steps 16, 17, and 18 for the 0.2 kg mass.

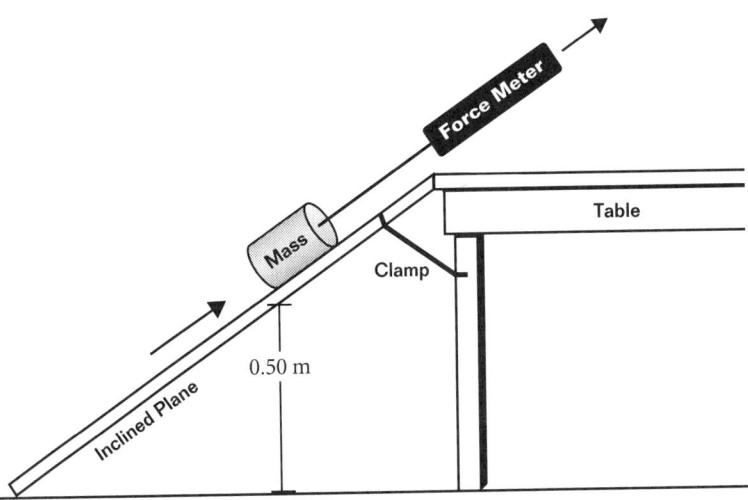

Analysis

H. Did you exert the same force on the 1 kg mass as you did on the 0.2 kg mass to move them an equal distance?

I. Did it require more force to lift the same mass 0.50 m along the inclined plane as it did to lift it 0.25 m?

J. What forces did you pull against?

K. Compare the force required to lift a mass using an inclined plane with the force required to lift the same mass to the same vertical displacement using only the force meter. Why are the values different?

L. How can you adjust the inclined plane so that moving the mass through the same vertical displacement requires less force?

Post-Chapter Activity 5 — HOLT PHYSICS Invention Lab

Bungee Jumping: Energy

NISKAYUNA HIGH ENGINEERING INC.
SCHENECTADY, NY 12309

December 10, 1999

Dr. John R. Kanga
1% Inspiration Laboratories
14557 West Post Road
Tempe, Arizona 85289

Dear Dr. Kanga:

Since the inception of bungee jumping nearly ten years ago, the development of equipment for this sport has been stagnant. Sheathed shock cords have been the only apparatus used in this activity. These cords lend no creativity in design for either application or appearance. As a result, there has been a decline in interest in the sport and, in turn, drops in the ride fees our clients can charge. It is our goal to promote new interest in the sport and to bolster sales by designing upgraded equipment for owners of current bungee-jumping operations.

We are seeking a new design for a bungee cord that will safely bring a diver to a smooth halt at the bottom of the flight. The new design should incorporate the use of our newly developed elastic bands and braided cords. Included in this mailing is the equipment that we have available for use in designing the new bungee cord. You must not include any other devices in the design, and you must use all the equipment enclosed.

To use humans in such experimentation is unwise and to perform a full size operation would not be practical, so a scaled-down model of the design is appropriate. Primarily, we must be certain that the diver would be safe. As a result, we require data from tests of your design. Your design, along with designs from other engineering firms, will be tested by our firm only once. A contract will be offered to the firm whose bungee cord stops the diver closest to the floor without touching the floor.

Sincerely,

Dr. Sun Nguyen

Dr. Sun Nguyen

More information about the design is on page 30.

1% Inspiration Laboratories

MEMORANDUM

Date: December 13, 1999
To: Development Team
From: Dr. John R. Kanga

The bungee-cord-design request from Dr. Sun Nguyen could lead to a big contract, so we will need to do careful planning. Before you go into the lab, prepare a plan for the design of the bungee cord. Your plan should include a list of materials needed and a diagram of the experimental setup. You will also need a data table for the mass, cord length, expected length of fall, and the spring constant of the elastic bands included in this kit. Remember to document all of your testing and development procedures in your lab notebook. I have included with this memo a newspaper clipping that may be helpful. Your plan should also include the following:

- a bungee-cord design that uses only the braided cord and the elastic bands provided in the kit. This means that you will need to justify the choice of bungee-cord length. Since this length depends on how much the elastic bands will stretch, you should also use equations to demonstrate how you will determine the spring constant of the elastic bands provided in the kit.

- recommendations of ways to bring the diver to a smooth halt. It may be helpful to consider the principle of conservation of energy in this situation.

I must approve your plan before you start work in the lab, so turn it in to me soon. You will receive the kit of braided cords and elastic bands when I approve your plan. After your work in the lab, prepare your report using the format of a patent application. Be sure your report includes all eight parts of the application. Good luck!

14557 West Post Road • Tempe, Arizona 8529

See next page for safety requirements, materials list, and more hints.

continued

MATERIALS

ITEM	QTY.
✔ clamps	3
✔ heavy cardboard	10 cm × 10 cm
✔ Hooke's law apparatus	
✔ meterstick	1
✔ set of slotted masses	1
✔ slotted mass holder	1
✔ suspension clamp	1

KIT INCLUDES:

ITEM	QTY.
✔ braided cords	1.5 m–2.0 m
✔ elastic bands	2 or 3
✔ hooked masses	0.2 kg, 0.25 kg or 0.5 kg

SAFETY

- Wear eye protection, and perform this experiment in a clear area, away from obstacles and people.
- Attach masses and cords securely. Swinging or falling masses can cause serious injury.

Plunge with a Bungee

Although bungee jumping has been a craze for almost a decade, many people are wondering just how safe such a plummet can be. A harnessed person secured to one end of a long elastic bungee cord attaches the other end of the cord to a high precipice, such as a bridge or a cliff. After summoning the courage, they plunge and are rewarded with the exhilarating free-fall acceleration of their body toward the ground. When the diver has fallen the length of the cord, the cord gives a little, much as a spring does. So it's important that designers know *exactly* how much the cord will give when they determine the length of the cord. Designers must also take into account the range of weights of different people. Although the fall is fun for many divers, some have complained about the jolt experienced at the end of the ride. When the cord cannot expand any further, it yanks the diver back up away from the ground—causing the diver to fall again and experience another, less harsh jolt. The entire experience is much like that of a bouncing ball.

30 HOLT PHYSICS Laboratory Experiments

Pre-Chapter Exploration 7
HOLT PHYSICS Discovery Lab

Circular Motion

SAFETY

- Wear eye protection and perform this experiment in a clear area away from electrical equipment or outlets. Clean up any spilled or splashed water immediately.
- The bands will break if they spin too quickly or in a figure 8. If the elastic bands break during the experiment, serious injury could result.
- Tie back long hair, secure loose clothing, and remove loose jewelry to prevent their being caught in moving or rotating parts.
- Rotating or swinging masses can cause injury.

MATERIALS
- 8 elastic bands, ⅛ in. wide
- balance
- meterstick
- plastic bottle marked at the 150 mL level
- 14 oz. plastic drinking cup with three equally spaced holes below the rim
- stopwatch

OBJECTIVES

- Distinguish between forces required to hold a variety of masses in a horizontal circular path moving at several speeds.
- Compare the circular motion of masses to the linear motion of masses.
- Discover the relationship between mass, speed, and the force that maintains circular motion.

Slow circular motion with a mass

Procedure

1. Push an elastic band through a hole below the rim of the plastic cup. Loop the band through itself as shown. This action should form a type of knot about the rim of the glass. Secure the knot tightly.
2. Repeat step 1 for each hole in the plastic cup.

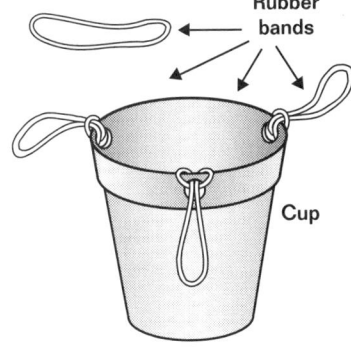

CHAPTER 7 **31**

3. Pull another elastic band through each knotted band on the cup's rim so that all three bands on the rim of the cup simultaneously loop around the fourth band. Make a knot similar to the one you made in step 1. This will knot all bands together and create a fourth band loop.

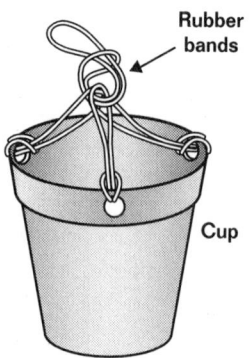

4. Loop another elastic band through the fourth band in the same way that you did in step 1. Then loop three more elastic bands end to end in a chain to lengthen the device. This device is referred to as a *cupsling*.

5. Carefully measure 150 mL of water into the plastic cup. Make sure that no water spills.

6. Place the cupsling on a balance, and record its mass using the appropriate SI units. Make sure to record all measurements to the precision of your balance.

7. Make sure the area is clear of obstacles, and warn other students that you are beginning your experiment. Holding the bands securely, slowly spin the full cupsling about you in a full circle. Slightly increase the speed until you can spin it so that the cup moves in a horizontal circle. Try to see how slowly you can spin the cupsling and still consistently maintain a horizontal circle. Be careful not to spill or splash any water.

8. With the stopwatch, a partner should time the 10 complete circles of the cup as you swing it *slowly* around in a *horizontal* circle.

9. A partner should use the meterstick to estimate the radius of the cup's horizontal path at this speed. Get as precise an estimate as possible. Always be aware of the position of the cupsling.

32 HOLT PHYSICS Laboratory Experiments

10. Using the appropriate SI units, record the radius of the circle and the total time it took to complete 10 horizontal circles of the cup in your notebook. Make sure to record all measured digits plus one estimated digit.

Analysis

A. Did you need to exert a force on the elastic band to start spinning the cupsling from rest?

B. Did you need to continue exerting a force on the elastic band to keep it spinning at a constant speed? How did you know?

C. When the cupsling moved in a circle, it was changing direction all the time. What caused the cupsling to change direction?

D. When the cupsling moved in a circle at a constant speed, did it accelerate? Explain your answer.

E. Where do you think the cup would go if the band were released while the cup was spinning?

F. What happened to the length of the elastic band as you increased the force to spin the cupsling in a horizontal circle?

G. How long did it take for the cup to complete one circle?

Circular motion with a mass

Procedure

11. Place the cupsling with 150 mL of water in the cup on a balance. Record its mass using the appropriate SI units. Make sure to record all measurements to the precision of your balance.

12. Holding the bands securely, slowly spin the full cupsling about you in a complete circle. Slightly increase the speed until you can spin it so that the cup moves in a horizontal circle. Spin the cupsling faster than you did in step 7 but not so fast that the bands will break. Remember to consistently maintain a horizontal circle throughout this experiment. Be careful not to spill or splash any water.

13. With the stopwatch, a partner should time the 10 complete horizontal circles of the cup.

14. Using the meterstick, a partner should estimate the radius of the cup's horizontal path at this speed. Get as precise an estimate as possible. Always be aware of the position of the cupsling.

15. Using the appropriate SI units, record the radius of the circle and the total time it took to complete 10 horizontal circles of the cup in your notebook. Make sure to record all measured digits plus one estimated digit.

Analysis

H. What happened to the length of the elastic band as the speed increased?

I. What happened to the force on the elastic band as the speed increased?

J. How long did it take for the cup to complete one circle?

Circular motion with an increased mass

Procedure

16. Place the cupsling with a total of 300 mL of water on a balance. Record its mass using the appropriate SI units. Make sure to record all measurements to the precision of your balance.

17. Make sure the area is clear of obstacles, and warn other students that you are beginning your experiment. Holding the bands securely, slowly spin the full cupsling about you in a full circle. Slightly increase the speed until you can spin it so that the cup moves in a horizontal circle. Try to see how slowly you can spin the cupsling and still consistently maintain a horizontal circle. Be careful not to spill or splash any water.

18. With the stopwatch, a partner should time the 10 complete circles of the cup as you sling it *slowly* around in a *horizontal* circle.

19. Using the meterstick, a partner should estimate the radius of the cup's horizontal path at this speed. Get as precise an estimate as possible. Always be aware of the position of the cupsling.

20. Using the appropriate SI units, record the radius of the circle and the total time it took to complete 10 horizontal circles of the cup in your notebook. Make sure to record all measured digits plus one estimated digit.

Analysis

K. What happened to the length of the elastic band when you increased the mass in the cup?

L. How did the increase in mass affect the force on the elastic band?

M. If a mass moves in a straight line and more mass is added, does the inertia increase, decrease, or stay the same?

N. Do you think that the same thing happens to a body in circular motion? Explain.

O. How long did it take for the cup to complete one circle?

Pre-Chapter Exploration 8

HOLT PHYSICS Discovery Lab

Torque and Center of Mass

SAFETY

- Attach masses securely. Swinging or dropped masses can cause serious injury.
- Tie back long hair, secure loose clothing, and remove loose jewelry to prevent their being caught in moving or rotating parts.

OBJECTIVES

- Discover what factors cause an object to rotate when a force is applied.
- Construct a model of the human arm, and examine the role of forces and rotation in its function.
- Locate the point about which an object that is free to rotate will pivot.

Rotational force and a wrench

Procedure

1. Secure a table clamp to the edge of the table. Use the table clamp to hold the wooden plank vertically. The wooden plank should not move when force is applied to it. Put the bolt through the hole in the wooden plank. Place the washer and the nut on the other side of the plank so that the bolt goes through the hole of the washer and then through the hole of the nut. Adjust the wrench so that it fits snugly around the nut.
2. Firmly grip the tail of the wrench, and use the wrench to tighten the nut. Make sure that the wrench does not slip and that your fingers do not get pinched or jammed.
3. Firmly grip the *head* of the wrench, and try to loosen the nut.
4. Firmly grip the tail of the wrench, and use the wrench to tighten the nut.
5. Firmly grip the *tail* of the wrench, and try to loosen the nut.

Analysis

A. Describe the force that causes the nut to turn when you tighten it. Draw a diagram of the setup showing the direction of the force as it is applied.
B. If you push the wrench into the bolt rather than rotate it, does anything happen?
C. Around which point does the motion of the nut and the wrench occur?

MATERIALS

- ✔ 1.25 cm diameter dowel rod, 0.5 m long
- ✔ 2 frozen-juice cans and lids
- ✔ 15 mm bolt, 5 cm long
- ✔ 15 mm nut
- ✔ 15 mm washer
- ✔ adjustable wrench
- ✔ apple
- ✔ clay
- ✔ cord, 1.00 m
- ✔ force meter
- ✔ masking tape
- ✔ masses, 20 g, 50 g, and 100 g
- ✔ plastic cup with handle
- ✔ support stand with clamps
- ✔ table clamp
- ✔ wooden plank with a drilled 15 mm hole

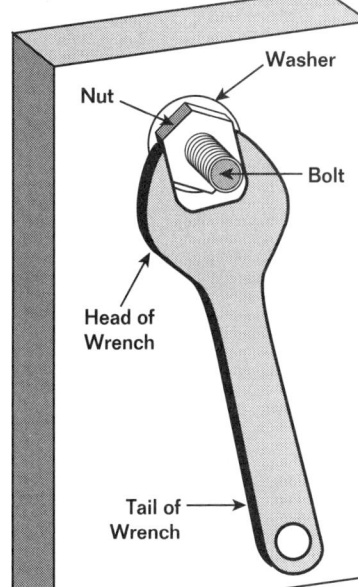

D. What angle between the wrench and the bolt is necessary for you to get the nut to turn the easiest?

E. Was it easier to loosen the nut with your hand by the head or by the tail of the wrench? Was it easier to loosen the nut by applying the force closer to or farther from the bolt?

F. Why do you think the nut stops turning?

Balanced rotational force and the human arm

Procedure

6. Set up the support stand as shown. Place one clamp 20 cm from the top of the stand and another clamp at the bottom of the stand. Make sure both clamps are perpendicular to the support stand.

7. Hook the force meter around the end of the top clamp. There should be at least 4 cm between the force meter and the support stand. Tie a piece of cord into a small loop 3 cm–5 cm in diameter. Hang the loop from the free hook on the other end of the force meter.

8. Thread the dowel rod through the hanging loop and clamp the end of the dowel to the support stand with the lower clamp. Adjust the clamped end of the dowel so that the dowel rod can move freely without falling out of the clamp. To do this, tape a piece of card to one side of the dowel as shown. Pull the cord tightly around the clamp and support rod, and tape the cord securely to the other side of the dowel rod.

9. Tie another piece of cord into a small loop 3.0 cm–5.0 cm in diameter. Hang this loop from the free end of the dowel rod and tape it securely to the dowel rod.

10. Hang a mass of 20.0 g from this loop.

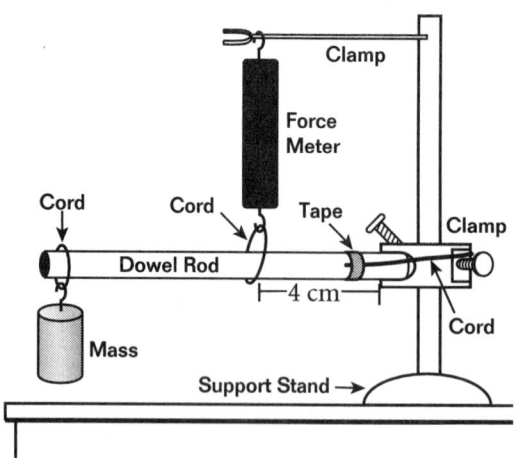

11. Adjust the entire setup so that the force meter and the mass are parallel to each other but perpendicular to the dowel rod. There should be about 4 cm along the dowel rod between the force meter and the clamp, as shown.

12. Observe the force measured on the force meter. Record the mass and the force in your lab notebook. Be sure to use appropriate SI units.

13. Add a 50.0 g mass to the 20.0 g mass, and repeat steps 11 and 12.

14. Add a 100.0 g mass to the 50.0 g and 20.0 g masses, and repeat steps 11 and 12.

15. Measure the distance to the masses from the clamp and the distance from the spring scale to the clamp. Record these values in your lab notebook using appropriate SI units. Be sure to record all digits plus one estimated digit.

Analysis

G. Look at your arm. What part of your arm is represented by the force meter in the model?

H. What part of your arm is represented by the dowel rod in the model?

I. What part of your arm is comparable to the clamp in the model?

J. About what point in the arm model does the rotation occur? What part of your arm does this correspond to?

K. What happens to the force meter when a mass is placed on the loop? Explain.

L. When does the dowel rod move?

M. At what point on the dowel rod is the force applied by the mass? Draw a diagram of the setup showing the direction of this force as it is applied.

N. What produces a force to balance the force due to a hanging mass and prevent the dowel from dropping downward? Draw the direction of the applied force on the diagram of the setup.

O. In which directions are the two forces exerted on the dowel rod?

P. What must happen with these two forces for the dowel rod to not move?

Q. From your observations of the model arm, do the actual forces always cancel each other out?

The pivot point of a freely rotating object

16. Pack clay firmly 1 cm–2 cm deep in one end of an empty frozen-juice can. Seal a lid on this can using masking tape.

17. Tie a 0.50 m cord securely around any part of the can so the can is free to swing. Suspend the can from a support stand and clamp.

18. Draw a line vertically from the suspended part of the cord down the side of the can. You may need to hold the can steady as you draw the line. You may use a ruler or a meterstick to guide you.

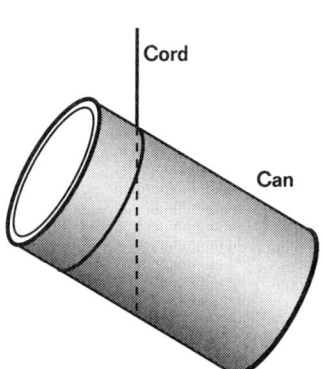

19. Tie the cord around a different part of the can, and suspend the can. Draw a vertical line from the suspended part of the cord down the side of the can. You may need to hold the can steady as you draw the line. You may use a ruler or a meterstick to guide you. Mark the place on the can where the vertical lines meet.

20. Repeat steps 17–19 for another empty frozen-juice can that has been fully packed from top to bottom with clay. Leave no air spaces. Seal a lid on this can using masking tape.

21. Repeat steps 17–19 for an apple on one end of a dowel rod, a pen, and a meterstick.

Analysis

R. Is the point at which the two lines meet the center of the object? Explain.

Post-Chapter Activity 8
HOLT PHYSICS Invention Lab

The Rotating Egg Drop

National Engineering Association
Tempe, Arizona

December 16, 1999

Mr. David Corricello
1% Inspiration Laboratories
14557 West Post Road
Tempe, Arizona 85289

Dear Mr. Corricello:

We are having an Engineering Fair in Wilkshire Mall on December 29 and 30 as part of an effort to inspire both children and adults to consider a career in the engineering industry. We are inviting all of the local engineering firms to set up educational exhibits in the mall. This would be a wonderful opportunity for your company to get some public exposure as well as to help foster awareness of engineering.

We would like to draw a crowd by having all the engineering firms set up an egg-drop exhibit. All egg-drop devices will be dropped from the second floor of the mall to land on the first floor. The object will be to protect the egg from breaking upon impact with the tile floor. To make the project more challenging, we are asking that all companies construct a frame around an egg using only toothpicks and glue. Note that the egg cannot be cooked in any way, nor can it be coated with glue. In addition, rotational motion must be taken into account in the design.

We would like this to be an educational effort as well, so all exhibits must provide a detailed explanation of why the design works. Each presentation should be in the form of a patent application. Each display must include a well-labeled drawing of the device and a sketch of the drop. Labels and captions should be placed below or within every picture.

The registration deadline is December 23. We can accept five entries from each firm. We wish you the best in your egg-drop design.

Sincerely,

Majesh Patel

Majesh Patel

More information about the design is on page 40.

1% Inspiration Laboratories

MEMORANDUM

Date: December 17, 1999
To: Development Team
From: David Corricello

This is a great opportunity to have our work displayed so that people can see it! Before you go into the lab, list the materials needed for the egg-drop device, draw the device's design, and sketch out the drop. Remember to label everything and to provide an informative caption beside each picture. I have jotted down some ideas and am including them with this memo. They might be helpful to your design and setup. You should also use your plan to do the following:

- Explain how Newton's laws of motion and the impulse equation apply to this situation. Use equations in your explanations, and describe how some details of your design influence the magnitude of the variables.

- Describe how rotational motion applies to the design of your egg-drop device.

- Comment on my comparison of the egg-drop device to a weather vane. State whether my ideas are correct, and explain your reasoning.

- Illustrate how the design of your egg-drop device incorporates concepts of rotational forces and torque.

I must approve your plan before you start work on your project, so turn it in to me soon. The five best egg-drop devices will be entered into the exhibit. After your work in the lab, prepare your report using the format of a patent application and include a complete explanation of why your design works. Be sure your report includes all eight parts of the application.

14557 West Post Road • Tempe, Arizona 852—

See next page for safety requirements, materials list, and more hints.

continued

MATERIALS

ITEM	QTY.
✔ glue	1 bottle
✔ raw egg	1
✔ toothpicks	1 box

SAFETY

- Wear eye protection, and perform this experiment in a clear area.
- Falling or dropped masses can cause serious injury.

> Problem: Orienting the egg-drop device so that I can predict how it will hit the ground.
> Is this related to how a weather vane operates?
> All weather vanes, which spin about a fixed axis, rotate to face into the wind as the air blows on them. If the weather vane is perpendicular to the wind, the air pushes equally on all parts of the vane. Because the tail of the vane is farther from the axis of rotation, there is more torque per unit area on the tail than on the head (because torque depends on the force and the distance from the rotation axis). So, there is a difference in torque on either side of the axis. This pushes the tail away from the wind and forces the head to face into the wind.
> Suppose I construct the device so that it has a toothpick tower on one side: If I drop the device horizontally, the air moves faster and faster as the device falls, and upward forces create a torque on both sides of the center of mass. The tower side is long, so forces on the far end of this side will produce large torque. This will push the tower side back, and the bottom of my egg-drop device should point toward the ground and land first!

HOLT PHYSICS Laboratory Experiments

Pre-Chapter Exploration 10
HOLT PHYSICS Discovery Lab

Temperature and Internal Energy

SAFETY

- Perform this experiment in a clear area.
- If a thermometer breaks, notify the teacher immediately.

MATERIALS

- ✔ 200 g copper shot
- ✔ 4 plastic-foam cups with lids
- ✔ balance
- ✔ hot tap water
- ✔ ice cubes of uniform size
- ✔ masking tape
- ✔ paper towels
- ✔ plastic container with a 100 mL mark
- ✔ sharpened pencil
- ✔ stopwatch
- ✔ thermometer
- ✔ weighing paper

OBJECTIVES

- Investigate the phenomenon of energy transfer by heat.

Melting ice cube contest

Procedure

1. Hold an ice cube in your hand so that it melts slower than anyone else's cube in the room.

Analysis

A. How did you hold the ice cube to cause it to melt slowly?

B. Did the heat from your hand influence how fast the ice cube melted?

Energy changes the temperature of copper

Procedure

2. Stack two sets of two plastic-foam cups so that one cup is inside the other cup. Tape each set of stacked cups together.

3. Twist a pencil to carefully bore a hole in the center of the bottom of the first stack of two cups so that the diameter of the hole is the same size as the thermometer. Do not use the thermometer to punch the hole. Make sure that the pencil punctures both cups and that the two holes align.

4. Use the balance to measure out 200 g of copper. Place the copper in the second set of stacked cups.

5. Place the first set of stacked cups upside down on top of the second set of stacked cups so that the rims are touching, as shown. Carefully and securely tape the cups together with masking tape. For the remainder of this lab, this device that contains the copper is called a *calorimeter*.

6. Find the mass of the stacked cups and the copper. Subtract the mass of the copper to find the mass of the calorimeter. Record this mass in your lab notebook. Push a thermometer into the calorimeter until the bulb is just inside the inner cup. Seal any cracks between the cup and the thermometer with tape.

7. Holding the thermometer in place, *slowly* invert the calorimeter so that the shot slides gently down to cover the bulb. Using the appropriate SI units, read and record temperatures at 5.0 s intervals until 5 consecutive readings are the same. Be sure to include all measured digits and one estimated digit.

8. Remove the thermometer from the calorimeter. Push one end of an unsharpened pencil through the thermometer hole until it just blocks the inner hole. Hold it in place with tape.

9. Shake the calorimeter so that the copper falls 425 times from the top of one cup to the bottom of the other cup.

10. Remove the masking tape from the outer cup. Carefully push the thermometer into the calorimeter. Tape any cracks between the cup and the thermometer.

11. Measure the temperature of the copper at the bottom of the calorimeter. Record the temperature in your notebook, using appropriate SI units. Be sure to include all measured digits and one estimated digit.

Analysis

C. How much did the temperature of the copper increase?

D. Use the physics concepts of work, energy, and force to describe what happened to the copper.

E. Were you surprised that the temperature increased? Explain.

Mass and changes in temperature

Procedure

12. Stack a pair of cups one inside the other and tape them together securely. This will make a calorimeter. Place the calorimeter with one lid on a balance and measure its mass. Record the mass in your notebook.

13. Add 200 g of copper shot to the inner cup and determine the mass of the calorimeter and copper. Record the mass in your notebook.

14. Carefully use a pencil to make a hole in the lid big enough to insert the thermometer. Place the lid securely on the inner cup. Insert the thermometer until the bulb touches the copper. Cover any holes in the lid with tape. When the temperature reaches a constant level, read the temperature of the copper using the appropriate number of significant figures. Record the temperature in your lab notebook.

15. Measure 100 mL of hot tap water into a container and measure its temperature. Record the temperature in your lab notebook.

16. Carefully remove the lid and thermometer from the calorimeter, keeping them together. Carefully add the hot water to the calorimeter and copper.

17. Immediately replace the lid and thermometer on the calorimeter and observe the thermometer. When the temperature reaches a constant level, measure the temperature of the copper and record it in your lab notebook.

18. Carefully remove the thermometer from the lid of the calorimeter, leaving the lid in place. Place the calorimeter, water, and copper on a balance and find its mass. Record the mass in your notebook.

19. Open the calorimeter, and carefully pour out the water. Place the wet copper in the container provided for this purpose. Dry the calorimeter carefully.

20. Repeat steps 13–19 using dry, unheated copper, and 200 mL of hot tap water.

Analysis

F. Did the temperature of the water increase or decrease?

G. Did the temperature of the copper increase or decrease?

H. How did using different amounts of water affect the temperature change?

Temperature change and phases of matter

Procedure

21. Stack a pair of cups one inside the other and tape them together securely. This will make a calorimeter. Place the calorimeter with one lid on a balance and measure its mass. Record the mass in your notebook.

22. Dry an ice cube with a paper towel and add the ice cube to the inner cup. Determine the mass of the calorimeter and ice. Record the mass.

23. Place the lid securely on the inner cup. Insert the thermometer until the bulb touches the ice. Cover any holes in the lid with tape. When the temperature reaches a constant level, read the temperature of the copper using the appropriate number of significant figures. Record the temperature in your notebook.

24. Measure 100 mL of cold tap water into a container and measure its temperature. Record the temperature in your lab notebook.

25. Carefully remove the lid and thermometer from the calorimeter, keeping them together. Add the cold water to the calorimeter and ice, being careful to avoid spilling any water.

26. Immediately replace the lid and thermometer on the calorimeter and observe the thermometer. When the temperature reaches a constant level, gently shake the calorimeter to make sure the ice is melted. Measure the temperature of the water and record it in your lab notebook. This should take about five minutes.

27. Carefully remove the thermometer from the lid of the calorimeter, leaving the lid in place. Place the calorimeter, water, and ice on a balance and find its mass. Record the mass in your notebook.

28. Open the calorimeter, and carefully pour out the water. Dry the calorimeter.

29. Repeat steps 22–28 using a fresh ice cube and 200 mL of cold tap water.

30. Repeat steps 22–28 using a fresh ice cube and 50 mL of cold tap water.

Analysis

I. As the ice cube melted, did the temperature of the water change?

J. How did using different amounts of water affect the final temperature of the water?

Post-Chapter Activity 10 — HOLT PHYSICS Invention Lab

Thermal Conduction

Schlachter Products
Bethel Park, PA

January 24, 2000

Dr. Katherine Loughrey
1% Inspiration Laboratories
14557 West Post Road
Tempe, Arizona 85289

Dear Dr. Loughrey:

It was good to speak with you last week at the Materials Science Conference. I am glad that you too are aware of the current environmental crisis facing our planet. For the past 15 years, my company has been producing personalized thermal products, such as ice chests and thermal stadium pillows. These products are durable, so they are preferable to disposable products that serve the same purpose. Unfortunately, the majority of these products use environmentally unfriendly materials, such as plastic foam. Our goal is to gradually phase out these constituents in favor of other materials without significantly raising our costs.

We are working to develop new environmentally safe polymers that will serve our needs, but we are primarily interested in finding currently available materials that can be used in our product line.

Basically, we are in need of materials that retain heat for long periods of time. We hope you can recommend appropriate materials or inform us of how simple, ecologically sound materials might be modified to retain heat better.

We are also interested in a similar project for a new product. We want to begin producing quick-thaw pans for frozen foods. We need to know of materials that radiate heat quickly. Your recommendations on this matter will be greatly appreciated.

I hope to speak with you soon. If you have any questions, please do not hesitate to send an E-mail or to call.

Sincerely,

Brian E. Clark

Brian E. Clark

More notes on testing procedures are on page 46.

1% Inspiration Laboratories

MEMORANDUM

Date: January 26, 2000
To: Materials Research Team
From: Katherine Loughrey

Attached is the work request from Schlachter Products. They seem to want both extremes: materials that retain heat for a long period of time and materials that radiate heat quickly. This seems like a fairly basic project, and I think we will be able to do one set of tests to solve both problems. Check out the materials supply list to see what we have available. Also, do some literature searching to find other materials that we might want to get in stock for testing. See me to order some samples; if they're available, test them as well.

Keep in mind that simple materials are less expensive. If modifications such as environmentally sound paint or coating can be made using easily obtained materials, so much the better. Cost is a factor here, so don't seek out exotic new materials. Also, remember that the surface area of the samples will affect the amount of radiated or absorbed energy—standardize your experimental controls. Also be sure to develop a standardized procedure: I have jotted down some ideas on a note card, so make sure you look them over before you prepare your plan.

Before you go into the lab and begin testing, I need to see your plan. Describe the tests you are going to perform in the lab. Include an explanation of how you chose the materials you are going to test.

When your tests are complete, prepare your report in the format of a patent application, describing the tests you performed and analyzing all your results. Your report should give specific recommendations for the materials to be used for the ice chests and also for the quick-thaw pans. Include relevant heating and cooling curves, and include a complete mathematical assessment.

14557 West Post Road • Tempe, Arizona 852—

See next page for safety requirements, materials list, and more hints.

continued

MATERIALS

ITEM	QTY.
✔ bulb and socket	1
✔ connecting wires and plug	1
✔ aluminum can	1
✔ black painted metal cup	1
✔ ceramic cup	1
✔ paper cup	1
✔ steel can	1
✔ stopwatch	1
✔ thermometer	2
✔ white painted metal cup	1

SAFETY

- Never put broken glass or ceramics in a regular waste container. Use a dustpan, brush, and heavy gloves to carefully pick up broken pieces and dispose of them in a container specifically provided for this purpose.

- Use a hot mitt to handle resistors, light sources, and other equipment that may be hot. Allow all equipment to cool before storing it.

- If a thermometer breaks, notify the teacher **immediately.**

- Do not heat glassware that is broken, chipped, or cracked. Use tongs or a hot mitt to handle heated glassware and other equipment because it does not always look hot when it is hot. Allow all equipment to cool before storing it.

- If a bulb breaks, notify your teacher immediately. Do not remove broken bulbs from sockets.

The most important thing is to make sure all tests are the same. I think we should use a light source to raise the temperature of each sample. While the sample is exposed to the light, keep track of how its temperature rises. Then remove the light source and measure how the sample's temperature drops. All samples should be the same size and should be placed at the same distance from the light source. Any factors in the lab that could affect one sample differently than others should be eliminated if possible.

HOLT PHYSICS Discovery Lab

Pre-Chapter Exploration 12

Pendulums and Spring Waves

SAFETY

- Attach masses securely. Perform this experiment in a clear area. Falling or dropped masses can cause serious injury.
- Tie back long hair, secure loose clothing, and remove loose jewelry to prevent their being caught in moving or rotating parts.

MATERIALS

- ✔ 5 metal washers
- ✔ cord, 1.00 m
- ✔ long, loosely coiled spring
- ✔ masking tape
- ✔ meterstick
- ✔ paper clip
- ✔ protractor
- ✔ stopwatch
- ✔ support stand and clamp

OBJECTIVES

- Determine the factors that influence the time interval required for a pendulum to complete one full swing.
- Investigate the nature of pendulum and wave motion.

The period of a pendulum

Procedure

1. Construct a pendulum like the one shown at right. Attach a bent paper clip to one end of a 1.00 m cord. Attach the other end of the cord to a clamp that is securely attached to a support stand so that the bottom of the paper clip hangs 0.50 m below the clamp. Securely clamp the support stand to the edge of the tabletop.

2. Hang a small metal washer from the paper clip. Bend the paper clip to hold the washer securely. Remove all obstacles nearby so that the washer is free to swing from side to side.

3. Lift the washer so that the cord is taut between the washer and the clamp. Raise it to a 20° angle from its resting position.

4. Release the washer. Begin the stopwatch the moment the washer is released. Stop timing when the washer completes 10 full swings (over and back). Divide the time by 10 to get the average time interval required for each swing.

5. In your notebook, record the angle, the total time, the number of swings, and the average time required for each swing. Be sure to use the correct number of significant digits and the appropriate SI units.

6. Lift the washer so that the cord is taut between the washer and the clamp. Raise it to a 15° angle from its resting position.

7. Release the washer. Begin the stopwatch the moment the washer releases. Stop timing when the washer completes 10 full swings (over and back). Divide the time by 10 to get the average time interval required for each swing.

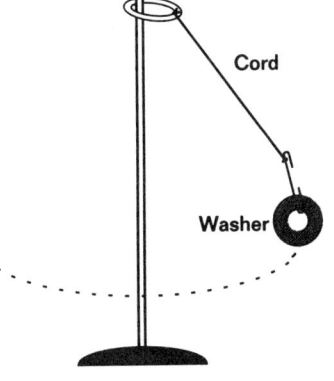

8. In your notebook, record the angle, the total time, the number of swings, and the average time for each swing. Be sure to use the correct number of significant digits and the appropriate SI units.

Analysis

A. How much time did it take for the pendulum to complete one full swing when it was raised to a 20° angle?

B. How much time did it take for the pendulum to complete one full swing when it was raised to a 15° angle?

C. Compare the number of seconds of each swing at each position. Which initial angle required the longest time interval to complete one full swing?

The length of a pendulum

Procedure

9. Adjust the cord in the clamp so that the pendulum is longer than 0.50 m but shorter than 1.00 m. Measure and record the length of the pendulum.

10. Lift the washer so that the cord is taut between the washer and the clamp. Raise it to a 20° angle from its resting position.

11. Release the washer. Begin the stopwatch the moment the washer is released. Stop timing when the washer completes 10 full swings. Find the average time interval for one swing.

12. Adjust the cord in the clamp so that the pendulum is longer than 10 cm but shorter than 20 cm. Measure and record the length of the pendulum. Repeat steps 10 and 11.

Analysis

D. How long did it take for each pendulum to complete one full swing?

E. Compare your observations for these pendulums with your observations for the 0.50 m pendulum. Plot your data on a graph of period versus length.

Building a pendulum with a specific period

Procedure

13. Based on your graph and your results above, adjust the length of the pendulum to create a pendulum that requires 1.0 s to complete one full swing.

14. When you have found the correct length, find the time required for a pendulum with the same length and a different mass to complete one full swing. Select two or three washers, and add them to the washer on the paperclip.

15. Measure the time required for the pendulum to complete 10 full swings, and find the average time for one full swing.

Analysis

F. How long was the cord for the pendulum that took 1.0 s to complete one full swing?

G. Did adding mass to the pendulum change the time required for one full swing?

H. To make a pendulum that requires 2.0 s for one full swing, would you lengthen or shorten the cord? Explain your reasoning.

Spring waves

Procedure

16. Hold a long, loosely coiled spring at one end. Have a partner hold the other end of the spring. Place the spring on the floor so that it is straight between both ends.
17. Quickly lift one end of the spring about 30 cm from the floor and place it on the floor again. You should do this in one second or less.
18. Observe the spring. Record your observations in your notebook. Draw a picture in your notebook of what you see. Clearly indicate the direction of motion.
19. Hold the spring at one end. Have a partner hold the other end of the spring. Place the spring on the floor so that it is straight between both ends.
20. Quickly move one end of the spring about 15 cm to the right and then 30 cm to the left. Make sure that the other end remains firmly on the floor.
21. Observe the spring. Record your observations in your notebook. Draw a picture of what you see in your notebook.
22. Hold the spring at one end. Have a partner hold the other end of the spring. Place the spring on the floor so that it is straight between both ends.
23. Quickly push one end of the spring forward and bring it back to its original place.
24. Observe the spring. Record your observations in your notebook. Draw a picture of what you see in your notebook.

Analysis

I. What did you observe when you quickly lifted the spring and set it back down again?
J. What did you observe when you quickly moved one end of the spring about 15 cm to the right and then 30 cm to the left?
K. What did you observe when you quickly pushed the spring forward and brought it back to its original place?

Post-Chapter Activity 12

HOLT PHYSICS Invention Lab

Tensile Strength and Hooke's Law

ORSINO DRUMS

February 3, 2000

Dr. Wes Graham
1% Inspiration Laboratories
14557 West Post Road
Tempe, Arizona 85289

Dear Dr. Graham:

I am writing in regard to my company, Orsino Drums. We are seeking a replacement for the springs used to provide resistance in the foot pedal of the drums we manufacture. The replacements need to be strong and reliable, and the displacement of the spring should be proportional to the force applied. I know that your company has done tensile testing of elastic and non-elastic materials in the past, and I hope that you will be able to provide such a service. I am enclosing a sample of the springs we use so that you can test it to determine what our needs are.

We also sell a low-end practice drum pedal, mostly for beginning drummers. In an effort to keep the prices of these pedals low, we are considering a move toward elastic bands, but we are not sure if their properties make them suitable for a drum-pedal spring. They need to show little sign of fatigue under normal use. I'm enclosing samples of these as well. I am very interested in your thoughts on their utility.

Thanks again for all your help. I look forward to hearing from your company.

Best wishes,

Mike Orsino

Mike Orsino, President

A picture of the drum pedal is on page 52.

1% Inspiration Laboratories

MEMORANDUM

February 4, 2000
To: Research and Development Team
From: Wes Graham

This letter is fairly self-explanatory. Test the springs and the rubber bands, and compare their performance. I need to see graphs and values for the spring constant. My hunch is that there is no way that a rubber band will be able to substitute for a spring, but I think that doubling the bands might give a reasonable substitute. Take a look at the marketing information they sent along, with a picture of the drum pedal. You can tell that there are basically two springs (or rubber bands) that provide resistance to the foot of the drummer.

Check this out during the next week, and let me know how the performance of the elastic bands compares with the performance of the springs.

P.S. Make sure you don't damage the spring samples. When the load is removed, the spring should return to its original length. Don't worry about damaging the rubber bands. In fact, you should try to find out how much force they can handle without breaking. Let me know as much as you can about the springs and the rubber bands.

14557 West Post Road • Tempe, Arizona 852—

See next page for safety requirements, materials list, and more hints.

CHAPTER 12 **51**

continued

MATERIALS

ITEM	QTY.
✔ extension clamp	1
✔ masking tape	1 roll
✔ mass hanger	1
✔ meterstick	1
✔ pad	1
✔ ruler	1
✔ sample elastic bands	2
✔ sample spring	1
✔ set of masses (50 g–1000 g)	2
✔ stopwatch	1
✔ support stand	1

SAFETY

- Attach masses securely. Falling or dropped masses can cause serious injury.
- Tie back long hair, secure loose clothing, and remove loose jewelry to prevent their getting caught in moving or rotating parts.
- Wear eye protection, and perform this experiment in a clear area. Falling or dropped masses can cause serious injury.

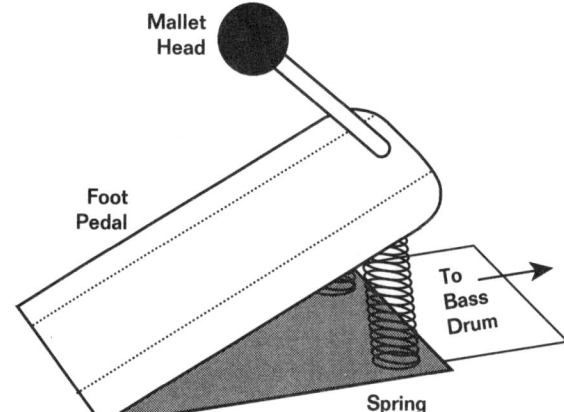

52 HOLT PHYSICS Laboratory Experiments

Pre-Chapter Exploration 13 — HOLT PHYSICS Discovery Lab

Resonance and the Nature of Sound

SAFETY

- Never put broken glass or ceramics in a regular waste container. Use a dustpan, brush, and heavy gloves to carefully pick up broken pieces and dispose of them in a container specifically provided for this purpose.
- Wear eye protection, and perform this experiment in a clear area. Falling or dropped masses can cause serious injury.

OBJECTIVES

- Explore the phenomenon of resonance in pendulums, and determine what conditions are necessary for resonance to occur.
- Explore the phenomenon of resonance with tuning forks, and determine what conditions are necessary for resonance to occur.
- Discover what variables affect the sound produced by an instrument.

MATERIALS

- ✔ adhesive tape
- ✔ aluminum support rod
- ✔ narrow-mouthed bottle
- ✔ pendulum bobs
- ✔ pendulum cord
- ✔ protractor
- ✔ right-angle clamp
- ✔ rubber tuning-fork hammer
- ✔ support stand and base
- ✔ tubes of different lengths
- ✔ pairs of tuning forks with resonance boxes

Resonance and pendulums

Procedure

1. Securely suspend two pendulums of different lengths from a flexible rod, as shown. The pendulums should be far enough apart that one pendulum can swing through 20° on each side without touching the other. The longer pendulum should be about 50 cm long. Use a slip knot to attach the pendulum bob to the cord.
2. Raise one pendulum to about a 20° angle so that the cord is taut.
3. Release the pendulum so that it swings freely.
4. Observe both pendulums for one minute as the released pendulum swings. Record your observations in your lab notebook.
5. Adjust the length of the longer pendulum using the slip-knot so that both pendulums are the same length. Make sure that one pendulum can swing without touching the other.
6. Raise one pendulum to approximately a 20° angle so that the cord is taut.
7. Release the pendulum so that it swings freely.
8. Observe both pendulums for one minute as the released pendulum swings. Record your observations in your lab notebook.

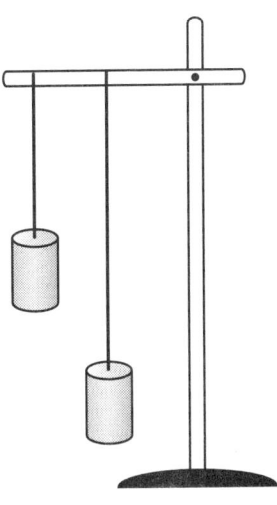

Analysis

A. When both pendulums were different lengths, what happened when one pendulum was raised and released? Describe what happened to the second pendulum.

CHAPTER 13 **53**

B. When both pendulums were the same length, what happened when one pendulum was raised and released? Describe what happened to the second pendulum.

C. When both pendulums were swinging, did they have the same frequency or different frequencies? Could you make them swing with different frequencies? Try it and record the results.

Resonance and tuning forks

Procedure

9. Place a tuning fork and resonator box on the table. Select a second resonator box with a tuning fork that is labeled with a different frequency, and place it in line with the first box, as shown. The open mouths of the boxes should be about 50 cm apart.

10. Use a rubber tuning-fork hammer to strike the first tuning fork. Strike the fork swiftly and firmly.

11. Listen to the sound produced by the tuning fork. Listen for any sound produced by the second tuning fork. Record your observations in your lab notebook.

12. Replace one of the tuning forks with another tuning fork that is labeled with the same frequency.

13. Use the rubber tuning fork hammer to strike the first tuning fork.

14. Listen to the sound produced by the tuning fork. Listen for any sound produced by the second tuning fork. Record your observations in your lab notebook.

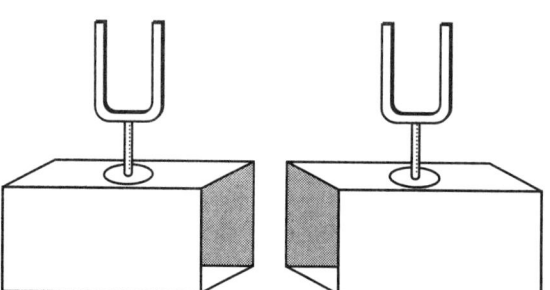

Analysis

D. When the tuning forks had different frequencies, what happened when one was struck? Did you hear any sound produced by the second tuning fork?

E. When the tuning forks had the same frequency, what happened when one was struck? Did you hear any sound produced by the second tuning fork?

Fundamental frequency

Procedure

15. Hold a narrow-mouthed bottle securely. Blow across the top of the bottle to make the bottle produce a whistling sound. Listen to the sound produced.

16. Select a short tube. Wrap masking tape around one end of the tube until the tube will fit snugly in the mouth of the bottle. Do not obstruct the end of the tube. Carefully push the tube firmly into place in the bottle.

17. Blow across the top of the tube in the bottle to cause it to produce a whistling sound. Listen to the sound produced.
18. Carefully remove the tube from the bottle and replace it with a longer tube. Blow across the top of the tube and listen to the sound produced.
19. Carefully remove the tube from the bottle and replace it with a longer tube. Blow across the top of the tube and listen to the sound produced.
20. Remove the tube from the bottle. Carefully pour water into the bottle to a depth of about 2 cm. Blow across the top of the bottle and listen to the sound produced.
21. Add more water to the bottle to a depth of about 4 cm. Blow across the top of the bottle and listen to the sound produced.
22. Continue to add water to the bottle in 2 cm increments until the bottle is full or no longer produces a sound. Listen to the sound produced by blowing across the top of the bottle after each addition.

Analysis

F. What happened to the sound as you added tubes of increasing length?

G. What happened to the sound as you added water to the bottle?

H. How did adding tubes affect the total length of the apparatus?

I. How did adding water affect the total length of the apparatus?

J. What is the relationship between the length of the apparatus and the sound produced?

Post-Chapter Activity 13 — HOLT PHYSICS Invention Lab

Building a Musical Instrument

EASTSIDE HIGH SCHOOL

February 17, 2000

Ms. Leslie Seecleff
Education Outreach Committee
1% Inspiration Laboratories
14557 West Post Road
Tempe, Arizona 85289

Dear Ms. Seecleff:

Thank you so much for the work you have done organizing the tutors and volunteers in the Education Outreach Committee here in town. Your volunteers have done a lot to help the students keep up with their school work, and I know you have also helped make learning fun!

We are getting ready for our annual Spring Science Fair, which will include students in grades K–12 from all the schools in our district. The volunteer tutors from your labs have always provided a lot of help with the science fair, but this year we have a special project for you. This year our physics classes have all focused on how physics is related to music. Throughout the year, students have attended special presentations about physics and music, including a workshop led by some of your tutors. The theme of the science fair this year is music, and we would like you to help us out by developing some instruments from basic physics principles. We will use these instruments, with reports explaining how physics concepts relate to the design of each instrument, as a special display at the science fair.

Because the focus of the display will be that physics determines how the instruments work, you don't need to worry about using special materials to make them. Simple household items will do. The fair will be held on April 29 in the Eastside High School gymnasium. Thank you so much for your continued support of our program.

Sincerely,

Calvin Saddleback

Calvin Saddleback

More information is on page 58.

1% Inspiration Laboratories

MEMORANDUM

Date: February 22, 2000
To: Education Outreach Committee
From: Leslie Seecleff

It's time for the school district's science fair again, and this year they have asked us to prepare a special exhibit for the students. I think it sounds like a lot of fun. As always, whenever we prepare exhibits for the fair we want to set a good example for the students to follow in their own work. To that end, I have drawn up some guidelines for the instruments.

Each instrument should be homemade and should meet the following requirements:

1. Each volunteer must make one musical instrument.
2. The instrument is to be made from common household materials.
3. The instrument must be capable of producing a complete octave.
4. Each instrument must be accompanied by a patent application that explains the workings of the instrument and describes in detail how physics principles apply to the instrument.

I have gone through the supply room and put together a list of materials that we have available. If you need something else, let me know; we may be able to find it. Before you begin work, please draw up a plan describing what kind of instrument you want to make and how you will use physics to meet the guidelines above.

Also take a look at the flyer for this year's fair. If the flyer is any indication, these students have really made the connection between physics and music this year, so the fair should be exciting.

Good luck and have fun!

14557 West Post Road • Tempe, Arizona 852—

See next page for safety requirements, materials list, and more hints.

continued

MATERIALS

ITEM
- ✔ adhesive tape
- ✔ bottles
- ✔ cans
- ✔ cardboard
- ✔ cord
- ✔ funnel
- ✔ glasses
- ✔ glue
- ✔ pipes of various lengths
- ✔ plastic combs
- ✔ plastic containers
- ✔ pots and pans
- ✔ rubber bands
- ✔ silverware/flatware
- ✔ stones
- ✔ tape
- ✔ wire
- ✔ wood blocks

SAFETY

- Review lab safety guidelines. Always follow correct procedures in the lab.
- Tie back long hair, secure loose clothing, and remove loose jewelry to prevent their getting caught in moving or rotating parts.

Tempe Public Schools

present

The Science of Music

Spring Science Fair 2003

April 29   7:00 P.M.

Eastside High School Main Gymnasium

SEE scientists and engineers build their own musical instruments.

HEAR the sounds they can produce.

TRY it yourself.

Pre-Chapter Exploration 14 — HOLT PHYSICS Discovery Lab

Light and Mirrors

SAFETY

- Secure all apparatus, and perform this experiment in a clear area. Swinging or dropped masses can cause serious injury.

OBJECTIVES

- Form images using mirrors.
- Locate images using different methods.

MATERIALS

- ✔ paper
- ✔ curved mirror
- ✔ eye charts, both normal and reverse
- ✔ meterstick
- ✔ mirror supports
- ✔ pencil
- ✔ protractor
- ✔ ruler or straightedge
- ✔ small flat mirror
- ✔ T-pin
- ✔ tape
- ✔ white paper

Virtual images

Procedure

1. Secure the normal eye chart to the wall using strong tape.
2. Choose any line on the chart, and step back just until the line can no longer be read clearly. Mark the position on the floor where you are standing with masking tape. Label it "reading point."
3. Measure the distance from the eye chart to the reading point with a meterstick. Record this distance in your notebook, using the appropriate SI units. Also record the number of the line that you were trying to read.
4. Secure a small flat mirror against the wall at chest level using strong tape.
5. Place the back of the reverse eye chart against your chest. Position the chart so that the line that you read appears in the mirror. Step back from the mirror, holding the eye chart against your chest until the image of this line is barely readable.
6. Mark the position on the floor where you are standing with masking tape. Label it "new point."
7. Measure the distance from the eye chart to the new point. Record this distance in your notebook, using the appropriate SI units.

Analysis

A. Describe the image of the reverse eye chart you saw on the surface of the mirror. Compare it with the appearance of the normal eye chart.

B. What distance did you measure between the mirror and the reverse eye chart?

C. What distance did you measure between the starting point and the eye chart on the wall?

D. Compare your answers in B and C. What is the relationship between the distances?

Flat mirrors

Procedure

8. Using two mirror supports, vertically stand one flat mirror on a table, away from the edge, as shown. Place a sheet of white paper on the tabletop so that the front of the mirror faces the paper. Tape the paper and mirror supports to the table so that they do not slide.

9. Using tape, carefully secure a T-pin on the tabletop, with the T side down in front of the mirror. Remove the eraser from a pencil. Secure the eraser on the pin to cover the point.

10. Wearing a pair of safety goggles, move your head to one side of the pin. Close one eye and place your open eye at the level of the tabletop. Observe the image of the pin in the mirror.

11. Use a ruler to draw a straight line on the paper from the image of the pin in the mirror to the position of your eye. Label it "outgoing beam." Use a ruler to draw a straight line from the object to the mirror's surface, connecting with the line labeled "outgoing beam." Label it "incoming beam."

12. Draw a line on the paper from the position of your eye perpendicular to the mirror's surface. Draw a line from the object perpendicular to the mirror's surface. Both lines should be parallel to each other. These lines will form angles with the lines you drew in step 11.

13. Measure the angle between the line labeled "outgoing beam" and the nearest perpendicular line. Measure the angle between the line labeled "incoming beam" and the nearest perpendicular line. Record these angles in your notebook, using the appropriate SI units.

14. Move your eye to a new position. Repeat steps 10–13.

15. Move your eye to a third position. Repeat steps 10–13.

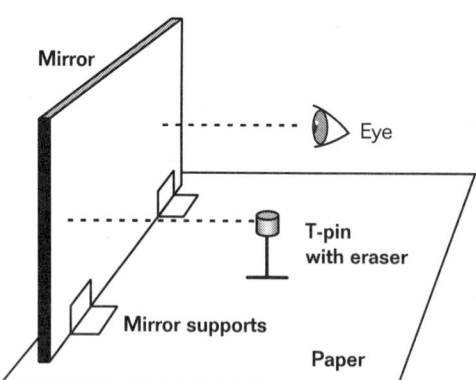

Analysis

E. Compare the two angles measured in step 13 for each position. What is the relationship between the angles?

F. In your notebook, draw the experimental setup as viewed from above. Include the lines and angles for each trial.

Curved mirrors

Procedure

16. Obtain a curved mirror. Use one mirror support to hold the mirror upright on the bench. Place the mirror so that you are facing the side that curves outward.
17. Place an object at various distances from the mirror. Look at the image of the object in the mirror.
18. Observe and record in your notebook how the image appears. Include the object's position (close to the mirror, far from the mirror), the size of the image (enlarged, small), and the orientation of the image (upright, upside down).
19. Turn the mirror around so that you are facing the side that curves inward.
20. Place an object at various distances from the mirror. Look at the image of the object in the mirror.
21. Observe and record in your notebook how the image appears. Include the object's position (close to the mirror, far from the mirror), the size of the image (enlarged, small), and the orientation of the image (upright, upside down).

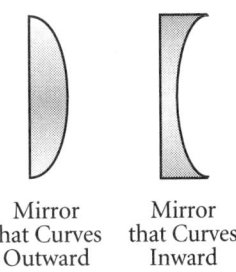

Mirror that Curves Outward   Mirror that Curves Inward

Analysis

G. How did the image appear when the object was in front of the curved-out mirror?
H. How did the image appear when the object was close to the curved-in mirror?
I. How did the image appear when the object was far away from the curved-in mirror?

Post-Chapter Activity 14
HOLT PHYSICS
Invention Lab

Designing a Device to Trace Drawings

Eastern Museum Press

March 29, 2000

Dr. Alexis White
Research and Development
1% Inspiration Laboratories
14557 West Post Road
Tempe, Arizona 85289

Dear Dr. White:

I am in charge of the publishing house here at the Eastern Museum. We publish art books as well as scientific and scholarly books and journals. Recently we have acquired a very old manuscript that is too delicate to be handled or exposed to bright lights.

This manuscript contains many scientific illustrations that we would like to reproduce in a new book. Obviously, this job calls for absolute accuracy. We have come to the conclusion that tracing may be the best method.

We are wondering if you could develop a piece of equipment that causes a virtual image of a picture to appear on a piece of paper next to an artist's real hand so that the artist can trace the image.

I would also greatly appreciate it if you could provide a clear explanation of how the device works so that I can explain its working mechanism to my colleagues. I look forward to hearing from you.

Sincerely,

Caroline Miller

Caroline Miller
Director

A diagram of a related device is on page 64.

1% Inspiration Laboratories

Memorandum

Date: April 1, 2000
To: Optical Design Staff
From: Alexis White

This project seems like one that we can handle. Please start by coming up with a plan for your device. Before you go into the lab, I would like to see a detailed plan including a materials list and a proposed design with ray diagrams.

Caroline's description reminds me of the structure of a periscope, so I suggest looking at the construction of one of these before you begin. I have included a diagram for you to look at while you come up with a plan.

I think you will need to include an eyepiece for the artist to look through during the tracing process. There are some materials on the list that will probably work for the eyepiece in the model. In your final report, include an explanation of why the eyepiece is needed. I would like to know if we could eliminate it and save some money.

In the lab, build a model out of materials that we have readily available. I have included a list of materials that we have on hand for this project. Wear goggles while you work. Your final report should be in the format of a patent application and should include all of the following:

- the model of the tracing device with instructions on how to use it, including information on how far it has to be from the object in order to trace it
- a drawing with objects and images showing how the device works
- an explanation of how the device works

14557 West Post Road • Tempe, Arizona 852—

See next page for safety requirements, materials list, and more hints.

continued

MATERIALS

ITEM
- ✔ adhesive tape
- ✔ cardboard
- ✔ converging lens
- ✔ craft knife
- ✔ diverging lens
- ✔ drinking straw
- ✔ glass
- ✔ light source
- ✔ mirror
- ✔ see-through mirror or one-way mirror
- ✔ support stands and clamps
- ✔ top from a sports-drink bottle
- ✔ various hollow cylinders

SAFETY

- Wear eye protection and perform this experiment in a clear area.
- Never put broken glass or ceramics in a regular waste container. Use a dustpan, brush, and heavy gloves to carefully pick up broken pieces and dispose of them in a container specifically provided for this purpose.
- Avoid looking directly at a light source. Looking directly at a light source may cause permanent eye damage.

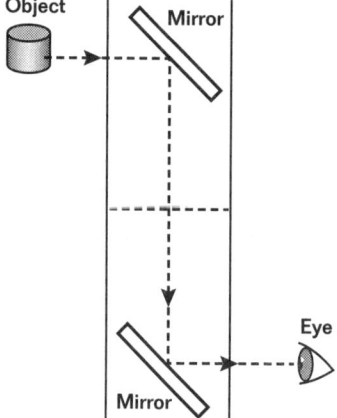

Periscope

Pre-Chapter Exploration 15 — HOLT PHYSICS Discovery Lab

Refraction and Lenses

SAFETY

- Secure all apparatus and perform this experiment in a clear area. Swinging or dropped masses can cause serious injury.
- Avoid looking directly at a light source. Looking directly at a light source may cause permanent eye damage. Always wear eye protection during this exercise.

OBJECTIVES

- Observe how light behaves as it passes from one substance to another.
- Observe images formed by different lenses.

MATERIALS

- ✔ coin
- ✔ drinking straw
- ✔ flashlight
- ✔ medicine dropper
- ✔ milk
- ✔ modeling clay
- ✔ opaque bowl
- ✔ pencil
- ✔ plastic electrical tape
- ✔ protractor
- ✔ ruler
- ✔ small, clear, rectangular container
- ✔ used chalkboard erasers
- ✔ various curved lenses

Principles of refraction

Procedure

1. Place a clean sheet of paper on the table. Secure it with tape so that it does not slide.

2. Place a small, clear plastic container on the paper. Carefully trace around the edges of the container, and then remove the container. Draw a line perpendicular to each side of the container. Throughout the lab, you will measure the angle of the incoming beam and the outgoing beam relative to these lines.

3. Carefully pour water into the container until it is half full. Add several drops of milk to the water, and stir carefully. Replace the container on the outline drawn on the paper.

4. Carefully cut a drinking straw so that it is 2.0 cm long. Tape the straw so that it is perpendicular to the flashlight's lens. Cover the rest of the flashlight's face with electrical tape so that light can only exit through the straw when the flashlight is turned on.

5. Use a ruler to draw a line at an angle to one of the perpendicular lines. The line should touch the side of the container.

6. Viewing from above, carefully place the flashlight on the tabletop so that the straw is aligned with the angled line and the beam enters the container. Gently tap two chalkboard erasers together once on each side of the container so that the beam is clearly visible. Observe where the light beam exits the container.

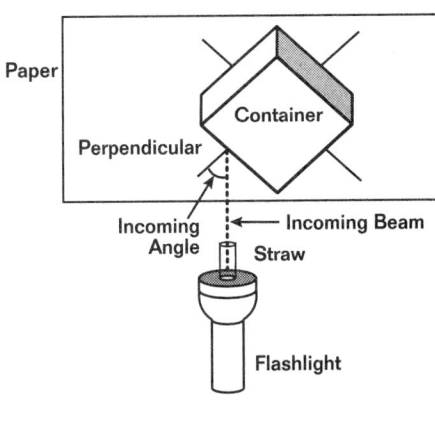

CHAPTER 15 **65**

7. Cut a drinking straw so that it is 5.0 cm long. Mount the straw on a small piece of modeling clay so that it is held horizontally at the same height above the table as the flashlight beam. Align this straw on the tabletop with the exiting beam by viewing the beam through the straw.

8. Observe from above the path of the light as it travels through the container. Draw a line on the paper to make the position of the straw. Measure the angle between the beam going into the container (incoming beam) and the perpendicular line with a protractor. Measure the angle between the beam going out of the container (outgoing beam) and the nearest perpendicular line with a protractor. Record your observations and the angles in your notebook.

Analysis

A. Draw the entire setup viewed from above. Include a ray diagram of the light beam and all angles in your drawing.

B. Do the straws lie in a straight line?

C. As the light traveled through the air before it reached the container, did it travel in a straight path or did it bend?

D. As light traveled into the container, did it travel in a straight path or did it bend?

E. As the light traveled through the milky water, did it travel in a straight path or did it bend?

F. As the light traveled from the container to the air, did it travel in a straight path or did it bend?

G. As the light traveled through the air after it left the container, did it travel in a straight path or did it bend?

Seeing around corners

Procedure

9. Place a coin in an empty bowl.

10. Lower your head until the coin goes just out of view. Hold your head in this position while your partner carefully fills the bowl with water without moving the coin.

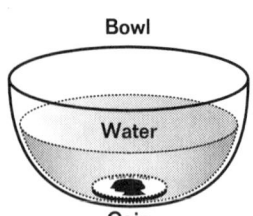

Analysis

H. Draw the view of the setup from the side. Include a ray diagram of the light beam from the coin to your eye in your diagram.

I. As the light traveled through the air before it reached the bowl of water, did it travel in a straight path or did it bend?

J. As light traveled into the bowl of water, did it travel in a straight path or did it bend?

K. As the light traveled through the water, did it travel in a straight path or did it bend?

L. As the light traveled from the bowl to the air, did it travel in a straight path or did it bend?

M. As the light traveled through the air from the bowl of water to your eye, did it travel in a straight path or did it bend?

N. The coin was out of view until the water was added. What do you think happened?

Lenses

Procedure

11. Obtain a lens that is thicker in the middle than at the edges.

12. Place an object at various distances from the lens. Look through the lens at the object.

13. Observe and record in your notebook how the image appears. Include the object's position (close to the lens, far from the lens), the size of the image (enlarged, small), and the orientation of the image (upright, upside down).

14. Obtain a lens that is thinner in the middle than at the edges.

15. Place an object at various distances from the lens. Look through the lens at the object.

16. Observe and record in your notebook how the image appears. Include the object's position (close to the lens, far from the lens), the size of the image (enlarged, small), and the orientation of the image (upright, upside down).

Lens that is thicker in the middle than at the edges.   Lens that is thinner in the middle than at the edges.

Analysis

O. How did the image appear when the object was far away from the lens that is thicker in the middle than at the edges?

P. How did the image appear when the object was close to the lens that is thicker in the middle than at the edges?

Q. How did the image appear when the object was in front of the lens that is thinner in the middle than at the edges?

R. Compare a curved lens with a curved mirror. What similarities and differences are there in the way that light behaves?

Post-Chapter Activity 15 — HOLT PHYSICS Invention Lab

Camera Design

DOLLAR A DOZEN PRODUCTS
25300 Villa Los Lobos
Albuquerque, New Mexico

April 11, 2000

Dr. Lincoln Chun
1% Inspiration Laboratories
14557 West Post Road
Tempe, Arizona 85289

Dear Dr. Chun:

We have just bought the inventory of a bankrupt optical company and are interested in using the lenses in a line of inexpensive cameras. The cameras will contain a single lens, and we will make use of the thin lens equation in their design. The logic of the design is based on the following theory.

For a camera to take quality photographs, it is necessary for a focused image to form on the film. The thin lens equation tells us that $1/p_0 + 1/q_i = 1/f$, where p_0 is the object distance from the lens, q_i is the image distance from the lens, and f is the focal length of the lens. This equation predicts that if an object is far away from the lens, the image will always form one focal length from the lens.

Because of this, we can design very inexpensive cameras if we place the film one focal length from the lens and instruct the photographer to use the camera only for pictures of distant objects. These cameras can be inexpensive because the lens never has to move with respect to the film, so no focusing apparatus is necessary, the photographer just points and shoots.

This is the theory. Our problem is that we do not possess any equipment for testing these lenses. For this reason, we would like you to develop a method to determine the focal length of our lenses. We also need a test apparatus so that we can set a screen one focal length from a lens and find the distance objects must be from the lens to form a focused image on the screen. Our lenses vary in diameter from 38 mm to 50 mm, so please design the apparatus to hold lenses spanning these dimensions.

Sincerely,
Maria Padilla
Maria Padilla

More information about camera design is on page 70.

1% Inspiration Laboratories

Memorandum

Date: April 14, 2000
To: Optical Design Staff
From: Lincoln Chun

I have found some disposable cameras that we can study to help us solve this problem. Take one apart and use the thin lens equation to analyze its design. Determine the focal length of the lens, the distance between the film and the lens, and the minimum distance an object must be from the lens for a focused image to appear on the film. Use an unfrosted light bulb as your object and tracing paper for a screen in this part of your investigation.

Finally, design an apparatus with a lens holder on the front and a screen on the back so that we can check out Dollar-a-Dozen's lenses. The apparatus should allow you to vary the screen's distance from the lens. The lens holder should also accommodate lenses of the sizes mentioned. One potential model would have the user simply place the lens in the holder, point the device at a distant object, and look into the screen on the back to see an image. By changing the distance between the screen and the lens you will be able to determine the focal length of each lens.

Before you go into the lab, prepare a plan describing the apparatus you will use and the tests you will perform in each part of the lab. After I have approved your plan, you can go into the lab and begin testing. When you are finished, prepare a report in the format of a patent application, describing your results.

14557 West Post Road • Tempe, Arizona 8529

See next page for safety requirements, materials list, and more hints.

continued

MATERIALS

ITEM	QTY.
✔ black construction paper	1 sheet
✔ black electrical tape	1 roll
✔ black paint (water-based)	1 pint
✔ cardboard box	1
✔ craft knife	1
✔ disposable camera	1
✔ double-sided tape	1 roll
✔ foamboard or mounting board	10 sheets
✔ lens and screen supports	4
✔ magnifier	1
✔ masking tape	1 roll
✔ matte acetate, 3 mL–5 mL	1 sheet
✔ medium-sized paint brush	1
✔ meterstick and supports	2
✔ support stand and clamp	1
✔ tracing paper	1 sheet
✔ unfrosted bulb and socket	1

SAFETY

- Avoid looking directly at a light source. Looking directly at a light source may cause permanent eye damage.
- Do not attempt this exercise with any batteries or electrical devices other than those provided by your teacher for this purpose.
- If a bulb breaks, notify your teacher immediately. Do not remove broken bulbs from sockets.
- Use a hot mitt to handle resistors, light sources, and other equipment that may be hot. Allow all equipment to cool before storing it.

Disposable Cameras: New Old Technology

Since the invention of the camera almost 150 years ago, cameras have come a long way. New technologies over the years have given us cameras with timers, cameras that take the red out of our eyes, and cameras that focus themselves.

Even with all these new developments, however, the basic design of a camera is really the same as it has always been—a camera uses a lens (or other optical device, such as a pinhole) to direct an image onto a light-sensitive material held in a light-proof container.

Because this design is so simple, there is a lot of room for making improvements and developing new features.

Most simple cameras have a fixed focus; this means that there is no way to adjust the focus for objects at different distances from the camera. This kind of camera can focus on most objects, as long as they are at least a certain distance away from the camera. This is the principle behind the new disposable cameras. The newest technology is really old news.

Disposable cameras are very similar to the earliest box cameras. They have a lens that is fixed in focus, and they can be used to take pictures of objects that are a little over 1 m away from the photographer.

After the roll of film has been used, the entire camera is returned to the processor. The film is developed, the pictures are printed, and the camera lens and other parts are recycled and made into new cameras.

Pre-Chapter Exploration 17
HOLT PHYSICS Discovery Lab

Charges and Electrostatics

SAFETY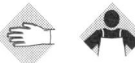

- Set up all the apparatus securely. Perform this experiment in a clear area. This exercise can produce sparks, so remove flammable liquids from the work area. Carefully handle metal with an insulating material such as rubber gloves to prevent shock.
- Tie back long hair, secure loose clothing, and remove loose jewelry. Roll back long sleeves because they may become charged.

OBJECTIVES

- Discover the electrical properties of metallic and nonmetallic objects.
- Construct an electroscope and investigate how it works.
- Observe forces between charged and uncharged objects.

MATERIALS

- ✔ 2 plastic-foam cups
- ✔ balloon
- ✔ comb
- ✔ felt cloth
- ✔ flannel cloth
- ✔ glue
- ✔ large aluminum pan
- ✔ large thick plastic drinking cup
- ✔ meterstick
- ✔ paper clip
- ✔ ruler
- ✔ sheet of aluminum foil
- ✔ silk cloth
- ✔ small aluminum pan

Constructing an electroscope

Procedure

1. Straighten the broad end of a paper clip. With the paper clip, carefully punch two holes 0.5 cm apart in the center of a small aluminum pan.
2. From a sheet of aluminum foil, cut out two 1 cm × 4 cm strips.
3. With the straightened end of the paper clip, carefully punch a hole 1 cm from one end of each aluminum foil strip.
4. Hook the narrow end of this paper clip through the holes in the strips. The strips should hang parallel to one another as shown.
5. Push the straightened end of the paper clip through a hole in the aluminum pan. Bend the paper clip back so that it can insert into the other hole in the pan. Push the end of the paper clip down through the hole. The paper clip and aluminum strips should hang below the pan.
6. Place a clear, thick plastic cup upright on a tabletop. Set the pan on top of the cup as shown. Throughout this lab, you will observe the movement of the aluminum-foil strips through the cup. This device is referred to as an *electroscope*.

Analysis

A. Did you observe a spark when you touched the aluminum pan?

CHAPTER 17 **71**

Determining whether objects are electrically charged

Procedure

7. Inflate a balloon until it measures at least 20 cm from its top to where the knot will be tied. Rinse the balloon with water. Dry it with a paper towel.

8. Vigorously rub the balloon with flannel. Move the balloon toward the electroscope. Closely observe the foil strips hanging from the paper clip. Record your observations in your lab notebook.

9. Touch the part of the balloon that was rubbed with flannel. Move the balloon toward the electroscope, and observe the foil strips. Record your observations.

Analysis

B. What did you observe as the balloon rubbed with flannel moved toward the electroscope?

C. What did you observe as the balloon that you touched moved toward the electroscope?

D. Based on your observations, did a force act on the foil strips? If so, was it a contact force or a field force? Explain.

Observing the effects of electric charge

Procedure

10. Move the aluminum pan toward the electroscope. Observe the foil strips hanging from the paper clip. Record your observations in your lab notebook.

11. Rub the pan with silk. Move the pan toward the electroscope, and observe the foil strips. Record your observations.

12. Glue a plastic-foam cup upside down to the inside of a small aluminum pan as shown. Glue the second plastic-foam cup to the inside of the large aluminum pan.

13. Pick up the small pan by the plastic-foam cup. Rub the pan with the flannel cloth. Move the pan toward the electroscope, and observe the foil strips. Record your observations.

14. Rub an inflated balloon with flannel. Holding only the plastic-foam cup, place the bottom of the small pan firmly against the balloon. Touch the pan once with your finger. Remove the pan from the inflated balloon.

15. Move the pan toward the electroscope, and observe the foil strips. Record your observations.

16. Rub an inflated balloon with flannel. Holding only the plastic-foam cup, place the large pan firmly against the balloon. Touch the large pan once with your finger. Remove the pan from the inflated balloon.

17. Move the large pan toward the electroscope, and observe the foil strips. Record your observations. Place a small ink mark on the edge of the pan's rim.

18. Rub an inflated balloon with flannel. Holding only the plastic-foam cup, place the small pan firmly against the balloon. Touch the small pan once with your finger. This time, place your finger on the plastic-foam cup before removing the small pan from the balloon. Remove the small pan from the inflated balloon.

19. Move the small pan toward the electroscope, and observe the foil strips. Record your observations.

20. Hold both of the pans by the cups. Move the small pan close to the large pan so that the small pan touches only the ink mark on the large pan. Observe what happens as the pans get very close.

21. Move the large pan horizontally toward the electroscope so that the ink mark is closest to the electroscope. Make sure the pan does not touch any part of the electroscope. Observe the foil strips when the large pan is 1 cm from the device.

22. Rotate the pan 180° so that the side of the pan opposite the ink mark is near the electroscope. Move the pan so that it is 1 cm from the electroscope.

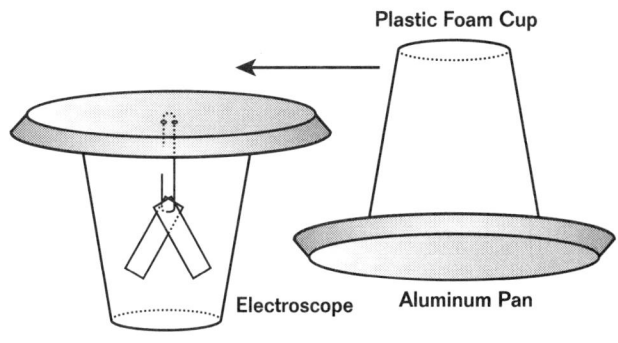

Analysis

E. What did you observe as you first moved the aluminum pan toward the electroscope?

F. What did you observe as the pan rubbed with silk moved toward the electroscope?

G. What did you observe as the pan that you touched moved toward the electroscope?

H. What did you observe as the pan rubbed with flannel moved toward the electroscope?

I. After placing your finger on the plastic-foam cup before removing the small pan from the balloon, what did you observe as the pan moved toward the electroscope?

J. What did you hear as the pans moved close to one another?

K. What did you observe as the ink mark on the pan moved toward the electroscope?

L. After rotating the large aluminum pan so that the ink mark was far from the electroscope, what did you observe as the aluminum pan moved toward the electroscope?

M. Based on your observations, do you think that a force acted on the foil strips?

N. Was this a contact force or a field force?

O. Did the foil strips of the electroscope ever move as you touched the pan?

P. Based on your observations, what was the plastic-foam cup used for?

Post-Chapter Activity 17 — HOLT PHYSICS Invention Lab

Levitating Toys

PARAMOUNTAIN STUDIOS
HOLLYWOOD, CA

April 19, 2000

Ms. Colleen Minks
1% Inspiration Laboratories
14557 West Post Road
Tempe, Arizona 85289

Dear Ms. Minks:

We are about to start filming *Hoop Screams*, a science fiction movie featuring small, hovering hoop-shaped structures that attack Earth. We are looking for a company to develop a levitating toy that we can market with the release of the film.

In the movie, the hoops enter other parts of the galaxy by flying through portals constructed out of material excavated from white dwarfs. The hoops can fly back and forth through the portals.

With this background in mind, we would like you to try to develop a toy with a levitating hoop that can be maneuvered around the room. The toy should also include large portals that the hoop can fly through.

If you feel that your company can supply us with this product, please contact me immediately. Thank you for your time. I look forward to hearing from you.

Sincerely,

Monali Jhaveri

Monali Jhaveri

Ideas for the design of the toy are on page 76.

1% Inspiration Laboratories

Memorandum

Date: April 20, 2000
To: Research and Development
From: Colleen Minks

I like the concept for this toy immensely. I think that you should be able to design and build this toy to use electrostatic repulsion.

The flying parts of the toy will have to be made from a lightweight material. We have a few space blankets in our storeroom that I think will be ideal. I have done a little research, and I think an electrophorus can be used to keep the pieces hovering. I have included a diagram of a simple model. The flying hoop and the electrophorus will have to have the same charge for this to work.

Start by constructing the levitating hoop. Construct it as neatly and symmetrically as possible. If you can get this small hoop to levitate, construct a portal for the hoop to hover through. For the best distribution of charge, the portal should not have any sharp edges. Determine whether the portal should be made from an insulator or a conductor, or if it should be grounded. To insulate the portal from its surroundings, hang it from some polyester thread.

If the hoop and portal work, spend some time maneuvering the hoop around the room and through both sides of the portal. Use your observations to make improvements to the design.

Before you go into the lab, give me a plan describing the procedure you will follow in the lab. Your plan should include the method you will use for charging the different parts of the toy.

When you are finished, I would like you to fill out a patent application for the finished toy. The report should include a short explanation of the electrostatic principles involved in the experiment and how they lead to the toy's failure or success. Include drawings showing the distribution of charges on the items.

14557 West Post Road • Tempe, Arizona 852

See next page for safety requirements, materials list, and more hints.

CHAPTER 17

continued

MATERIALS

ITEM	QTY.
✔ plastic-foam plate or polystyrene board	1
✔ new unsharpened pencil with eraser end	1
✔ plastic-foam cup	1
✔ aluminum pie pan	1
✔ wool flannel	1 piece
✔ space blanket	1 small piece
✔ coat hanger	1
✔ polyester thread	1 m
✔ rubber cement	1 jar
✔ meterstick	1
✔ craft knife	1
✔ cardboard or poster board	1 piece

SAFETY

- Tie back long hair, secure loose clothing, and remove loose jewelry to prevent their getting caught in moving or rotating parts.
- Do not attempt this exercise with any batteries, electrical devices, or magnets other than those provided by your teacher for this purpose.
- Do not eat or drink anything in the laboratory. Never taste chemicals or touch them with your bare hands.

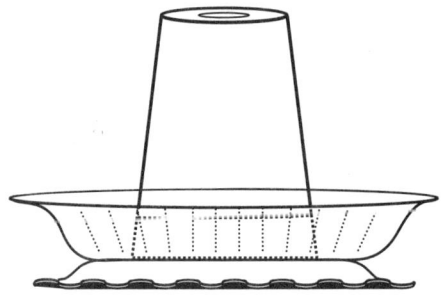

Electrophorus

> The electrophorus shown in this diagram is constructed from a plastic-foam dinner plate, an aluminum pie pan, and an insulating handle. The handle may be made by gluing a plastic-foam cup upside down on the inside of the pie pan. Charge the plastic-foam plate by rubbing it with a wool cloth. Place the pie pan onto the charged foam, then touch the pie pan with your finger. The pan is now charged and can be used for electrostatic experiments.

Pre-Chapter Exploration

HOLT PHYSICS
19 Discovery Lab

Resistors and Current

SAFETY

Never close a circuit until it has been approved by your teacher. Never rewire or adjust any element of a closed circuit. Never work with electricity near water; be certain that the floor and all work surfaces are dry.

If the pointer on any kind of meter moves off scale, open the circuit immediately by opening the switch.

Do not attempt this exercise with any batteries or electrical devices other than those provided by your teacher for this purpose.

MATERIALS

✔ 6 battery holders for D-cells
✔ 6 D-cell batteries
✔ light bulb and socket
✔ 2 multimeters or 1 dc ammeter, 1 ohmmeter, and 1 voltmeter
✔ graph paper
✔ insulated connecting wires
✔ 2 resistors
✔ switch

OBJECTIVES

- Measure current, resistance, and potential difference across various resistors.
- Graph the relationship between the potential difference and current for various resistors.
- Interpret graphs relating potential difference and current for various resistors.

Potential difference and current in a resistor

Procedure

1. Use the multimeter or ohmmeter to measure the resistance of the resistor. Hold the plastic part of the resistance meter probes. Place the probes across the terminals of each resistor in turn by touching the metal part of the red probe to one terminal and the metal part of the black probe to the other terminal. Read the values for the resistance across the resistors, and record the values in your lab notebook using the appropriate SI units.

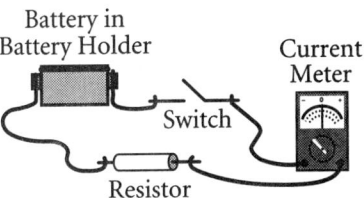

2. Using the resistor with the larger value, set up the apparatus as shown. Use one wire on each end of the battery holder to connect the switch and the resistor as shown. Connect the switch to one post of the current meter. Connect the other post of the current meter to the resistor. Carefully connect one post of the voltage meter to one side of the resistor, and connect the other post of the voltage meter to the other side of the resistor.

3. Carefully place a battery in the battery holder. ***Do not close the switch until your teacher approves your circuit.***

4. When your teacher has approved your circuit, close the switch. Read the value for the current in the resistor, and record the value in your lab notebook using the appropriate SI units.

CHAPTER 19 **77**

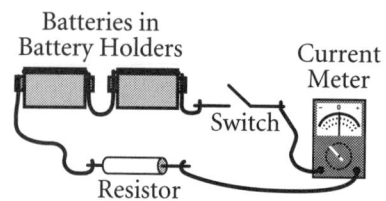

5. Use the multimeter or voltage meter to measure the potential difference across the resistor, and record the value in your lab notebook using the appropriate SI units. Open the switch.

6. Disconnect one side of the battery holder, and add another battery holder to the setup using another wire as shown. Carefully place a battery in the empty battery holder. **Do not close the switch until your teacher approves your circuit.**

7. When your teacher has approved your circuit, close the switch. Measure the current and the potential difference as in steps 4–5.

8. Disconnect one side of the battery holder, and add a third battery in a row with the other two as in step 6.

9. When your teacher has approved the circuit, close the switch. Measure the current and the potential difference as in steps 4–5.

10. Disconnect one side of the battery holder, and add a fourth battery in a row with the other three as in step 6.

11. When your teacher has approved the circuit, close the switch. Measure the current and the potential difference as in steps 4–5.

12. Replace the resistor with the second resistor, and repeat steps 2–11.

Analysis

A. How did adding more batteries to the setup affect the potential difference measured across the resistor?

B. How did adding more batteries to the setup affect the current measured in the resistor?

C. For each data set, divide the potential difference by the corresponding current. Record these ratios in your lab notebook.

D. Compare the value of the ratios for each resistor. What do you notice?

E. For each resistor, make a graph current on the *x*-axis and potential difference on the *y*-axis. Label each axis with the appropriate SI units.

F. Determine the slope of each graph. To do this, choose one point at the beginning of the graph and one point at the end. Find the change in potential difference and the change in current between these two points. Divide the difference in potential difference by the difference in current.

G. Compare the value for the slope with the resistance that you measured. Are there any similarities?

H. Compare the value for the slope with the ratios found. Are there any similarities?

Potential difference and current in a light bulb

Procedure

13. Place a light bulb securely in a socket. Holding the plastic part of the probes, carefully touch the resistance meter probes across the posts of the socket. Read the value for the resistance across the light bulb, and record the value in your lab notebook using the appropriate SI units.

14. Set up the apparatus as shown. Connect the switch, the battery holder, and the light bulb as shown. Connect one post of the current meter to the switch. Connect the other post of the current meter to one post of the light bulb socket. Carefully connect one post of the voltage meter to one post of the light bulb socket, and connect the other post of the voltage meter to the other post of the light bulb socket.

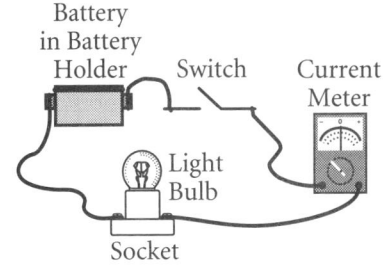

15. Carefully place three batteries in the empty battery holder. **Do not close the switch until your teacher approves your circuit.**

16. When your teacher has approved your circuit, close the switch. Measure the current in the light bulb, and record the value in your lab notebook using the appropriate SI units.

17. Use the voltage meter to measure the potential difference across the light bulb, and record the value in your lab notebook.

18. Disconnect one side of the battery holder, and add another battery holder to the setup. Carefully place a battery in the empty battery holder. **Do not close the switch until your teacher approves your circuit.**

19. Measure the current and the potential difference as in steps 16–17.

20. Add a fifth battery in a row with the other two as in step 18.

21. Measure the current and the potential difference as in steps 16–17.

Analysis

I. How did adding more batteries to the setup affect the potential difference measured across the light bulb?

J. How did adding more batteries to the setup affect the current measured in the light bulb?

K. For each data set, divide the potential difference by the corresponding current. Record these ratios in your lab notebook.

L. Compare the value of the ratios. What do you notice?

M. Graph your data with current on the *x*-axis and potential difference on the *y*-axis. Label each axis with the appropriate SI units.

N. Compare the graph with the graphs in E. Are the shapes similar?

O. Determine the slope of the graph. To do this, choose one point at the beginning of the graph and one point at the end. Find the change in potential difference and the change in current between these two points. Divide the change in potential difference by the change in current for the same interval.

P. Compare the ratios with the resistance that you measured. Are there any similarities?

Q. Compare the value of the slope with the ratios found. Are there any similarities?

Post-Chapter Activity 19 — HOLT PHYSICS Invention Lab

Battery-Operated Portable Heater

Leaping Lizards
2378 Whippoorwill Road
Bethel, Maine 04217

April 16, 2000

Dr. Ryan Williams
Research and Development
1% Inspiration Laboratories
14557 West Post Road
Tempe, Arizona 85289

Dear Dr. Williams:

My pet store specializes in reptiles and amphibians. In the store, all our cages and aquariums are equipped with hot rocks, heating pads, and basking lights. We need a way to keep the animals warm when they are moved from cage to cage and when they are taken home by their new owners. We are looking for a company to design a small battery-powered cage heater for our lizards and other coldblooded animals. These heaters will be used to heat the animals' carrying cases during cool weather. They can also be used as backups in case we lose power during a winter storm.

I have enclosed some information that we give to new owners, describing how to care for lizards. This information provides the ideal temperature range and some ideas for providing heat and light in the animals' cages. The cage heaters should maintain temperatures somewhere within the temperature range described in the information.

Thank you very much for your attention to this matter. These heaters will solve a serious problem for us and our customers.

Sincerely,

Terry Murphy

Terry Murphy

Information on lizard cages is on page 82.

1% INSPIRATION LABORATORIES

MEMORANDUM

Date: April 18, 2000
To: Research and Development
From: Ryan Williams

I think that we should be able to design these little heaters. The simplest approach is probably to use batteries to provide current in a high-resistance wire placed in the lizard's cage. You should start by controlling the size and number of batteries—use two new D-cell batteries to power the circuit. This will allow you to focus your experiments on determining the length and type of wire necessary to achieve an appropriate temperature. Terry Murphy sent some information on the best temperature range for most of their animals, so refer to that while you work. Let's assume that cool weather is around 10° C and design the heater to raise the temperature 10° C–15° C above the ambient temperature.

Before you begin work, I will need to see your plans for building and testing the device. Make sure you include plans to measure the temperature level of the wire when there is current. Describe how you will raise and lower the temperature to bring it to the appropriate level. Once you discover how to obtain a suitable temperature, you will need to develop a plan for using the wire and batteries safely and effectively in a small animal carrier.

Because raising the temperature of the wire requires a lot of current, you should keep track of the number of times that the batteries are used and approximately how hot the wire gets on each trial. Batteries can be used up very rapidly when they are used to bring wire to high temperatures, so keep careful track of this while you work.

When you are finished, submit your final design to me in the form of a patent application. Your application should include a discussion of the physics principles that describe how the heater works, as well as some explanation of how different types of wire could be used to make similar heaters.

14557 West Post Road • Tempe, Arizona 852—

See next page for safety requirements, materials list, and more hints.

CHAPTER 19 **81**

continued

MATERIALS

ITEM	QTY.
✔ Nichrome wire	2.5 m
✔ insulated connecting wire	1.5 m
✔ battery holder for 2 D-cell batteries	1
✔ D-cell batteries	2
✔ felt, 20 cm × 60 cm	1
✔ masking tape	
✔ connectors for wire	
✔ multimeter or dc ammeter with connecting leads	1
✔ thermometer or CBL system with temperature probe	1
✔ liquid crystal thermometer strip	1 (opt)
✔ cardboard box	1
✔ bare copper wire	1 m
✔ wire leads with alligator clips	2
✔ insulating materials	
✔ stopwatch	1

SAFETY

Wire coils may heat up rapidly during this experiment. If heating occurs, open the circuit immediately and handle the equipment with a hot mitt. Allow all equipment to cool before storing it.

Never close a circuit until it has been approved by your teacher. Never rewire or adjust any element of a closed circuit. Never work with electricity near water; be sure the floor and all work surfaces are dry.

If the pointer on any kind of meter moves off scale, open the circuit immediately.

Do not attempt this exercise with any batteries or electrical devices other than those provided by your teacher for this purpose.

Caring for your pet lizard

Now that you have your lizard, there are a few things you need to know to make sure your pet lives a happy and healthy life. You are responsible for meeting the dietary, temperature, and habitat needs of your pet. Some lizards, such as iguanas, can live to be over thirty years old, so this is a serious commitment!

Your lizard needs a terrarium that contains places to climb and hide, a water bowl that is easy to get in and out of, and a heater or basking light. A branch or shelf placed directly below the basking light will allow the lizard to quickly raise its body temperature. Lizards also need regular exposure to sunlight or UVB lighting.

Most lizards are active during the day and rest during the night. The ideal temperature range is from 18°C –24°C at night and 21°C –26°C during the day, with a basking area of 29°C –32°C.

HOLT PHYSICS
Pre-Chapter Exploration 20 — Discovery Lab

Exploring Circuit Elements

SAFETY

Never close a circuit until it has been approved by your teacher. Never rewire or adjust any element of a closed circuit. Never work with electricity near water; be certain the floor and all work surfaces are dry.

Do not attempt this exercise with any batteries or electrical devices other than those provided by your teacher for this purpose.

If a bulb breaks, notify your teacher immediately. Do not remove broken bulbs from sockets.

MATERIALS
- 1.5 V flashlight batteries, 2 or 3
- 5 miniature light bulbs
- 5 miniature light sockets
- 20 connecting wires
- capacitor
- rubber bands or tape

OBJECTIVES
- Construct circuits using different combinations of bulbs, batteries, and wires.
- Observe the effects of an electric current.
- Compare your observations from different trials to discover how relationships are affected by changing one or more variables.
- Classify and analyze your observations.

Simple circuit

Procedure
1. Place the bulbs securely in the sockets. Using one light bulb, a battery, and wires, connect the bulb to the battery to produce light.
2. Observe how brightly the bulb is lit. Also make observations of other qualities—temperature, sound, smell, color, motion, and anything else you observe. Hold your finger against the insulated part of the wire to test for motion in the wire.
3. Disconnect the battery. In your lab notebook, write a brief description of the bulb's brightness and of your other observations.

Analysis
A. How would you describe the brightness of the bulb?
B. Develop a system for comparing the brightness of different bulbs. Explain how your system would work in different situations, such as in a dark room and in direct sunlight.
C. Other than light, what effects did you observe when the bulb was lit?
D. Based on your observations, how can you detect the presence of current?

Circuit with bulbs in series

Procedure

4. Connect all three sockets of bulbs in a side-to-side row using two wires as shown. Use an additional wire on each end to connect the unattached ends to the battery so that all the bulbs light. (Hint: You may need to use more than one battery to get the bulbs to light.)

5. Compare the bulbs in terms of brightness and other qualities, and then compare the bulbs with the single bulb you observed earlier.

6. Disconnect the battery to sketch your circuit, and briefly describe your observations and comparisons in your lab notebook.

7. Reconnect the battery to light all three bulbs. Unscrew one bulb, and observe the effects on the other bulbs. Try this with the other bulbs to see if the position of the bulb makes a difference.

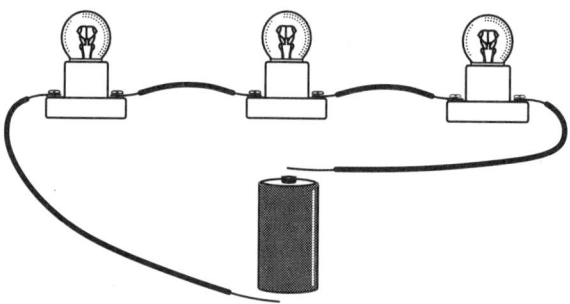

Analysis

E. When all three bulbs were lit, how did the brightness of the bulbs compare? How did the brightness of the bulbs compare with the brightness of the one-bulb system you observed before?

F. What happened when you unscrewed one of the bulbs? Did it matter which bulb you removed? Explain why or why not.

G. Based on your observations, what do you think would happen to the brightness of the bulbs if you added two more bulbs? Explain your reasoning. If time permits, get your teacher's permission and try it.

H. If the brightness of each bulb depends on the current, what do your observations tell you about the current in each bulb in the three-bulb circuit? Is the current the same in each bulb? Why or why not?

I. Suppose that a light bulb provides resistance to the current. How does using more than one light bulb affect the total resistance of the entire circuit? How does it affect the total current?

Circuits in parallel branches

Procedure

8. Connect all three sockets of bulbs in a column, with two wires connecting each pair of sockets, as shown. Each post will be connected to two wires. Using two more wires, connect the posts of the socket to the end of the battery so that all three bulbs light.

9. Observe the brightness and other qualities of the bulbs. Compare the bulbs with each other, and with the bulbs you have already observed.

10. Disconnect the battery and record your observations. Draw your circuit in your notebook.

11. Reconnect the battery so that all three bulbs relight. Unscrew one bulb and observe the effects on the other bulbs. Try this with the other bulbs to see if the position of the bulb in the circuit makes a difference.

12. Disconnect the battery and record your observations.

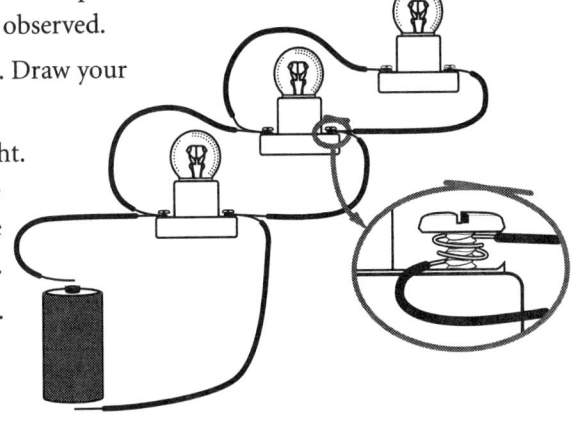

Analysis

J. When all three bulbs were lit, how did the brightness of the bulbs compare? How did the brightness compare with that of other systems you have observed?

K. What happened when you unscrewed one of the bulbs? Did it matter which bulb you removed? Explain why or why not.

L. Based on your observations, what do you think would happen to the brightness of the bulbs if you added two more branches with bulbs? What if the bulbs were different wattages from the bulbs you are already using?

M. If the brightness of a bulb depends on the current, what do your observations tell you about the current in each bulb? Is the current the same in each bulb? Why or why not?

N. Suppose that a light bulb provides resistance to the current. How does using a different branch for each bulb affect the total resistance of the entire circuit? How does it affect the total current?

Circuit with a capacitor

Procedure

13. Your teacher will supply you with a capacitor. Connect the capacitor and a light bulb with wires as shown.

14. Connect the battery to the bulb and capacitor so that the bulb lights. Leave the battery connected until the light goes out. Record your observations.

15. Next, remove the battery and connect the ends of the wires to each other. Observe what happens. Record your observations in your notebook.

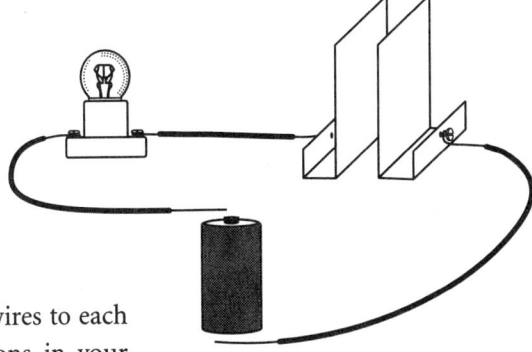

Analysis

O. Describe your observations of the brightness of the bulb when the bulb and capacitor were connected to the battery. Give an explanation of what happened.

P. What happened when the battery was removed and the wires were connected to each other? Explain.

Q. Based on your observations, do you think the current remained constant in this circuit? Explain your answer.

R. What do you think happened to the current when you removed the battery and reconnected the wires? Explain.

Post-Chapter Activity 20
HOLT PHYSICS Invention Lab

Designing a Dimmer Switch

Greenville Historical Science Foundation
Greenville, North Carolina

April 21, 2000

Dr. Kelly Maxwell
1% Inspiration Laboratories
14557 West Post Road
Tempe, Arizona 85289

Dear Dr. Maxwell:

We are restoring the home of Seelie Charles, an inventor who lived in our town during the turn of the century. We are planning to open the house as a historical museum. To promote interest in Ms. Charles's inventions and to give an idea of her vision of the future, we are incorporating many of her inventions and patents into the design of the house.

During the renovation of the laboratory, we came across the enclosed page of Ms. Charles's notebook. After conducting a patent search, we came to the conclusion that Ms. Charles was never able to develop her ideas for a dimming light switch. We would like to use these switches in the house. Electricity will be supplied to the house by means of a DC generator and rechargeable batteries, much like the ones Ms. Charles implemented in 1886 when she became the first citizen in Greenville to use electric lighting in her house.

Because of the high quality of your work, we would like you to develop a lighting design based on Ms. Charles's ideas. Unfortunately, the Foundation is unable to pay for your services, but you will maintain ownership of any patent issued on your design and we will credit you with a plaque at the house, as well as a formal mention in all of our advertising and promotional materials.

Please let me know as soon as possible if you will be able to complete this work on these dimmer-switch lighting systems. Thank you very much for your time.

Sincerely,

K. Azielinski

K. Azielinski

The page from Ms. Charles's notebook is on page 88.

1% INSPIRATION LABORATORIES

MEMORANDUM

Date: April 24, 2000
To: Development Team
From: Kelly Maxwell

I am a real history buff, and this looks too good to pass up. The publicity will be great, and if we get a patent, that could turn out to be profitable too. Ms. Charles has provided us with several good hints, but there are still several pieces to fit together before we start testing. Before you go into the lab, prepare a plan for each of the three designs mentioned in Ms. Charles's notebook:

- a light that can shine at three different brightness levels, with the amount of current controlled by the potential difference supplied
- a light that can shine at three different brightness levels, with the amount of current controlled by the amount of resistance in the circuit
- a light that stays on for a short amount of time, gradually growing dimmer until it is completely dark

I will approve your plan before you start work in the lab, so get this to me as soon as possible. For each design, your plan should include a list of materials needed, a diagram, and a one- or two-sentence explanation of what you expect to happen. I have included a list of the electrical components and equipment we have available. If you need something that you can't find on the list, be sure to ask about it; there may be more equipment available.

You will prepare your report in the form of a patent application. Remember to document all your testing and development procedures in your lab notebook. Good luck!

14557 West Post Road • Tempe, Arizona 85281

See next page for safety requirements, materials list, and more hints.

continued

MATERIALS

ITEM	QTY.
✔ metal paper clips	1 box
✔ rubber bands	1 box
✔ tape	1 roll
✔ 1.5 V flashlight battery and battery holder	3
✔ 6.0 V lantern battery	1
✔ capacitor—1 F	1
✔ resistor—390 kΩ	3
✔ resistor—180 kΩ	3
✔ resistor—10 Ω	2
✔ miniature light bulbs, 1.5 V	2
✔ miniature light sockets	2
✔ miniature light bulbs, 2.5 V	2
✔ miniature light bulbs, 6.3 V	2
✔ connecting wires with alligator clips	20
✔ single-throw knife switch	3
✔ double-throw knife switch	2

SAFETY

Never close a circuit until it has been approved by your teacher.

Never rewire or adjust any element of a closed circuit.

Never work with electricity near water—be sure the floor and all work surfaces are dry.

Do not attempt this exercise with any batteries or electrical devices other than those provided by your teacher for this purpose.

May 19, 1901

Idea 1: Design lights that are not always the same brightness, but can be made brighter or dimmer depending upon mood or activity.

Principle: The brightness of a light depends on the amount of current in the circuit, which depends on voltage and resistance.

Design: A circuit could be constructed that contains a different amount of current depending upon the position of a switch. This can be constructed by providing different resistance or different potential difference.

Idea 2: Design a light that will "turn off by itself"—this will be perfect for use in bedrooms, corridors, etc., wherever it is now necessary to walk across a darkened room or use a candle.

Principle: The duration of a light depends on the current in the circuit, which depends on the voltage.

Design: A circuit could be constructed in which the potential difference gradually becomes equal to zero; the current therefore decreases and the light gradually goes out.

Pre-Chapter Exploration 21
HOLT PHYSICS Discovery Lab

Magnetism

SAFETY

Perform this experiment in a clear area. Falling or dropped masses can cause serious injury.

Do not attempt this exercise with any batteries, electrical devices, or magnets other than those provided by your teacher for this purpose.

Never place fingers between the poles of magnets.

OBJECTIVES

- Investigate the properties of the field surrounding a magnet.
- Relate distance and field strength of a magnet.

MATERIALS

- ✔ 2 bar magnets with labeled poles
- ✔ 4 large, rectangular erasers
- ✔ aluminum foil strips
- ✔ cardboard, 1 sheet
- ✔ compass, 1.8 cm diameter
- ✔ graph paper
- ✔ iron filings in a shaker
- ✔ paper
- ✔ paper clips
- ✔ plastic pen
- ✔ plastic cup
- ✔ rubber band
- ✔ metric ruler
- ✔ scissors
- ✔ staples

The nature of magnets

Procedure

1. In each hand, hold a bar magnet by its center. Point the ends labeled *N* toward each other. Slowly move them close together, but do not let them touch. Observe what happens, and record your observations in your notebook.

2. Point the ends labeled *S* toward each other. Slowly move them close together, but do not let them touch. Observe what happens, and record your observations in your notebook.

3. Still holding the magnet by its center, rotate one magnet 180° and point the N end toward the S end of the other magnet. Slowly move the magnets close together, but do not let them touch. Observe what happens and record your observations in your notebook.

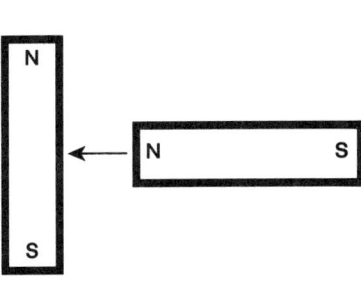

4. Rotate one magnet 90° so that the magnets are perpendicular to one another, as shown. Point the N end of one magnet toward the center of the other magnet. Observe what happens, and record your observations.

5. Repeat step 4, pointing the N end of one magnet toward several different points along the side of the other magnet. Observe what happens, and record your observations in your notebook.

6. Repeat steps 4–5, pointing the S end of one magnet toward the center of the other magnet. Observe what happens, and record your observations in your notebook.

7. Move one end of the magnet toward a paper clip. Observe what happens, and record your observations in your notebook.

8. Repeat step 7 with a variety of different objects, including a plastic cup, a pen, staples, aluminum foil, a rubber band, a pair of scissors, and paper.

Analysis

A. Do the magnets have to be in contact to interact?

B. Was the interaction stronger between the magnets when they were perpendicular or when the magnets were held with their ends facing one another?

C. Which ends of the magnet repelled one another?

D. Which ends of the magnets attracted one another?

E. Classify the objects that were attracted and repelled by the magnet. What did the objects attracted to the magnet have in common?

Mapping a magnetic field

Procedure

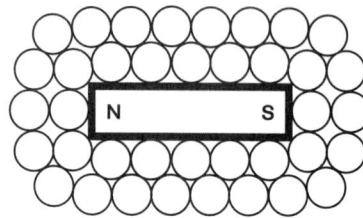

9. Place a sheet of paper on a nonmetallic tabletop. Place a bar magnet in the center of the paper so that the N end of the magnet points to the right. Make sure that the magnet is far away from any other magnets. Trace around the magnet and label the ends *N* and *S* on the paper.

10. Place a small compass on the paper beside the magnet. Trace a circle around the compass with a pencil.

11. Move the compass to a new position beside the magnet, and repeat step 10. Continue until you have traced a pattern of circles around the magnet as shown.

12. Move the compass far away from the magnet. Observe which way the needle points.

13. Place the compass in one of the circles on the paper. Mark the edge of the circle to indicate the direction that the needle points. Remove the compass. Draw an arrow in the circle to represent the position of the compass needle. The tip of the arrow should touch the mark on the edge of the circle, and the tail of the arrow should pass through the center of the circle.

14. Repeat step 13 until all the circles contain arrows.

Analysis

F. Does the compass needle always point the same direction?

G. Does the compass needle always point to the same end of the magnet?

H. Which end of the bar magnet does the compass needle point toward? Which end of the bar magnet does the needle point away from?

I. What kind of force causes the compass needle to change direction, a contact force or a field force?

The shape of a magnetic field

Procedure

15. Place the bar magnet on a nonmetallic tabletop. Make sure that the magnet is far away from any other magnets. Place a sheet of cardboard on top of the bar magnet so that the magnet is under the middle of the cardboard. Support the cardboard at the edges with rectangular erasers so that it remains level. Place one sheet of paper on top of the cardboard.

16. Carefully sprinkle iron filings on top of the paper over and around the magnet.
17. Carefully tap the cardboard a few times. When the filings settle into position, observe the pattern formed.
18. Draw the pattern of iron filings in your lab notebook.

Analysis

J. Compare the pattern made by the iron filings with the pattern of the arrows made by the compass needle. Does the iron-filing pattern have any relationship to the pattern of the arrows?

K. Did it require a force to move the iron filings into position? If so, was it a contact force or a field force?

The strength of a magnetic force

Procedure

19. Place a sheet of graph paper on a nonmetallic tabletop. Place a bar magnet in the center of the graph paper. Make sure that the magnet is far away from any other magnets.
20. On the graph paper, mark positions next to the magnet, as shown. Label these positions A–G.
21. Move a compass to each position on the graph paper. Observe how quickly the compass needle moves at each position. Using the words *strong*, *medium*, and *weak*, label how the force that moves the compass needle varies at each position.
22. On the graph paper, measure and mark a distance of 3.0 cm from each marked position, as shown.
23. Place a paper clip on a position marked 3.0 cm from the magnet. Point the end of the paper clip toward the magnet.
24. Slowly move the magnet toward the paper clip until the paper clip begins to move toward the magnet. Mark the position of the magnet on the paper. Using appropriate SI units, measure the distance the magnet was from the paper clip. Record the measurements in your lab notebook.
25. Repeat steps 23–24 for each position marked 3.0 cm from the magnet.

Analysis

L. Is the strength of the force the same everywhere, or does it vary along the length of the magnet? Explain.

M. Is the force that caused the paper clip to start moving a contact force or a field force?

Post-Chapter Activity 21
HOLT PHYSICS Invention Lab

Designing a Magnetic Spring

AQUACHEX ENVIRONMENTAL SERVICES
2240 Arena Drive
Evergreen, CO 80436

May 20, 2000

Dr. Belinda Fu
Product Development
1% Inspiration Laboratories
14557 West Post Road
Tempe, Arizona 85289

Dear Dr. Fu,

Aquachex Environmental Services specializes in monitoring lakes, streams, and other bodies of water. We have developed a sampling probe that remains in the water for 24 hours at a fixed depth and absorbs certain pollutants. The probe is then recovered and replaced. The used probe is brought to our laboratory for analysis.

Our problem is that the probe frequently hits the bottom too forcefully. This damages the probe and causes the samples to be contaminated with mud. Using a spring at the bottom of the line to slow the probe has failed because the spring corrodes after a few months in the water, especially in more-polluted locations.

We hope that you can develop a magnetic device that will act like a spring to slow the probe as it approaches the bottom and hold it about 20 cm above the bottom.

We are also having difficulty recovering the probe after the 24-hour testing period because the line we use to pull the probe to the surface often becomes tangled with the anchor line or with weeds. We would like your design to include something we can lower to retrieve the probe, so that the line does not have to be left in place during the testing period.

We would like to solve these problems as quickly as possible. We look forward to seeing your design soon.

Sincerely,

Cecil Dawkins

Cecil Dawkins

A page from the Aquachex Field Manual is on page 94.

1% INSPIRATION LABORATORIES

MEMORANDUM

Date: May 25, 2000
To: Product Development Team
From: Belinda Fu

I know we have a good supply of ring magnets in stock. I think we can solve both the spring problem and the retrieval problem using magnets; we can use repulsion between magnets for the spring and attraction between magnets for a hook to grab the probe during retrieval. Write a plan for your design and testing procedures. I will approve your plan before you go into the lab.

In the lab make a model of the probe described in the *Aquachex Field Manual*, and use clay to simulate the resin packages. The finished probe should have a mass of 120 g, just like the real one.

The probe is designed for water 0.5 m to 2.0 m deep, so test your spring design by having the probe slide down a vertical anchor line for 2.0 m in the lab. Remember that the probe will fall faster in air than in water, so any system that works well in air will have an added safety factor when used in water. Test your retrieval system on the same anchor line.

Try several combinations of magnets to optimize both spring force and support height. To keep the cost of the final device down, don't use more than eight ring magnets in your design. If you decide to attach magnets to the probe, remember to make them easily removable so they can be reused when the rest of the used probe is disposed of.

When you are finished, submit your report in the form of a patent application.

14557 West Post Road • Tempe, Arizona 852—

See next page for safety requirements, materials list, and more hints.

continued

MATERIALS

ITEM	QTY.
✔ bar magnets	6
✔ ceramic-ring magnets	8
✔ clay	150 g
✔ cord	5 m
✔ craft knife	1
✔ glue	1 tube
✔ heavy plastic cup, 14 oz	1
✔ lids for 12 oz plastic-foam cups	2
✔ meterstick	1
✔ plastic drinking straw	1
✔ plastic water pipe	15 cm
✔ plastic-foam hot drink cup, 12 oz	1
✔ rare earth magnet	1
✔ self-adhesive plastic tape	1 roll
✔ slotted masses, 10 g–500 g	1 set
✔ steel screw	2
✔ waterproof tape	1 roll

SAFETY

- Attach masses securely. Perform this experiment in a clear area. Swinging or dropped masses can cause serious injury.

- Magnets can generate strong forces. Never place your fingers between two magnets.

Aquachex Field Manual

An inexpensive probe using a plastic-foam hot-drink container has been developed.

Cut three slots 65 mm long and 12.5 mm wide in the body of the container. Two small holes 2 mm in diameter are made in the centers of the container bottom and the snap-on lid so that the probe can slide along the anchor line. The retrieval line is knotted through another hole in the lid.

Three packages of *ChexSorb II* resin are fitted inside the probe. The probe is 120 mm high, 95 mm diameter, and has a mass of 120 g.

A weighted anchor line is lowered until the weight rests on the bottom. A probe is threaded onto the anchor line, and a buoy is attached to the top.

The free end of the retrieval line is tied to the buoy. To retrieve the probe, untie the retrieval line and raise the sample to the surface.

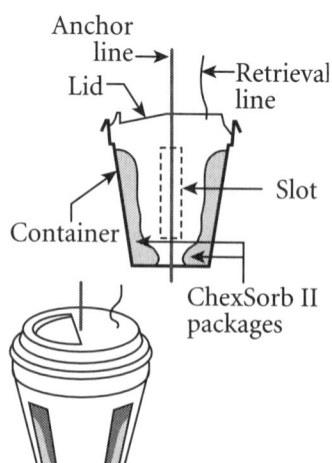

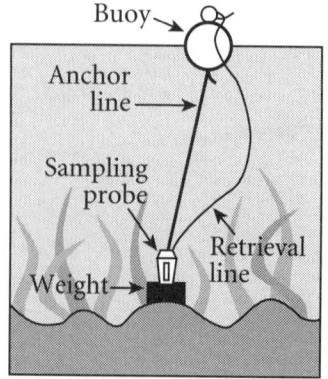

Pre-Chapter Exploration 22
HOLT PHYSICS
Discovery Lab

Electricity and Magnetism

SAFETY

Never close a circuit until it has been approved by your teacher. Never rewire or adjust any element of a closed circuit.

Never work with electricity near water; be certain that the floor and all work surfaces are dry.

Do not attempt this exercise with any batteries, electrical devices, or magnets other than those provided by your teacher for this purpose.

OBJECTIVES

- Observe the effects of a current through a wire.
- Discover how the core of an electromagnet affects the magnet's strength.
- Construct a simple speaker.

Exploring magnetic fields around wires

Procedure

1. Leaving a 20 cm tail, as shown below, wind 1.5 m of insulated wire around a cylindrical pen to create 40 tight coils. The coils should touch each other but should not overlap. Leave another 20 cm tail on the other end of the coils, as shown.

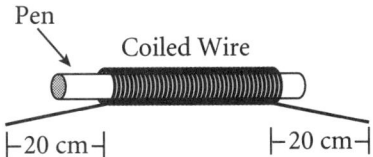

2. Keeping the wire coiled, carefully remove the wire from the pen.
3. Using leads with alligator clips, connect the coil to the posts of the battery holder as shown. Carefully insert the batteries in the battery holder.
4. Place the compass directly under the wire leading from the battery to the coil. Observe the position of the compass needle, and record your observations in your lab notebook.
5. Move the compass to a position directly above the wire leading from the battery to the coil. Observe the position of the compass needle, and record your observations in your lab notebook.

MATERIALS

- ✔ headphone plug
- ✔ 2 D-cell batteries
- ✔ brass screw or bolt
- ✔ steel screw or bolt
- ✔ brass nut
- ✔ steel nut
- ✔ battery holders for 2 D-cell batteries
- ✔ ceramic disk magnets
- ✔ cylindrical plastic pen
- ✔ electrical tape
- ✔ film canister with a hole in the bottom
- ✔ magnet wire
- ✔ insulated wire
- ✔ insulated connecting wires with alligator clips
- ✔ masking tape
- ✔ meterstick
- ✔ paper clips
- ✔ portable battery-powered radio
- ✔ metric ruler
- ✔ small compass
- ✔ wire cutters

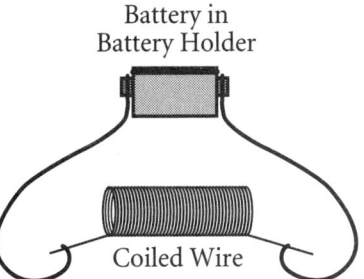

6. Place the coil horizontally on the desk. Touch the compass to one opening of the coil. Observe the position of the compass needle, and record your observations in your lab notebook.

7. Touch the compass to the other opening of the coil. Observe the position of the compass needle, and record your observations in your lab notebook.

8. Move the compass from one end of the coil to the other end while keeping it in contact with the side of the coil. Observe the position of the compass needle, and record your observations in your lab notebook.

9. Place 5 or 6 paper clips on the table near the coil. Without moving the battery, carefully move the coil close to the paper clips. Observe the paper clips, and record your observations in your lab notebook.

10. Remove the batteries from the battery holder. Disconnect the coil from the posts of the battery holder.

Analysis

A. Describe how a compass needle responds to a current-carrying wire when the compass needle is below the wire, when the compass needle is above the wire, and when the compass moves from above the wire to below the wire.

Electromagnet cores

Procedure

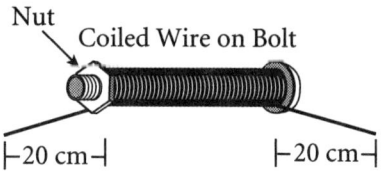

11. Insert a steel bolt through the wire coil. Insert the tip of the bolt protruding from the coil into a nut. Screw the nut clockwise, securing the coil on the bolt as shown.

12. Using leads with alligator clips, connect the coil to the posts of the battery holder. Carefully insert the batteries in the battery holder.

13. Touch the compass to one end of the bolt. Move the compass from one end of the bolt to the other end while keeping it in contact with one side of the coil. Observe the position of the compass needle and record your observations in your lab notebook.

14. Place five or six paper clips on the table near the coil. Without moving the battery, carefully move the coil close to the paper clips. Observe the paper clips, and record your observations in your lab notebook.

15. Remove the batteries from the battery holder. Disconnect the coil from the posts of the battery holder.

16. Replace the steel bolt with a brass bolt and repeat steps 11–15.

17. Remove the batteries from the battery holder. Disconnect the coil from the posts of the battery holder.

Analysis

B. Did the wire coil with the bolt have the same effect as the wire coil alone? Explain.

C. What happened as the bolt moved toward the paper clips?

D. Did the coil with the steel bolt pick up the paper clips as effectively as the coil with the brass bolt did?

Constructing a simple speaker

Procedure

18. Leaving a 40 cm tail, wind 2.0 m of magnet wire around a film canister with a hole in its base. The coils should touch each other but should not overlap. After five coils, tape the wire so that it does not fall off the canister. Wrap until you are 0.5 cm from the base of the canister. Carefully tape the coils to the side of the canister so that they do not unravel. Leave another 40 cm tail on the other end of the coils.

19. Place the uncoiled tail of the wire coil on a piece of cardboard. Using the wire cutters, carefully remove the enamel coating on the last 3.0 cm of each end of the wire.

20. Unscrew the casing from the phone plug. Thread both ends of the wire through the hole in the casing. Move this casing 25 cm up the wires.

21. Connect one wire to each of the metal posts of the phone plug. Make sure that opposite wires and posts do not touch. Wrap tape around one of the wires so that it does not touch the other wire.

22. Move the casing back down the wires. Screw the casing onto the metal part of the phone plug.

23. Move to a quiet area. Stack the ceramic magnets flat on the table. Place the film canister over the magnets so that it rests on the table.

24. Tune the portable radio to a station, and decrease the volume to its minimum. Insert the phone plug into the headphones slot on the portable radio.

25. Position your ear on the hole at the film canister base. Slowly increase the volume setting on the radio. You should be able to hear the radio. If not, reopen the phone plug and check the connections.

Analysis

E. What powers the electromagnet in the speaker?

F. Different parts of a speaker must pull and push on each other to produce sound waves that travel to your ear. Describe how different parts of this speaker produce sound.

G. Describe some ways to get the speaker to produce a louder sound.

Post-Chapter Activity 22 — HOLT PHYSICS Invention Lab

Building a Circuit Breaker

Miriam Parsa
20350 Via Subida
San Diego, California 92117

May 4, 2000

Dr. Shana Gillis
1% Inspiration Laboratories
14557 West Post Road
Tempe, Arizona 85289

Dear Dr. Gillis:

While looking through a trunk filled with my deceased mother's belongings, I came across a lab notebook with instructions for a circuit breaker. I am excited about this find because the breaker she designed appears very cheap to make; it can be made from materials commonly found around the home. It also should sell well because a circuit breaker usually works much better than a fuse.

I am enclosing all the instructions that my mother left for the working part of the circuit breaker. The problem is that her instructions are incomplete, and I have not been able to build this device or test it in a working circuit. I need your help in completing the breaker and in figuring out how to install it in a circuit. I do know that a moving part is missing from the design. I also know that the moving part must somehow connect and then disconnect the current-carrying wires. Can you and your staff help me? Please let me know as soon as possible. Thank you so much for your time.

Sincerely,

Miriam Parsa

Miriam Parsa

The page from the notebook is on page 100.

98 HOLT PHYSICS Laboratory Experiments

1% INSPIRATION LABORATORIES

MEMORANDUM

Date: June 21, 2000
To: Research and Development
From: Shana Gillis

The notes provide us with a good start on the solenoid. First, write up a plan for building the circuit breaker and fitting it in the circuit.

After I approve your plan, go into the lab and follow these steps:

1. Make the part of the solenoid described in the notes. Follow the directions carefully.

2. Decide what material to use for a plunger, and determine how the plunger should be shaped.

3. Get the solenoid-and-plunger device to work when power is applied directly to it.

4. Mount the solenoid and plunger onto a piece of cardboard, and wire the device in a circuit consisting of a bulb and a battery pack. Show that the circuit works well under normal conditions but that when a short circuit occurs and there is too much current, the solenoid shuts off the current.

I would like a drawing of the complete circuit and a short explanation of what you expect to happen. I have included a list of equipment that we have available.

You will prepare your report in the form of a patent application.

14557 West Post Road • Tempe, Arizona 852—

See next page for safety requirements, materials list, and more hints.

CHAPTER 22 **99**

continued

MATERIALS

ITEM	QTY.
✔ large metal paper clips	1 box
✔ magnet wire	1 roll
✔ plastic drinking straw	1
✔ cardboard	1
✔ battery pack for 2 D-cells	1
✔ D-cell battery	2
✔ lamp board with 5 miniature sockets	1
✔ miniature bulb (3 V)	5
✔ craft knife	1
✔ electrical tape	1 roll
✔ scissors	1
✔ aluminum foil	1
✔ modeling clay	1
✔ connecting leads with alligator clips	3
✔ switch	1
✔ bare copper wire	70 cm

SAFETY

Wire coils may heat rapidly during this experiment. If heating occurs, open the switch immediately and handle the equipment with a hot mitt. Allow all equipment to cool before storing it.

Never close a circuit until it has been approved by your teacher. Never rewire or adjust any element of a closed circuit. Never work with electricity near water; be sure the floor and all work surfaces are dry.

Do not attempt this exercise with any batteries or electrical devices other than those provided by your teacher for this purpose.

Date: October 27, 1957

A solenoid consists of many coils of wire neatly wrapped around a hollow cylinder. A thin piece of magnetic metal (such as iron, steel, or nickel) is then placed partly in the cylinder. This metal acts as a plunger. When current is put through the coils of wire, the magnetic field created pulls the plunger completely into the cylinder. I think I can use this device to make a circuit breaker.

Measure and mark 6 cm from the end of a plastic drinking straw. Measure a 10 cm tail at the end of a magnet wire, and bend the wire 90°. Tape the tail to the long part of the straw so that the bend is at the 6 cm mark. Wind tight, even coils of wire from the bend to the free end of the straw, making sure the coils touch each other. Count the coils as you wrap. Tape the coils down at regular intervals. When you reach the end, place tape over the first layer of coils, and begin wrapping in the opposite direction. Continue wrapping back and forth down the length of the straw until you have 200 coils (this should make at least four layers of wire on top of the straw). Leave a 5 cm tail of wire when you finish. Now take a